Treasures for Scholars Worldwide

浙江省档案馆藏
中国旧海关瓯海关税务司与
海关总税务司署往来机要函

Semi-official Correspondence Between Wenchow Commissioners and the Inspectorate General of Customs in Zhejiang Provincial Archives

主　编｜赵 伐　周彩英

本册编译｜何习尧

3

广西师范大学出版社
·桂林·

提 要

本册收录了浙江省档案馆藏1922年至1924年瓯海关税务司与海关总税务司署总税务司及铨叙科、秘书科等税务司的往来机要函(亦称半官函)。信函如包含有附件,则用符号( )将附件名称列在该信函标题之后。为简化每封信函的标题起见,信函的责任者与受文人只写人名的中文译名,其英文原名、职务、供职单位集中在以下表中列出。

姓名	职务
安格联(F. A. Aglen)	海关总税务司署总税务司
包罗(C. A. V. Bowra)	海关总税务司署代理总税务司
贺伦德(G. C. F. Holland)	海关总税务司署铨叙科税务司
丹安(B. Phillips-Denham)	海关总税务司署秘书科税务司
熊乃哲(P. N. Shone)	海关总税务司署署襄办秘书科副税务司
郝乐(B. E. F. Hall)	海关总税务司署署襄办秘书科副税务司
阿拉巴德(E. Alabaster)	瓯海关税务司
威立师(C. A. S. Williams)	瓯海关署税务司

Contents
目　录

1922 年

1月6日，丹安致阿拉巴德：已收到其第238号半官函（S/O） ································· 3

1月12日，安格联致阿拉巴德：就商人因民船船钞征收向中央政府请愿一事表明需妥善处理不应放弃（S/O） ·· 4

1月14日，阿拉巴德致安格联：汇报就民船船钞与当地利益相关方的交涉、与民食维持会代表就防止大米走私的交流情况、新监督尚未到任、职员近况等（S/O 240）（L060-001-0183-098） ·· 5

1月28日至2月22日，阿拉巴德与安格联：就台、宁、温、绍、闽船商代表要求退还暂征民船船钞一事作汇报和回复（附台、宁、温、绍、闽船商代表的请愿书）（S/O 241）（S/O）（L060-001-0183-099） ·· 9

2月9日至2月20日，阿拉巴德与熊乃哲：就民船船钞征收的最终解决方案、新监督将到任、按造册处税务司的要求整理总税务司通令作汇报和回复（S/O 242）（S/O）（L060-001-0183-100） ·· 16

2月27日至3月20日，阿拉巴德与安格联、熊乃哲：就新监督到任、三等验货 Garwood 考虑结婚、华员同文供事 Chang King-shuen 因病在休假结束后无法返岗、关医队伍人手充足作汇报和回复（S/O 243）（S/O）（L060-001-0183-101） ·· 19

3月9日至3月30日，阿拉巴德与安格联：就非海关建造灯塔是否应纳入海政局各关海江警船示册、为防海盗船商成立护商协会、当地县议会和参事会等机构建立、前任及现任海关监督情况作汇报和回复（附省道修建条规）（S/O 244）（S/O）（L060-001-0183-102） ············ 22

3月30日，阿拉巴德致安格联：汇报海关监督离温赴沪、整理总税务司通令的进展、鸦片销毁和搜查、职员 Chang King-shuen 在患病的情况下赴沪（S/O 245）（L060-001-0183-103） ··· ·· 30

4月18日至5月23日，阿拉巴德与安格联：就监督滞留上海、商会就民船自用大米配额请愿、拒绝日籍船只按内港行轮章程从事贸易的请求、茶叶贸易可能复兴、常关税收增加、员工近况等作汇报和回复（S/O 246）（S/O）（L060-001-0183-104） ………………………………… 32

5月6日至5月27日，阿拉巴德、安格联与威立师：就税务司职权交接、职员包德士已到岗等事宜作汇报和回复（S/O 247）（S/O）（L060-001-0183-105） ………………………… 37

5月20日至6月5日，威立师与安格联、熊乃哲：就威立师到岗及职权交接、拜访当地官员、县议会开始运作、鸦片收缴、外海水上警察逮捕并枪毙7名海盗、永嘉筹金赎路会联合学生开展向日本赎回胶州铁路的游行（附相关传单）（S/O 248）（S/O）（L060-001-0183-106） … ……………………………………………………………………………………………… 39

6月3日至6月19日，威立师与安格联：就旅客携带钱币通关的限额、海晏号船员打伤苦力引发罢工、民船被海盗劫掠情况、建议浙江沿海新建无线电站并增派快船打击海盗、员工宿舍建造等事宜作汇报和回复（S/O 249）（S/O）（L060-001-0183-107） ……………………… 46

6月16日至7月3日，威立师与安格联：就租用英领事馆房屋情况、外交使团反对征收印花税、建议提高出租给邮局房屋的租金、铜钱出口管制规定、出口货物检验、职员情况、当地多数医生未参加政府组织的医师资格考试等事宜作汇报和回复（S/O 250）（S/O）（L060-001-0183-108） …………………………………………………………………………………… 52

7月1日至7月12日，威立师与安格联：就当地政府批准美孚石油公司购地兴建储油池及后续影响、认为中国政府应裁员增效并建议裁撤监督委员一职、对卢永祥和当前局势的评估、放行出口的赈灾米、当地中学生欲报考税务专门学校等事宜作汇报和回复（S/O 251）（S/O）（L060-001-0183-109） ……………………………………………………………………… 59

7月15日至7月28日，威立师与安格联：就对裁厘加税的看法、亚细亚火油公司拟建储油池、建议向亡故的听差之子发放身后赏金、浙江电报局脱离交通部、龙舟赛期间道桥护栏倒塌造成伤亡、当地大米丰收作汇报和回复（S/O 252）（S/O）（L060-001-0183-110） ………… 66

7月29日至8月16日，威立师与安格联：就填围前滩空地工程的进展、杭州关和浙海关税务司对裁厘加税的看法、查获一批日本假币、本地大米假借赈灾名义出口及处置办法、监督赴沪作汇报和回复（S/O 253）（S/O）（L060-001-0183-111） ……………………………… 74

8月12日至9月7日，威立师与安格联：就华籍船员罢工对瓯海关的影响、员工调任及工作情况、地产购置、建议修改常关税则、当地官吏调任、民众对赈灾米去向的怀疑、卢永祥拟在浙江沿海兴建无线电站并招募兵士、当地火灾、当地拟拆除城墙筑路作汇报和回复（S/O 254）（S/O）（L060-001-0183-112） ………………………………………………………………… 80

8月26日至10月4日，威立师与安格联：就当地台风和暴雨的情况及造成的损失、当地与外界交通有所恢复、因受灾情影响无税款可汇解、已购地产的修建计划等作汇报和回复（S/O 255）（S/O）（L060-001-0183-113） ……………………………………………………… 88

9月14日至10月21日，威立师与安格联：就台风给瓯海关关产造成的破坏、缙云及丽水等地发生洪灾、与上海船运恢复但电报不畅、海盗在大头山抢劫金源丰号民船、当地商店火药爆炸、发现常关税则的错误等作汇报和回复（S/O 256）（S/O）（L060-001-0183-114） …… 93

9月28日至10月28日，威立师与安格联：就关产修复费用估算、建议购地兴建帮办宿舍、询问《汉语隐喻手册》的销售情况、当地方言特点、职员中文学习情况、档案整理等作汇报和回复（S/O 257）（S/O）（L060-001-0183-115） ………………………………………… 100

10月13日，威立师致安格联：询问新购置关产的登记方式、申请维修因台风受损的关产、汇报台风导致城墙倒塌造成损失、当地官吏要求海关支持其成立华洋义赈温处支会、文案和录事要求加薪（附1919年和1922年温州生活必需品价格对比表）（S/O 258）（L060-001-0183-116） ……………………………………………………………………………………………… 107

10月28日至11月13日，威立师与安格联、包罗：就关产维修、参与受灾地区调查、批准赈灾大米的运出、海盗活动猖獗等作汇报和回复（S/O 259）（S/O）（L060-001-0183-117） … 114

11月11日至12月6日，威立师与安格联：就近期海盗猖獗、应日本水道部要求将在当地开展磁力观测、受损关产修缮情况、为筹款赈灾商办轮船招商局将沪温间船费提高10%、台球桌的使用、地产购置等作汇报和回复（附瓯海关致三都澳关税务司的信函）（S/O 260）（S/O）（L060-001-0183-118） …………………………………………………………………… 119

11月23日至12月23日，威立师与安格联：就海盗再次劫掠臻祥号、磁力观测队已到达、文案和录事的加薪事宜、监督胡惟贤赴新加坡筹资赈灾、交通部为参加国际航海大会要求报送航船标志的信息、缉获鸦片情况、当地火灾等作汇报和回复（S/O 261）（S/O）（L060-001-0183-119） …………………………………………………………………………………… 126

12月9日，威立师致安格联：汇报磁力观测队已完成任务、募捐赈灾工作艰难、外海水上警察炮舰在追击海盗时触礁沉没、Keith Smith就其驾驶水上飞机由温州前往日本的计划询问相关信息、建议购置英领事馆的房产（S/O 262）（L060-001-0183-120） ………………………… 132

12月23日，威立师致安格联：汇报购置英领事馆房产的计划、温州轮船公司成立、当地官吏近况、温州民船商会请求交通部打击海盗、关产修缮进展等（附英驻宁波领事给瓯海关税务司的信函）（S/O 263）（L060-001-0183-121） ……………………………………………… 137

1923 年

1月6日，威立师致安格联：汇报1922年常关和海关的税收均创新高、建议对几处常关关产调整或修缮、信件和电报费率调整、客轮乘客溺水身亡、市中心房屋被烧毁等（S/O 264）（L060-001-0184-001） ……………………………………………………………………… 145

1月8日，安格联致威立师：要求就购买英领事馆房产的计划以公文请示（S/O）（L060-001-0183-120） …………………………………………………………………………………… 149

1月16日，安格联致威立师：表明可为购买英领事馆房产支付7000海关两（S/O）（L060-001-0183-121） …………………………………………………………………………………… 150

1月20日，威立师致安格联：汇报沈致坚接任道尹、商办轮船招商局与当地船公司的竞争、帮办宿舍需重新购置、司秤Lin Yin-li被指控吸食鸦片而受传唤、日本船只绑架人质和贩卖儿童的嫌疑、税务司公馆附近发生火灾（S/O 265）（L060-001-0184-003） ……………… 151

— 3 —

2月3日，威立师致安格联：汇报1月出口贸易改善税收增加、运货代理商对内港行船章程不满、二等同文供事后班柯呦苹病愈、司秤 Lin Yin-li 的举报人试图对其敲诈勒索、申请增派一名试用同文供事等（S/O 266）（L060-001-0184-005） 156

2月9日，安格联致威立师：认为即使厘金取消沿海常关的重要性也不会削弱（S/O）（L060-001-0184-002） 159

2月15日，安格联致威立师：就日本船只涉嫌绑架妇女和贩卖儿童一事认同铃子手救回人质的行为（S/O）（L060-001-0184-004） 160

2月22日，安格联致威立师：认为若在出口增加的同时能作税则调整税收将更好、表明海关不再任命试用同文供事（S/O）（L060-001-0184-006） 161

2月24日，威立师致安格联：汇报当地春节庆祝情况、监督正返回温州、上海一家银行破产及其对温州的影响、对在山间所购地产的维护、对调走头等总巡后班葛韩师表示不舍并希望继任者尽早到岗（S/O 267）（L060-001-0184-007） 162

3月10日，威立师致安格联：汇报2月税收增加、调查温州出口的赈灾米粮是否被高价转卖、瓯海关文案房的工作量、威立师因《汉语隐喻手册》受到法兰西文学院的嘉奖（S/O 268）（L060-001-0184-009） 165

3月12日，郝乐致威立师：已收到其第267号半官函（S/O）（L060-001-0184-008） ... 168

3月24日，威立师致安格联：汇报浙江省将对烟草征税20%、对温州出口的赈灾米粮是否被高价转卖的调查遇到困难、对档案的整理情况（附浙江省军务善后督办处及省长公署布告第15号）（S/O 269）（L060-001-0184-011） 169

4月5日，安格联致威立师：要求对浙江省的烟草税持保留态度（S/O）（L060-001-0184-012） 177

4月7日，威立师致安格联：汇报1季度税收上涨、Feiching 号运输4箱烟草印花税票要求免检免税通关、当地示威游行要求废除21条、海盗仍然猖獗、当地火灾、员工情况等（S/O 270）（L060-001-0184-013） 178

4月12日，包罗致威立师：通知将增派供事至瓯海关、祝贺威立师受到法兰西文学院的嘉奖（S/O）（L060-001-0184-010） 181

4月12日，威立师致安格联：汇报若土货复进口半税废除对瓯海关的税收和员工工作量不会造成太大影响（S/O 271）（L060-001-0184-014） 182

4月21日，威立师致包罗：说明对持过期护照出口的大米不予退税的详情、未签署监督所撰写的棉花出口禁运布告、请求对进口烟草印花税票的指示、汇报向中外赈灾委员会申请大批赈灾款、军队动向、与当地官员关系良好、当地抵制日货活动等（S/O 272）（L060-001-0184-015） 184

4月27日，贺伦德致威立师：通知调任帮办黄厚诚至三都澳关其职务由朱金甫接替（S/O）（L060-001-0184-017） 189

5月1日，郝乐致威立师：已收到其第270、271、272号半官函（S/O）（L060-001-0184-016） 190

5月5日，威立师致包罗：汇报4月税收同比增长、外班人手紧缺请求增补、监督胡惟贤携赈灾款返温、县丞张濂由张鹏翊暂代、监考英美烟草代理商行经纪C. A. Wolf 的汉语考试、当地民众对高价转卖赈灾米粮不满（附《新瓯潮》所刊文章摘录）（S/O 273）（L060-001-0184-018） ……………………………………………………………………………………… 191

5月19日，郝乐致威立师：已收到其第273号半官函（S/O）（L060-001-0184-019）… 195

5月19日，威立师致包罗：汇报更改木筏测量制度、亚细亚火油公司建造储油池的计划、当地发生火灾、若干盐务署外籍职员到达温州、已停止对内河航行的轮船征收樑头税（S/O 274）（L060-001-0184-020） …………………………………………………………………………… 196

6月1日，包罗致威立师：说明海关出版物中有关于木筏测量的有相关规定、就亚细亚火油公司建造储油池要求不予以协助、就停征内港行船樑头税要求以公文汇报（S/O）（L060-001-0184-021） …………………………………………………………………………………………… 200

6月2日，威立师致包罗：汇报因进出口量较前一年翻倍故与商办轮船招商局商量扩建其货栈、监督建议更改部分往来于温沪间夹板船的航行路线、对发往乐清的部分客船征收樑头税、贸易和关员情况、当地民众要求杭州当局调查高价转卖赈灾米粮的行为（附民众请愿书）（S/O 275）（L060-001-0184-022） ……………………………………………………………………… 202

6月12日，包罗致威立师：询问瓯海关贸易激增的原因、就对部分客船征收樑头税要求以公文请示、确认海关职员柯呦苹的首次任命时间（S/O）（L060-001-0184-023） ……………… 208

6月16日，威立师致包罗：汇报建筑师检验关产及相关情况、因樑头税收入不高认为可以取消、监督不再建议更改部分往来于温沪间夹板船的航行路线、希望北京局势平稳（S/O 276）（L060-001-0184-024） …………………………………………………………………………… 209

6月23日，包罗致威立师：表明现阶段暂不需要瓯海关关产购建的计划书、海关不会购买威立师的私人房产（S/O）（L060-001-0184-025） ……………………………………………… 213

6月30日，威立师致包罗：请示能否开凿自流井、希望工程局能提供瓯海关改建计划图纸的复件以便和当地官员磋商、请示是否批准钤子手Coxall去莫干山别墅度假、员工及天气情况等（S/O 277）（L060-001-0184-026） ……………………………………………………………… 214

7月10日，包罗致威立师：要求就瓯海关改建计划以公文汇报、说明若莫干山别墅还有空房间Coxall可以入住（S/O）（L060-001-0184-027） ……………………………………………… 219

7月14日，威立师致包罗：就关产的购建计划阐明看法、汇报整理瓯海关档案的进展、建议批准Coxall休假、职员情况、当地官员动向等（S/O 278）（L060-001-0184-028） ………… 220

7月28日，包罗致威立师：因资金紧张暂不批准房屋建造、支持裁减常关职员但要求以公文汇报（S/O）（L060-001-0184-029） ……………………………………………………………… 226

7月28日，威立师致包罗：汇报已炸毁Hanyang Maru号沉船、常关华员被控受贿及勒索、将就十字绣的征税问题以公文请示、大米丰收等（S/O 279）（L060-001-0184-030） ………… 227

8月13日，威立师致包罗：汇报两次台风接连过境造成的破坏及应对措施、A. C. Akehurst途经温州调查浙南地区的水文情况以应对水灾、欲购的英领事馆房产详情、对财政部要求提供本关的详细统计数据表示难以应对、常关录事和验货人员申请涨薪、威立师申请离温赴沪（附职员请愿书）（S/O 280）（L060-001-0184-032） ……………………………………………… 229

8月18日，郝乐致威立师：已收到其第279号半官函（S/O）（L060-001-0184-031） ··· 241

8月27日，包罗致威立师：就海关监督根据财政部通知要求提供详细统计数据说明可告知无总税务司批准不便提供相关数据、允许威立师9月暂时离岗（S/O）（L060-001-0184-033） ·· 242

8月27日，威立师致包罗：汇报在拒绝瓯海船舶公会允许夹板船进入内陆的提案后海关监督仍转发相关请愿、申请拨款修复帮办宿舍、建议购买外滩房产、申请补偿台风给本关水手造成的损失、询问工学院学生生产的袜子可否享受出口税收优惠（S/O 281）（L060-001-0184-034） ·· 243

9月8日，威立师致包罗：汇报使用舢板的首月常关缉私收效显著、尚未收到对几封呈文的回复、就所购英领事馆房产希望在过户前能免除租金、已做好暂时离岗的相关安排、说明处理广东劣等辅币难度较大且费时费神（S/O 282）（L060-001-0184-036） ·············· 248

9月12日，包罗致威立师：就购置帮办宿舍要求以公文汇报、拒绝赔偿水手和引水员在台风中所受损失、拒绝向工学院学生生产的袜子提供出口税收优惠（S/O）（L060-001-0184-035） ·· 254

9月21日，包罗致威立师：告知对几封瓯海关呈文的归档及回复情况、认为应支付租金给英领事馆（S/O）（L060-001-0184-037） ·· 255

9月24日，威立师致包罗：汇报已休完短假返岗、当地部队在无陆军部批准的情况下强制运输军火和军需品通关、税务司公馆已完全翻新、修缮帮办宿舍的安排、申请任命一名长聘的泥水匠、计划到各常关分卡巡查等（S/O 283）（L060-001-0184-038） ················ 256

10月4日，包罗致威立师：就帮办宿舍的修缮认为不必从上海派遣工师相关事务可由税务司及总巡敲定、拒绝瓯海关长聘一名泥水匠（S/O）（L060-001-0184-039） ·············· 261

10月4日，威立师致包罗：汇报税收持续增长、商人希望尽早解决十字绣的征税问题、外班职员要求加薪、对帮办包德士的调离表示不舍、帮办宿舍修缮的进展、因商会抗议扣押广东劣币建议没收两成并将余额发还、威立师加入当地的汉语文学社、800名华籍难民从日本抵达（S/O 284）（L060-001-0184-040） ·· 262

10月18日，威立师致包罗：汇报前三季度海关和常关税收的增长情况、就向财政部提交统计数据的方案提出建议、缴获鸦片、学生参与抵制日货、未收到有关印花税票的通知、建议对D账户的分项作调整、未收到所购英领事馆地产免租的回复、关产和员工近况、与监督的来往、浙江省仍保持独立（S/O 285）（L060-001-0184-042） ·············· 268

10月31日，包罗致威立师：对瓯海关税收增加表示嘉许、不确定税务处是否会派专员来海关收集数据、此前已回复所购英领事馆房产的租金问题、同意对D账户的分项作调整、因经费紧张无法满足关于帮办宿舍的要求（S/O）（L060-001-0184-043） ·················· 279

11月2日，威立师致安格联：汇报与地方当局协商设立工程部收取码头捐用于扩建关厂、当地抵制日货情况、9月和10月近5000名难民由日本返还、三井物产株式会社的代理前来温州采购物资、海盗猖獗、就警察和士兵登上港内停靠的船只搜查提出抗议、询问是否查抄福建铸造的钱币、希望配置汽艇以加强缉私工作、关员健康状况等（S/O 286）（L060-001-0184-044） ·· 281

11月12日，郝乐致威立师：已收到其第284号半官函（S/O）（L060-001-0184-041） ······ 291

11月17日，威立师致安格联：询问是否需在监督同意后再通知其他口岸和领事馆本地爆发的疫情、县丞张濂病逝、认为应划清海关和当地政府部门的职权范围、帮办卜郎表现良好、推荐柯呦苹升为帮办、表扬录事黄聘珍等（S/O 287）（L060-001-0184-047） ………… 292

11月26日，安格联致威立师：就瓯海关与地方当局协商设立工程部收取码头捐用于扩建关厂说明若对洋货征收需取得相关国家的同意、赞同裁减冗员（S/O）（L060-001-0184-045） ……………………………………………………………………………………… 297

12月1日，威立师致安格联：申请批准从宁波进口的货物卸到保税货仓、表明对出口货子口税制度的看法、安排图书馆给邮务长办公、请示是否免税放行运往杭州的军用大米、汇报将被扣押船只的相关文件移交给地方法院、当地官员动向、轮船公司在相互竞争后就收费标准达成一致、火灾情况、道尹收到省府指令调查偷运大米案、关产修复情况等（附浙江军务善后督办处及省长公署给瓯海道尹的指令）（S/O 288）（L060-001-0184-049） ………… 298

12月7日，安格联致威立师：就防疫工作的程序进行解释（S/O）（L060-001-0184-048） ……………………………………………………………………………………… 309

12月13日，安格联致威立师：通知不没收福建所铸钱币（附江海关、浙海关给总税务司的半官函）（S/O）（L060-001-0184-046） ………………………………………… 311

12月15日，威立师致安格联：申请配备汽艇及为水手提供住所、熔化缉获的广东劣质银币的成本及不便之处、监督建议海关采取印花税制度、认为对从内陆进口的酿酒用糯米应征收从价税、将研究改进常关工作的方法、当地官员动向、50里外常关已取消附征贩捐、与亚细亚火油公司就其储油池的选址及火油载运的交涉情况、缴获鸦片等（S/O 289）（L060-001-0184-051） ……………………………………………………………………… 314

12月17日，安格联致威立师：批准从宁波进口的货物可以由内陆船只卸到保税货栈、暂时不处理出口货子口税制度一事、表扬税收增长（S/O）（L060-001-0184-050） ………… 324

12月29日，威立师致安格联：汇报自治会商讨并通过扩充外滩以修建验货厂、整理修订家具清单、抵制日货的学生与进口日货的商人起冲突、郝旭东任温处台部队司令、缉私关员以手写证词代替出堂作证等（S/O 290）（L060-001-0184-053） ……………… 325

1924年

1月8日，安格联致威立师：就瓯海关申请配备汽艇说明需考虑资金问题、要求汇报引水服务每年给瓯海关带来的收入、认为海关应摆脱熔化劣等银元的责任、反对海关采用印花税制度、认为难以对酿酒用糯米征收从价税、要求按违规处理亚细亚火油公司从轮船上卸下所运汽船的行为等（S/O）（L060-001-0184-052） …………………………………………… 333

1月15日，威立师致安格联：汇报当地警察悬赏抢劫钱庄的青红帮成员、日本地震后大量船只前来运输木材和煤炭、法国炮舰抵港、船只相撞、就县丞下令更换浙江省印花税票作请示、被缉获劣等银元的民众向税务处请愿、销毁所缉获的鸦片、对常关税则的调整、查获欲走私至日本的雷管、引水服务每年给瓯海关带来的收入等（S/O 291）（L060-001-0184-055） …… 335

1月16日，安格联致威立师：说明作为起诉方除非法庭接受手写证词否则海关不能拒绝派员出庭作证（S/O）（L060-001-0184-054） ··· 342

1月31日，威立师致安格联：就派员出庭作证提出疑问、就财政部派专员赴各海关搜集相关数据请示如何应对、赈灾工作情况、认为税务处在处理两件商人请愿免税案上未给予海关足够支持、就英美烟草公司华员抗议海关收缴其剪刀说明后续的处理、军方组织海岸巡防行动、道尹沈致坚前往杭州等（S/O 292）（L060-001-0184-057） ··· 343

2月1日，安格联致威立师：要求对新浙江印花税票不予过问、认为税务处在免税案上处理不当、指示可用瓯海关的引水收入为引水员配备所需设施但不应超支（S/O）（L060-001-0184-056） ··· 350

2月11日，安格联致威立师：询问是否知悉浙江督军卢永祥通过日本代理商购进德国武器一事（S/O）（L060-001-0184-060） ·· 352

2月15日，威立师致安格联：建议向鸦片走私者处以罚款以支付缉私奖金、就常关罚没数据填报的统一性提出意见、监督向中央政府建议实行海关印花税制度、常关的选址情况、已就税则提交疑问、尚无卢永祥购进德国武器的相关消息、温处台部队的司令官离开温州（附瓯海关监督胡惟贤给税务处等部门的呈文）（S/O 293）（L060-001-0184-059） ··················· 353

2月19日，安格联致威立师：重申中国法庭有权传唤目击证人、允许向财政部专员提供所需非机密信息、赞许威立师的赈灾工作、表明可建议监督对免征牡蛎常关税设时间限制（S/O）（L060-001-0184-058） ·· 364

2月29日，威立师致安格联：建议将对1919年修订进口税则的说明性文字加入1922年税则、汇报当地报纸发表文章希望能从福建免税免护照进口大米、购买英领事馆房产遇到的波折、认为卢永祥若要秘密进口武器则不会选择在口岸通关、对所售常关关产作估价、外商和乘客可能反对海关印花税制度、在贸易报告中加入当地的气候信息、四等帮办卜郎患流感、税务司公馆的火灾情况、监督不愿意就牡蛎壳的免税问题抵触税务处、税务处要求500吨以上的轮船安装无线电设备等（附《新瓯潮日报》所刊文章摘录）（S/O 294）（L060-001-0184-062） ······
··· 366

3月15日，威立师致安格联：汇报对超载木炭的日本船只没收并转卖超载品、巡役存在渎职现象、龙泉宝剑在税则上的归类问题、常关私货仓库被盗、在子口税票管理上的不规范之处、与监督就鸡蛋征税权的沟通情况、金源行号夹板船船主因输掉官司怀恨在心而向税务处举报海关、收到通知海关不必再熔化所缉获的劣质银币、常关没收县丞所运木料、浙江省开征煤油附加税等（S/O 295）（L060-001-0184-064） ·· 376

3月26日，安格联致威立师：不赞同向鸦片走私者处以罚款以支付缉私奖金、就常关罚没数据填报的统一性要求以备忘录形式呈报建议、指示采取巧妙手段阻止实施海关印花税制度的计划、就税务处要求500吨以上的轮船安装无线电设备一事告知在收到总税务司通知之前不采取任何行动（S/O）（L060-001-0184-061） ·· 385

4月1日，威立师致安格联：汇报第1季度税收增加、与班达公司就鸡蛋的子口税票问题进行沟通、没收5艘民船所载物品及后续处理、与监督就海关印花税制度的沟通情况、所购英领事馆地产的草图测绘情况、询问外班职员要求加薪的请愿是否能得到处理、索取安格联的画像以挂在图书馆内、据悉接下来5年英国领事在税收问题上将减少对中国政府的干预等（S/O 296）（L060-001-0184-066） ·· 387

4月10日，安格联致威立师：说明海关设置巡役一职的必要性、认为龙泉宝剑的传说与亚瑟王的传说很相似、表明税务处将对剑鞘是否征税作出裁决、希望各支所能加强对子口税票的查验、认为后续会有更多类似煤油附加税的税种、表示将设法取得税务处关于劣等银元的指示等（S/O）（L060-001-0184-065） ……………………………………………………………………… 394

4月15日，威立师致安格联：汇报监督极力推动海关印花税制度及自己的反对意见、阐述向鸦片走私者施以罚款的合理性、已完成对所缉获的民船载运私货的处理、建议除非监督要求否则不逐月向其提供海关运行的相关信息、当地医院申请1斤所缉获的鸦片、对华商保税货栈的检查情况、与当地官员协商扩充关厂的情况等（S/O 297）（L060-001-0184-068） ………… 396

4月28日，安格联致威立师：说明所购英领事馆地产在产权上存在的不明确之处并作相关指示（S/O）（L060-001-0184-063） …………………………………………………………………… 401

5月1日，威立师致安格联：汇报购置英领事馆地产的进展、英领事帮助亚细亚火油公司获批修建储油池、为方便铃子手Coxall领取退伍津贴为其签字作见证、希望验估处能够修订关于税则的说明、因井水不稳定支持当地成立供水公司、当地照明公司进口所需设备等（S/O 298）（L060-001-0184-069） ……………………………………………………………………………… 404

5月6日，安格联致威立师：说明将适时考虑为常关外班职员加薪、告知可向上海一家照相馆索要所需的总税务司照片、批准向鸦片走私者处以罚金但应谨慎行事、就扩充关厂一事认为资金来源是大问题等（S/O）（L060-001-0184-067） ……………………………………………… 409

5月15日，威立师致安格联：汇报谭安此前已呈交关于茶叶货运稽查处的报告、监督对推行海关印花税制度的信心产生动摇、对所缉获的劣等银元的处理、对英领事馆内的书籍和文件的处理情况、对袭击铃子手的苦力处以罚款、申请割草机的零件、听说监督收到通知上交其罚没收入的三成给财政部、部分俄罗斯人由上海经温州前往南方各港口等（S/O 299）（L060-001-0184-070） ………………………………………………………………………………………… 411

6月2日，威立师致安格联：汇报购置英领事馆地产的进展、在认识到印花税票制度不可行后监督建议效仿浙海关、乡绅请愿禁止木炭出口、申请加高税务司公馆花园的东墙、监督胡惟贤将赴沪、尚未收到总税务司第1239号训令（S/O 300）（L060-001-0184-072） ………… 416

6月9日，安格联致威立师：希望能顺利购置英领事馆地产、不反对威立师为铃子手Coxall领取退伍津贴的签字作见证、要求就当地供水工程以公文汇报、表明在抵制监督关于海关印花税制度的建议时应为其留足面子、就财政部要求监督上交其罚没的三成一事认为恐难以实现等（S/O）（L060-001-0184-071） ……………………………………………………………… 419

6月16日，威立师致安格联：汇报已就所辖常关的工作制度及整改意见提交公文、正在酝酿给海关监督留面子的方式、葡萄牙纵帆汽船希望扩充其航行路线至海门、金宝康号夹板船遭海盗劫掠、《字林西报》刊登本关去年贸易报告、亚细亚火油公司的员工来温调查相关信息以修建储油槽和货栈、新任职的俄籍盐运使抵温、仍未收到总税务司第1239号训令等（S/O 301）（L060-001-0184-073） ……………………………………………………………………………… 421

7月1日，安格联致威立师：告知总税务司第1239号训令与第1238号训令一起寄出、认可其在收到监督的回复前暂拒葡萄牙纵帆汽船扩充其航行路线至海门的请求（S/O）（L060-001-0184-074） ……………………………………………………………………………………… 426

7月1日，威立师致安格联：汇报英国帆船护送盐船抵港、帮办朱金甫申请调往上海、向美国驻上海领事提供注册船公司的名单、认为常关后续可能独立于海关因此需要专人负责、询问可否从华籍帮办中任命监督、税务司公馆险些被盗、烧毁走私鸦片、放行两箱军需医用物品等（S/O 302）（L060-001-0184-075） 427

7月15日，威立师致安格联：汇报上半年税收情况、监督对给其留面子的措施表示满意、美国班达公司询问是否可用江海关监督所颁发的子口税票运输鸡蛋和家禽通关、Ruxton 抵温巡视盐课、请示能否打赏到访的当地官员扈从、海警局抓获海盗、台风影响航运、当地成立新商轮公司、县议会重新运营等（S/O 303）（L060-001-0184-076） 432

7月31日，安格联致威立师：告知已获悉帮办朱金甫申请调往上海、不认为常关和海关将分离、说明海关监督是政治任命而非由海关招聘、表明从未授权打赏到访官员的扈从（S/O）（L060-001-0184-077） 437

8月1日，威立师致安格联：汇报得知政府会为打击海盗配备无线电台和汽船、中国政府在温州船运商会于交通部注册之前暂不会对软木板材降税、说明常关总关改址的必要性、监督胡惟贤突然死亡、询问是否认可对出口茶叶的处理方式、县议会同意征收码头捐以扩充关厂、各商会要求由其管理进港民船及自己的反对意见、就购买英领事馆的房产提出看法等（附《新瓯潮日报》所刊文章摘录）（S/O 304）（L060-001-0184-078） 439

8月13日，安格联致威立师：就打击海盗一事认为沿海巡逻难以由地方政府完成、表明总税务司不会干涉税务处对监督的任命、反对商会要求由其管理进港民船等（S/O）（L060-001-0184-079） 449

8月15日，威立师致安格联：汇报将渔船发现的日本鱼雷移交给军方、担心商办轮船招商局的广济号更改航线会对税收造成影响、省政府指示当地警察对广告征税、蒋邦彦被任命为瓯海关监督、购置英领事馆房产的进展等（S/O 305）（L060-001-0184-080） 450

9月1日，威立师致安格联：汇报浙江与邻省的矛盾及军队动向、上海的银行拒绝接受温州商户汇款导致贸易停滞、新监督到任及工作情况、希望道尹为农民降低护照发行费、已就统捐局效仿海关对乘客的行李征税提出抗议、温州茶叶货运稽查处的情况、在推行口岸间内河运货关税征收新规上遇到的困难、铃子手 Coxall 因婚事希望调任到大的港口等（S/O 306）（L060-001-0184-082） 454

9月6日，安格联致威立师：说明发现鱼雷一事不属于缉私因此难以发放奖金并询问鱼雷的后续处理情况（S/O）（L060-001-0184-081） 462

9月15日，威立师致安格联：汇报当地实施军管及部队动向、鱼雷已交还给日舰但军方拒发奖金、申请派遣建筑师实地考察常关总关选址、监督拒绝葡萄牙纵帆汽船扩充其航行路线至海门的请求、50 里外常关加征赈灾附加税、追问铃子手 Coxall 的调任问题、征收码头捐以改善港口设施的方案仍在修订中、天气情况等（附浙江温处防军兼戒严司令官布告等）（S/O 307）（L060-001-0184-083） 463

10月1日，威立师致安格联：汇报就当地暴乱采取的应对措施、因税务司公馆旁边的建筑有火灾隐患申请灭火器、监督熔化劣等银元的火耗比海关高出三四倍、当地商轮公司的船只在运木炭至日本的途中沉没、员工情况、申请给华员发放身份证明等（附闽海关给华员发放的身份证明）（S/O 308）（L060-001-0184-085） 489

10月7日，安格联致威立师：表明要等到次年才能安排 Coxall 的调任、表明可放行军用大米并做好记录（S/O）（L060-001-0184-084） 495

10月15日，威立师致安格联：汇报军阀彭德铨控制温州后的治理手段及军阀混战的情况、巡役刘子春因战乱在休假结束后未能按期到岗、吸毒者Hartman[n]来温州欲取道赴厦门、就亚细亚火油公司为修建储油池而需要与地方政府达成协议提出相关建议等（S/O 309）（L060-001-0184-086） ··· 496

11月1日，威立师致安格联：汇报温州仍在军事管制中但局势稳定、为华员发放身份证明、与新监督杨承孝的来往情况、吸毒者Hartmann已离温赴厦门、冬季海盗猖獗、英领事来温处理地产移交手续及英国国民被捕案、亚细亚火油公司因拒缴手续费而被阻止修建防洪堤、申请尽快在瓯江入海处为引水员修建住处、请示如何处理作为缉私奖励所得的劣质银币、就所购领事馆房产的整修发表意见、建议尽快派建筑师来温州确定常关总关的建造方案等（S/O 310）（L060-001-0184-088） ··· 504

11月7日，安格联致威立师：说明在亚细亚火油公司与地方政府达成一致之前应暂不批准其在储油池的选址处卸建筑材料（S/O）（L060-001-0184-087） ································ 512

11月15日，威立师致安格联：汇报浙江省军政情况、当地设立禁毒局、就修建瓯江入海处的引水员住处的详细方案作说明、税务司公馆内常用器皿的配备情况、没收劣等银元的政策引发不满、近期火灾频发、有人试图走私大米获利等（S/O 311）（L060-001-0184-089） ······ 514

12月1日，威立师致安格联：汇报在处理劣等银元上的难处、亚细亚火油公司的经纪就修建浮桥与当地乡绅的往来情况、铃子手从日本船只救回被绑架孩童、威立师被任命为禁毒局顾问、当地开始供电照明、当地官员变动及火灾情况等（S/O 312）（L060-001-0184-090） ······ 521

12月13日，贺伦德致威立师：要求就关于四等铃子手前班卢诗和的指控作调查（附相关指控信、瓯海关头等总巡关于卢诗和情况的说明）（S/O）（L060-001-0184-094） ················ 526

12月15日，威立师致安格联：汇报监督插手常关税收、尚未移交缉获的劣等银元给监督、法院要求营救孩童的铃子手出庭作证、认为对外班员工的指控不实、当地政府人事变动、禁毒局举行游行、法国船只来温停留3日、一艘新轮船下水在温州附近水域运营等（S/O 313）（L060-001-0184-091） ··· 529

12月27日，威立师致安格联：认为对四等铃子手前班卢诗和的指控不实（附相关指控信）（S/O 314）（L060-001-0184-095） ·· 534

12月31日，安格联致威立师：希望禁毒局不是打着幌子的鸦片专卖局、说明不再为税务司公馆提供刀叉（S/O）（L060-001-0184-092） ··· 538

12月31日，安格联致威立师：要求按照第1292号训令处理劣等银元、认同监督的频繁更换不利于海关的发展（S/O）（L060-001-0184-093） ·· 539

1922年

4.—42]

INSPECTORATE GENERAL OF CUSTOMS,

PEKING, 6th Jan. 1922.

Dear Sir,

I am directed by the Inspector General to inform you that your S/O Letter No. 538, dated 6/12/21, has been duly received.

Yours truly,

B. Phillips D'Eby
Private Secretary.

V. Alabaster, Esquire

Wenchow

INSPECTORATE GENERAL OF CUSTOMS,

PEKING, 12th, January, 19 22.

Dear Mr. Alabaster,

I have duly received your S/O letter No.239 of the 28th December, 1921.

<u>Merchants' appeal to Peking against payment of Junk Dues.</u> This appealing to Peking, very possibly for interest motives as you suggest, is a nuisance but we have to make the best of it. I am replying to your despatch in a few days and I hope we shall be able to get matters settled. In any case dont let go.

Yours truly,

[signature]

—————ster, Esquire,
WENCHOW.

CUSTOM HOUSE,

S/O No. 240.

Wenchow, 14th January 1922.

Dear Sir Francis,

This is becoming slack towards the Lunar New Year and for a week or ten days we shall be without steamer communication.

Dues: interview merchants.

The junk interests desired to see me a week or so ago on the matter of Junk Dues revision and I accordingly interviewed them on the day they wished. I asked them how it came that they did not appear, when duly arranged for over a month ago. They expressed regret that they had not appeared. I reiterated what I had already told them - i.e. that their cooperation was what we particularly wished - and I further stated that in the absence of their cooperation, however, a very generous revision

FRANCIS A AGLEN K. B. E.,
Inspector General of Customs,
    PEKING.

revision embodying certain of their wishes, and certain proposals, had been submitted to Peking, in whose hands the matter now rested. I did not enter into details beyond telling them that very considerable reductions had been proposed, a statement which appeared to afford them satisfaction. I am afraid that I have found them to be a very slippery lot! And I daresay it will not be long before they set up some kind of taxing establishment under some safe name. The Superintendent tells me they told him that we would collect over Tls. 10,000 a year from the Junk Dues, whereas our statistics show that, without revision, we should collect under Tls. 4,500! As revised - on the present basis - we should collect rather over Tls. 2,500 annually. The chief, if not the sole reason for the agitation raised about a comparatively small sum is the hope of discharged <u>hu shang</u> employés to set up a profitable financial organ.

A representative (one of the teachers in the Methodist College here and

a

...tion of food
...: interview with
...entative of
... <u>re</u>.

3.

a respectable young man) of a local society for the "protection of the food supply" interviewed me a few days ago relative to joint search along with the Native Customs of I.W.S.N. steamers with a view to stopping rice smuggling. I told him that, while appreciating the excellent motives guiding the society, the Customs was unable to assent to any such joint search. I also told him that anything in the nature of information we would of course welcome and act on at once. He is the mandarin teacher, as I gathered later, of one of the Tidewaiters here (Mr. Cammiade), and I referred him to the latter, also informing Mr. Cammiade of the interview. As a matter of fact there is probably much rice smuggling, but the smugglers carefully avoid a route lying through Maritime Customs auspices. The Maritime Police exercise considerable vigilance, too, according to their lights - in some cases leading to affray, as in an instance at Pingyang lately - but with, of course, collusion is a rule.

The

4.

ials: Superintendent   The present Superintendent's delegate
aoyin.   here tells me that the new Superintendent is
                        not over anxious to come here from Wuhu.
                        I invited both the Superintendent and the
                        taoyin to lunch the other day. I have for
                        long owed the taoyin return hospitality, but
                        his somewhat hurried departure in the summer
                        threw arrangements out: the Superintendency,
                        unfortunately, was not represented at my
                        meal as the delegate was down with influenza.

influenza: N.C.   I have had a touch of influenza,
er.   of which there is much about of a persistent
                        type: but I appear to be better now. It
                        only kept me one day away. Otherwise every
                        one seems well. - Mr. Christophersen has
                        been up-country for a few days, visiting
                        one of the great scenic sites of China (Yen-
                        t'ang (雁蕩) not far from here). -
                        Nothing further has come up concerning the
                        charge against the N.C. Examiner referred to
                        in my S/O No. 237, and it looks as if the
                        matter had fallen through.

                                                Yours truly,

CUSTOM HOUSE,

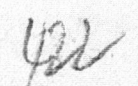

S/O NO. 241.   Wenchow, 28th January 1922.

Dear Sir Francis,

Dues:
On receipt of your telegram of the 17th - received prior to your despatch of the 14th - I saw the Superintendent, and explained matters to him as instructed. I interviewed the junk representatives on the 23rd instant, explained my instructions in detail, and was informed by the representatives that they accepted the present Ningpo rates, rules and procedure which they understood as being ordered by the Shui-wu Ch'u. Arrangements accordingly are being made in consultation with the Superintendent. I referred them to the appendices of your despatch No. 1067 regarding refund of dues paid and requested from them an explanation.

They

FRANCIS A AGLEN K. B. E.,
Inspector General of Customs,
    PEKING.

2.

They admitted that no such undertaking as to refund of dues had been either given or accepted by me, and that the statement was false: and they claimed no refund whatsoever. (There was a statement made by me, but it was not to the above effect: my statement was merely that should the number of levies under the Provisional Regulations be reduced by revision after the three months, whatever levies the junks had paid would be taken into consideration. Thus should the number of levies be reduced from ten to six, and should the junks have paid two or three during the provisional period, those two or three would be considered as subtracted from the six. That was all). On the termination of this interview I telegraphed to yourself on the 24th (in reply to yours of the 23rd instant) and wrote to the Superintendent. On the 26th I received a petition from the junk interest of which I append a copy, accepting the Ningpo Regulations and procedure but claiming the refund and thereby repudiating

insofar

3.

insofar and in that respect what they had already stated as above before a witness. I have, accordingly seen the Superintendency which had also been petitioned, and the latter informs me that the Shui-wu Ch'u has been telegraphed to reporting this lack of faith, and asking for instruction. I sincerely trust that the Shui-wu Ch'u will not entertain the request of the merchants for a refund. As distinct from refund, however, it will be correct to take into consideration what the junks have already paid under the Provisional Regulations, when levying on them under the about to be introduced Ningpo Rules and procedure. Inasmuch as under the latter we shall derive so very little it will not be easy to arrange this to the satisfaction of the traders. But I am fixing to see the latter and will endeavour to arrange something satisfactory. It being Lunar New Year period, and no mails running I may probably have to wire to you insofar.

I

4.

I am sorry that you have been troubled with this matter: various factors have unaided simplification: (one being that, when all is said and done, there was no available suitable official procedure for collecting these Junk Dues: another the appreciation by the traders that more was to be got out of Peking than from us: and a third a certain clever and plausible twisting of facts in their representations). The rain of petitions and telegrams must have been calculated, even in this comparatively small case (with, however, its larger possibilities) to unsteady the Shui-wu Ch'u in general Chinese conditions. Probably the best medicine for the appellants is less attention to their requests at face value, and something rather strong. Anyway, the more they get, the more they want, not unnaturally two or three of the five junk representatives have no "interest" in the junks at all and are merely special pleaders working for a fee. And if they get the refund, they
would

5.

would divide the proceeds as their share of the spoil. What the merchants would doubtless have preferred - short of non-collection by us at all - even more than the adoption of the present Ningpo Tariff and procedure would be their own interpretation of the above Tariff. I am glad, at least, that the Shui-wu Ch'u has not given sanction to this: though to work the present Ningpo procedure here, and although the merchants have accepted it, will still probably involve certain modifications. Anyway we can now fix up things here locally definitely on the general lines of the instructions.

Pending official report, I am sending to you the above details. I am sorry that force of circumstances has proved too much for the Provisional Regulations.

Yours truly,

APPEND.

具禀台甯溫紹閩船商代表王煦壹周梓文陳芝鴻徐子楷邱世藩等禀為絃經決定請將暫征銀兩批准如數給領事竊緣前奉暫征船鈔稅一條本年一月二十三日承邀代表等到關當奉

貴稅務司

監督諭以此案現經

財政部

稅務處指令准照浙海關辦法每年每船征收一次等因代表等遵即轉知各船商僉以既奉

處部決定祗得遵照浙海關章程完納但此案現在始奉核准成立所有上年十月一日起算至核准以前試辦期間內暫收此種稅銀當然發還以平法律等語除禀

監督外為此據情具禀伏乞

稅務司監核迅賜查案准將此項暫收稅銀如數批准給領公感上禀

中華民國十一年一月　　日

INSPECTORATE GENERAL OF CUSTOMS,

S/O.

PEKING, 22nd February 1922,

Dear Mr. Alabaster,

I have duly received your S/O letter No. 241 of the 28th January.

Junk Dues: the many telegrams sent from Wenchow in connection with this case may have unsteadied the Ch'u's judgement on general conditions.

Once the Shui-wu Ch'u is brought into such matters they *ipso facto* pass out of my sole control.

Yours truly,

E. Alabaster, Esquire,
Wenchow.

CUSTOM HOUSE,

S/O NO. 242.

Wenchow, 9th February, 1922.

Dear Sir Francis,

Dues.

I have interviewed the merchants twice since my last letter and, as telegraphed, have arranged things with them, no refund being allowed, and the Dues already paid being taken into consideration when collecting under the present Ningpo procedure. This latter procedure, throughly explained to the merchants (but which will need a few changes in detail to fit it to local conditions) will forthwith be operated, and a joint Notification of myself and Superintendent is being issued. The case is now concluded: and I am reporting its conclusion, including the above refund matter, more specifically officially. The petition of the merchants

FRANCIS A AGLEN K. B. E.,
Inspector General of Customs,
PEKING.

merchants as to the latter was in the nature of a "try-on": feeling that they had gained considerably, they desired to gain more

ials:
intendent.

The new Superintendent is expected to assume office here on the 16th: but has not yet arrived. I hope he will soon appear, as a more or less transitional period of this sort is apt to prove awkward.

Circular
Medium.

I am progressing very fairly with this, and now practically all my material is sorted out; but not pasted in, which takes the longer time. Moreover revision in various respects is required: I have devised a plan to meet the requirements of keeping up-to-date on the loose leaf system as proposed by the Statistical Secretary.

Yours truly,

[A.—42]

INSPECTORATE GENERAL OF CUSTOMS,

PEKING, 20 February. 1922.

Dear Sir,

I am directed by the Inspector General inform you that your S/O Letter No. 242, dated 9th February. 1922, has been duly received.

Yours truly,

P. Shone
Actg. Private Secretary.

E. Alabaster Esquire
Wenchow.

CUSTOM HOUSE,

S/O NO. 243.   Wenchow, 27th February, 1922.

INITIALS.
Arrival of new
Superintendent.

Mr. Garwood contem-
plates marriage:
Mr. Chang King-shuen
still ill.

Dear Sir Francis,

  The new Superintendent arrived on the 22nd instant, and we have exchanged visits. He seemed friendly: somewhat apprehensive of the general situation: and relieved to find that no questions remained over for him. After some time without the presence locally of a Superintendent it is something of a novelty to possess one.

  Mr. Garwood, Assistant Examiner, contemplates marrying the woman (Macanese) with whom he lives, in the interest of his child I gather. He will shortly report his intention. — We are all well. — Mr. Chang King-shuen — Chinese Clerk on 4 months sick leave — has passed his leave here and shows no improvement. He understands that he is expected to report

SIR FRANCIS A AGLEN K. B. E.,
Inspector General of Customs,
 PEKING.

2.

report at Shanghai at the close of ~~this month,~~ March

K)UES.

Nothing further has transpired: and I have arranged matters with Ningpo.

Dr Plummer is returning shortly to the Methodist Mission here, I understand, together with a trained nurse: and as Dr. Bury is also still here (waiting a steamer for England in June) assisting Dr. Stedeford, we are somewhat unusually well-off in this department.

Yours truly,

[A.—42]

INSPECTORATE GENERAL OF CUSTOMS,

S/O

PEKING, 20 March 1922.

Dear Sir,

I am directed by the Inspector General to inform you that your S/O letter No. 243, dated 27th February 1922, has been duly received.

Yours truly,

P. Shone

Actg. Private Secretary.

E. Alabaster, Esquire

Henchow.

S/O NO. 244.

CUSTOM HOUSE,

Wenchow, 9th March, 1922.

Dear Sir Francis,

ficial Light
chow despatch
648).

The Coast Inspector's comments of 2nd instant do not make it quite clear whether or not he recommends that a Notice to Mariners should be issued. Seeing that the light in question is visible 20 miles off, according to the master of the S.S. "Haean", the location and general nature of the light, and the fact that it is not under Maritime Customs administration, ought I think to be publicly notified generally - especially with the approach of the typhoon season - to avoid any possibility of confusion or accident. One of the Chuang brothers visited the Custom House the other day with his Chinese charts.

Association,
tion of, in view
evalent piracy.

The local newspaper (cutting attached) reports the formation of a Junk Association here

SIR FRANCIS A AGLEN K. B. E.,
    Inspector General of Customs,
        PEKING.

2.

here, protection against the prevalent piracy being an object mentioned in this connexion. This looks like a preliminary to the resurrection of the hu shang chü under some other name as anticipated by me: for it is as sure as anything can be that fees will be collected. The ineffectiveness of official action against pirates - although somewhat greater activity appears to have been displayed of late - gives plausibility to this undertaking. But the conception at bottom is, I am sure, money making. I should not be surprised if the fee collecting by the promoters of the above unofficial light proved to be an additional incentive. These things constitute trespass on administrative prerogative: but of course it is the administration itself which ultimately is responsible. We have got our Junk Dues anyway, if somewhat shorn: but I will watch developments closely.

Operation of
 ict Deliberative
 ns.

With a view, no doubt, to establish a vent for any surplus democratic sentiment two District bodies - originally authorised by the Central Government but not so far operated under the military régime, and being

a

3.

a local duplication of the Central Government and Provincial Civil representative mechanism insofar - have now been established here, as elsewhere in Chekiang, and in some other Provinces. The body of first instance is the District Assembly (縣議會) with popularly elected local representatives, in ratio to population, each member receiving $40 a month. From the District Assembly affairs pass to the Consultative Council (參事會) composed of a limited number of members, half elected by the District Assembly, and half nominated by the District Magistrate. Council meetings are to be held in the Magistrate's office with the Magistrate as Chairman. Whether these measures will suffice to enable the Administration to keep touch of the popular pulse in reality, remains to be seen. I am inclined to doubt it: and there are bound to be clashes between the official and unofficial representatives in the Council. Funds for upkeep are derived from the Local Account of the District Magistracy.

The

4.

The up roar in Hongkong gives these in authority to pause even in this Sleepy Hollow - not so sleepy, though, with the number of schools there are about.

9.	There is no doubt that satisfactory impetus is being created for the development of these, which are more particularly necessary in the mountainous southern and western parts of Chekiang with the absence of water routes. Soldiers are being employed, which is also satisfactory. I hear the use of the monorail is being advocated, somewhat at the expense of ordinary motor transit. I remember, about ten years since, the monorail was advocated in Anhwei: in a way - in other than the Brennan type, I think - it is specially suited for mountainous tracts, as deep cutting and tunnelling is thereby avoided largely. But motor transit and transport has vastly improved in ten years, so I hope the Road Authority will not be led away by others with, doubtless, an axe to grind. On this subject I append a translation of a set of the guiding Rules.

10.	Various local fatal cases which
appear

5.

ials: ex-Superin-
nt: new Superin-
ent.

appear to be plague have lately occurred and are now the subject of medical investigation.

I hear the ex-Superintendent is to engage in commercial undertakings at Hsin Hsü Chou [Kiangsu]. The new man is nervous re the Peking Government and perhaps uncertain as to whether or not he shall place his money on the Anfu - Chang Tso-lin - South combination.

Yours truly,

Haburo W C.

Append

6.

APPEND.

Concise Rules regarding the building of a Provincial Road by soldiers and workmen under the supervision of the District Magistrate, presented by the Provincial Road Bureau (省道籌備處), to the Military and Civil Governors.

ROUTE: Hangchow - Hsiao Shan (蕭山) - Ch'eng Hsien (嵊縣) - Hsin Ch'ang (新昌) - Tien T'ai (天台) - Lin Hai (臨海) - Huang Yen (黃巖) - Wen Ling (溫嶺) - Yotsing (樂清) - Yung Chia (永嘉) - Jui An (瑞安) - Ping Yang (平陽) - Fukien border.

RULES: 1. These rules are drawn up by reason of the Magistrate also being appointed special official delegate for Road Construction (修築省道特派員).

2. It is the duty of the Magistrate to purchase land, etc.: and no other delegate is appointed by the Bureau.

3. Should trouble arise between soldiers and people, it is for the Magistrate to settle it in co-operation with the chief military officer on duty.

4. Should the local people create trouble, the Magistrate shall adjust such conjointly with the District Engineer.

5

7.

5. Should personal advice and inspection be required, the Magistrate will have to arrange accordingly.
6. In addition to the various reports addressed to the Military and Civil Governors a copy is required for the Provincial Road Bureau.
7. The services of Special Delegates are honorary: $50.00 as travelling expenses will however be allowed by the Provincial Road Bureau calculated from the time of beginning work until its completion in the particular district.
8. These rules will operate from the date of issue.

INSPECTORATE GENERAL OF CUSTOMS,

PEKING, 30th March 19 22.

S/O.

Dear Mr. Alabaster,

I have duly received your S/O letter No. 244 of the 9th March.

<u>Unofficial Light (Wenchow Desp. No. 3648): C.I's comments do not make it quite clear whether or not he recommends that a notice to Mariners be issued.</u>

I myself think that a notice to Mariners is called for. Please raise the question with the C.I. if you are in doubt.

Yours truly,

E. Alabaster, Esquire,
    Wenchow.

CUSTOM HOUSE,

S/O NO. 245.   Wenchow, 30th March 1922.

Superintendent:
Departure of, for
Shanghai for few
days.

Dear Sir Francis,

    The Superintendent has gone to Shanghai for a few days, he tells me. I wonder if he will adopt his predecessor's method, and remain permanently at that place. Possibly the political pulse needed closer personal investigation. I find him personally pleasant and accommodating: and of course as he has been so much abroad he understands foreign ways and customs. He appears to rely a good deal on his Office manager, a Mr. Shen Ming (沈銘), who graduated at the Customs College and was formerly in the Customs at Shanghai.

Compendium.

    This takes up most of my spare time, and is now getting a considerable move on.

We

SIR FRANCIS A AGLEN K. B. E.,
   Inspector General of Customs,
      PEKING.

2.

**um Burning and
  oking.**

We shall shortly have to have a small burning of the drug. There is any amount of smoking locally, but very little of the drug comes our way. I hear that two detectives paid a visit to the Acting Manager (Clerk) of the C.M.S.N. Co. here the other day. The detectives made a search of the premises and took possession of various opium smoking requisites: a bribe, however, settled the case, but not before the work of the Company's Office had been seriously incommoded, and the S.S. "Haean" delayed. The actual Wenchow Manager of the Company is usually in Shanghai.

**Chang King-shuen left
  r Shanghai.**

Mr. Chang King-shuen left for Shanghai on the 22nd, in a very bad state.

Yours truly,

CUSTOM HOUSE,

S/O NO. 246.   Wenchow, 18th April 1922.

Dear Sir Francis,

erintendent.   The Superintendent has not yet returned from Shanghai: he went there, partly, to meet his brother (the Minister in Japan) en route to Peking.

antile organisations:
tivity of: rice for
nk's use.   The Chamber of Commerce, and individual merchants (gingered up by that organisation) have lately been getting restless again, the latest enquiry being as to the number of bags of rice allowable for junk's use. The Port rule is a fixed number of bags per vessel - the latter divided into large, medium or small; irrespective however of distance, or number of crew. In some cases this allowance might prove to be too little: but in others, also, too liberal. I am looking into this question, which has

several

SIR FRANCIS A AGLEN K.B.E.,
    Inspector General of Customs,
        P E K I N G.

several sides to it, with a view to meet the desires of the traders as far as is reasonably possible, and I may have to report to you. The Junk Dues procedure appears to be operating without incident: though occasionally traders come to me enquiring as to certain points. I deal with all such personally. Indeed much of my time is given up to seizure cases so as to ensure by thorough enquiry that absolute justice is done. Cases of reputed substitution, in particular, need close examination and, not seldom, reference to the Shanghai Appraiser.

anese sailing vessel th auxiliary motor wer desires to rade inland under W.S.N. Rules.

The Chinese agent of a Japanese sailing vessel (of 112 tons) with auxiliary motor power, asked me for permission to trade under I.W.S.N. Rules. In view of your Circulars Nos. 2,767, 1761, 1734 I told him that I could not give him such authority. I understand he has now given up the idea: and that no question is to be raised with the Legation.

trade.

There seems to be some possibility of revival of our tea trade. I hear that four

3.

four new tea firms have opened and that orders for some 1,600 tea chests have been given by them. Possibly some hopes are entertained of American enquiries.

de and Revenue.
The Native Customs trade and Revenue show some improvement for the year to date, and make a better showing than the Maritime Customs. Contrasted with the unfortunate situation last year, we are now exporting rice.

ff: Messrs Hirano
d Garwood.
I am keeping Mr. Hirano until his successor arrives and gets some sort of grip of the work. - Mr. Garwood, Assistant Examiner, is reporting his intention to marry. His fiancée is the woman with whom he is living: and he is, I believe, marrying her in the interest of his child (see S/O No. 243) for although we have not in our law legitimatio per subsequens matrimonium. Mr. Garwood thinks his child will by his marriage enjoy a better position.

ness.
There is a good deal of cerebro-spinal-meningitis current.

-Christian
itation.
I hear three emissaries of the
anti-Christian

Anti-Christian Organisation have arrived and are endeavouring to stir up trouble.

Yours truly,

INSPECTORATE GENERAL OF CUSTOMS,

PEKING, 23rd May 1922.

S/O.

Dear Mr. Alabaster,

I have duly received your S/O letter No. 246 of the 18th April.

<u>Junk Dues procedure operating without incident.</u>

I hope everything will go on smoothly after you leave and that they will not take the opportunity of a change of Commissioner to raise the question now happily settled !

Yours truly,

E. Alabaster, Esquire,
  Wenchow.

CUSTOM HOUSE,

S/O NO. 247.   Wenchow, 6th May 1922.

Dear Sir Francis,

I expect Mr. Williams and family to-morrow, and we shall be leaving this port on or about the 10th for Shanghai. Dentistry will detain us a few days in the latter place and I anticipate arriving in Chinkiang on or about the 17th instant.

re: arrival of Mr. de Bodisco.

Mr. de Bodisco arrived on the 29th April. He is in the General Office. He appears to be a gifted man: and a nice fellow. He is taking up Chinese seriously.

I trust no untoward developments are occurring at Peking. It must be a trying time.

Yours truly,

E. Haburs W.

FRANCIS A AGLEN K. B. E.,
Inspector General of Customs,
    PEKING.

INSPECTORATE GENERAL OF CUSTOMS,

PEKING, 27th May 1922

S/O.

Dear Mr. Williams,

I have duly received Mr. Alabaster's S/O letter No. 247 of the 6th May.

<u>Commr. hopes that no trouble has been caused by the fighting round Peking.</u>

No: we have never been in any danger.

Yours truly,

C. Williams, Esquire,
WENCHOW.

CUSTOM HOUSE,

S/O No. 248.   Wenchow, 20th May 1922.

Dear Sir Francis,

tival.
    I arrived on the 7th instant, accompanied by my wife, three children, and nursery governess. My eldest son remains at school in England. We were detained in Shanghai for several days until a steamer was available. All the family are well, and we have settled down comfortably in our house.

rge.
    Since taking over charge on the 9th, I have been chiefly occupied in studying the local regulations.

nese Officials.
    Mr. Alabaster personally conducted me on a round of visits to the Superintendent's Secretary, officiating in the absence of the Superintendent, the Magistrate, and the Taoyin, and they have duly returned my calls.

                                Superintendent

FRANCIS A AGLEN K.B.E.,
Inspector General of Customs,
    PEKING.

Superintendent Hu Wei-hsien (胡惟賢) returned on the 17th, when I sent in my card, and he called on me yesterday.

trict Assembly.
The District Assembly (縣議會) - vide Mr. Alabaster's S/O No. 244 of 9th March - started to function on the 1st instant.

um seizure.
A seizure of 10 taels of native opium was made by Watcher Lin T'ing-fang (林廷芳) from a Chinese passenger on S.S. "Kwangchi" on the 10th instant. The passenger was detained and handed over to the Superintendent, who asked that the seizing officer should be sent with the opium to the local court when the case was to be tried on the 16th. I sent the opium, in accordance with the instructions of I.G. Circular No. 3118, and asked for its return when the case was settled, but stated that unfortunately the Watcher could not be spared from his duties.

ates.
Seven pirates, captured by the Wenchow Maritime Police (外海水上警察) off Pei

3.

al efforts for
overy of Shantung
lway.

Pei Lu Island (北鹿), were shot in the south-east corner of the city on the 15th, and not, as in former cases, within view of the Commissioner's house!

On the 16th instant there was a demonstration on the part of the students of the 10th Normal School,&c.and some of the gentry, who paraded the streets with flags, and styled themselves 永嘉籌金贖路會 . They distributed leaflets inviting subscriptions for the purpose of raising funds for the redemption of the Shantung Railway from Japan.

Yours truly,

C.A.S. Williams

INSPECTORATE GENERAL OF CUSTOMS,

PEKING, 5th June, 1922.

ar Sir,

I am directed by the Inspector General form you that your S/O letter No. 248, 20th May 1922, has been duly ved.

Yours truly,

B. Stone

Ass't. Private Secretary.

J. Williams, Esquire.

Wenchow.

永嘉籌金贖路會游行大會底宣言

我們現將今日游行底目的，大略說明一下，並要請大家注意。

你們還記得那年為了山東問題去抵制劣貨嗎？這個爭持累年的懸案，到了去年華會開幕的時候，我國以全國人民的奔走呼號，政府及國民代表的折衝樽俎；和英美各國的善意調停；繞得若強人意的結果。因為山東問題的焦點，全在膠濟鐵路；日人已先許於五年期內，由中國用三千萬圓，把該路贖回。——這不是很可欣喜嗎？現在的政府，天天在那裏鬧窮，那裏籌得出這許多款子，只好聽國民備款贖回，把該路作為民有；從此這種偉大的責任，都要我國民擔負了；這種特殊的權利，此要歸我國民享受了。

但是到了限期，若籌不出這宗鉅款來，不但貽笑外邦，增人家的蔑視，且使國際的地位，國民的人格，都要到萬劫不復的地步，這真是可為寒心啊！然而國民有了熱熱的愛國心，努力進行，鉅款並不難集；現在京津滬杭各處，已經有許多人從事募款；我們同是國民，應當和全國各界，取一致的行動。此次籌款贖路，並不是慈善事業，也不是等於納稅；簡直是一種經營事業的性質。膠濟鐵路的所在地，都是富饒繁盛之區。——自濟南至膠州長約七百餘里——日人在那裏經營許怎嗎了，現在的政府，天天在那裏鬧窮，那裏籌得出這許多款子，只好聽國民備款贖回，把該路作為民有；從此這種偉大的責任，都要我國民擔負了；這種特殊的權利，此要歸我國民享受了。

但是到了限期，若籌不出這宗鉅款來，不但貽笑外邦，增人家的蔑視，且使國際的地位，國民的人格，都要到萬刼不復的地步，這真是可為寒心啊！然而國民有了熱熱的愛國心，努力進行，鉅款並不難集；現在京津滬杭各處，已經有許多人從事募款；我們同是國民，應當和全國各界，取一致的行動。此次籌款贖路，並不是慈善事業，也不是等於納稅；簡直是一種經營事業的性質，取一致的行動。此次籌款贖路，膠濟鐵路的所在地，都是富饒繁盛之區。——自濟南至膠州長約七百餘里——日人在那裏經營許多年，賺了不少的利質。我們贖回之後，這種特殊的權利，都要歸我們享受；要是放棄了責任，現在捨不得出錢，將來想「不勞而獲」，那是不可能的事！

我們聯合各團體，今天出發遊行，就是以最誠懇的意思，作普徧的宣傳；促大家真正的覺悟；踴躍投資，務達贖回膠濟鐵路底目的。你們須知歷來的「愛國」運動，仍然不是實力的運動，只是紙面上的筆墨運動，和口頭上的口舌運動。——這是中國人的大病！祇有贖路這一件事，正是國民掃除積弊試驗實力的絕妙時機！我的可愛的同胞們！你們不願意隨落人格嗎？起！起！！起！！！快來擔任這實驗愛國的運動，博中華民國無上底光榮！

最後我們還要聲明一句：今天的大遊行，只是擔任宣傳，並不經收款項。你們若踴躍輸將，自有銀行存貯。將來還有詳細的辦法奉告，現在不重贅了。

今天为什么大游行呢？因为劝告我父老兄弟姊妹们快去筹金。为什么要筹金呢？就是要向日本赎回胶州诸位读者这条铁路是山东的门户，也是我们中国最重要的交通机关。所以去年太平洋国会议的时候，我们中国的代表就提议收回这路的问题。当时已经各国赞成，日本不得己要中国以五千三百万马克之欵（申中国三千五百余万元赎回但是我们政府没有这许多的金钱难能凑足了，那笔欵只好由我们人民担此责任，募捐集股，好把这个目的达到了。如果不能够赎回，恐怕连跌利远给日本占有了。那么我同胞还争什么利权，要雪什麽国耻呢？所以今天特地劝我们父老兄弟姊妹们努力！猛着！

省立第十师校全体启

S/O No. 249.

CUSTOM HOUSE,
Wenchow, 3rd June 1922.

:intendent.

:r Coins.

Dear Sir Francis,

I have established cordial relations with the Superintendent, and have duly returned his visit referred to in my last s/o.

With reference to my despatch No. 3662, in which I recommended the continuation of the application of the Currency Bureau's Rules (I.G. Circular No. 3300) to the Native Customs as heretofore, I have just received a despatch from the Superintendent transmitting the Shui-wu Ch'u's ruling that the passengers allowance in Chekiang province is not to exceed 1,000 1-cent pieces (vide I.G. despatch No. 1020/84,127), but, as before, no mention is made of the Native Customs. I anticipate further Circular instructions in this matter.

A

FRANCIS A AGLEN K.B.E.,
Inspector General of Customs,
PEKING.

2.

e strike.

A seizure of 6,480 copper cents was made by the Native Customs on the 25th May ex S.S. "Pingyang", and I duly notified the Superintendent as directed in I.G. Circular No.3296, N.C. No. 281.

On the 27th May at 9 a.m. a member of the crew of C.M.S.N. Co's S.S. "Haean" (海晏) struck a coolie working cargo and severely injured him, with the result that all the other coolies went on strike. The offender was sentenced to two months imprisonment, and the coolies returned to work on the following day.

y.

I received a petition on the 1st instant from the owner of the Lorcha "Chin Jui K'ang" (金瑞康) who reported that on the 22nd May the vessel was boarded off Shih p'u (石浦) by 20 pirates, who took her to a place near P'ingyang (平陽), where they went ashore and attacked an alum factory, etc. A considerable amount of booty - including some money from the A.P.C. agency - was put on board the lorcha, and four natives of the place were held for ransom. The

3.

The lorcha was then taken to Taichow Bay where the four prisoners and the booty were transferred to small junks, and the lorcha released; she entered here minus 14 boxes of soap, a bag of sugar, etc., her Tonnage Dues Certificate, and her Manifest. I transmitted a copy of the petition to the Superintendent, for the information of the Maritime Police. I think there should be more wireless stations on the Chekiang Coast, in communication with a fleet of fast motor vessels, armed with machine guns, to deal effectively with the pirates infesting the archipelago, and they could also put down the growing of opium in the islands.

Bungalow.   With reference to my despatch No. 3666 proposing the provision of a staff bungalow, Mr. Alabaster has just written to me saying that Mr. Heywood, of the Methodist Mission, Wenchow, informed him that the mission recently acquired a fair sized hill site for $30, though no doubt he had a slight pull. Mr. Alabaster further-more remarked that he would have urgently requested
you

4.

464

you to sanction the building of a bungalow, probably on the knoll just above the missionaries' site, had he remained on at this Port.

As land is so cheap, the C.I.M. are trying to get some to build on, and now is the opportunity for us to get our pick first. It seems that it is government land, rented for a nominal sum to the farmers for growing sweet potatoes, and it might even be possible to get some for nothing! It is probable, however, that the influx of outsiders may slightly raise the values, and it will be necessary to do a little levelling.

I paid a visit of inspection with the Tidesurveyor to the site proposed, which is about 1,400 feet high, just above the Methodist bungalow on the Ta Tien Mountain (大田山) across the river, and it adjoins a good spring and a swimming pool. It takes about two hours to get there. I may mention that the Customs doctor goes up frequently during the summer, and he strongly recommends the position. It commands a fine view down the river, while the sea, 20 miles away, is

sometimes

sometimes visible. Given a summer bungalow, this should be a good place to send married men to. Now that salaries are increased, there will be more married employés to be provided for.

I sincerely hope that you will favourably consider this scheme, and perhaps a Clerk of Works could be sent up to report on it.

Yours truly,

INSPECTORATE GENERAL OF CUSTOMS,

PEKING, 19th June 1922.

S/O.

Dear Mr. Williams,

I have duly received your S/O letter No. 249 of the 3rd June.

<u>Piracy on the Chekiang Coast: Commr. suggests that more Wireless Stations in communication with a fleet of fast armed motor vessels are necessary to keep piracy in check.</u>

How is a bankrupt Government going to pay for such things?

Yours truly,

C.A.S. Williams, Esquire,
    WENCHOW.

CUSTOM HOUSE,

S/O No. 250. Wenchow, 16th June 1922.

Closing of British Consulate.

Dear Sir Francis,

I received a letter last week, dated 30th May, from Mr. V.L. Savage, H.B.M.'s Consul for Ningpo and Wenchow, saying that the British Government has decided to abolish their Consular Office at Wenchow. He proposed to come here, accompanied by his wife, to close the Office, and asked me to have crates made to pack up all the Office furniture.

I replied offering to put up Mr. and Mrs. Savage during their stay (I knew him 18 years ago in Hankow), and said I would be glad to have the crates made for him. They were due to arrive last Sunday, but I hear they missed their connection in Shanghai, and therefore have to wait another week.

The

FRANCIS AGLEN K.B.E.,
Inspector General of Customs,
  PEKING.

2.

The Consulate here is at present rented for $60.00 a month for the use of the Tidesurveyor, two rooms being retained as Consular Offices, and we made an offer to buy it for $7,500.00 which was refused. When the Office is definitely closed, I shall write to H. B. M.'s Office of Works and propose a reduction of rent to $40.00 in accordance with the suggestion made in I.G. despatch No. 1077/88,378.

When the Office is formally closed I shall report to you officially.

Tax objected to plomatic Body.

Mr. C. Cance, local agent for the British American Tobacco Co., circulated a Consular Notification, by request of the British Consul at Ningpo, on the 10th inst., which reads as follows:-

"The Diplomatic Body having objected as
"regards their respective nationals to the
"collection, by means of stamps, of
"revenue not provided by Treaty in the
"way of surcharges in connection with the
"Railways, Telegraphs, Post-offices and
steamship

3.

"steamship lines of China, British
"subjects and the subjects of other
"Treaty Powers at Ningpo are hereby
"warned that they are in no way called
"upon to pay such surcharges. Any
"attempt to enforce the collection of
"such illegal surcharges should be
"reported to the undersigned, who has
"already addressed a protest to the
"Local Authorities on the subject."
I presume this refers to the Stamp Tax,
which I believe has been instituted by the
Chiao-t'ung Pu to secure funds for famine
relief. What should be our attitude in
regard to this question?

Post Office.   With reference to my despatch No.3669
proposing an increase of the nominal rent
paid by the Chinese Post Office for two
rooms on our premises, I had a visit from
the Chinese Postmaster on the 8th inst. I
did not mention the matter of rent, but I
elicited from him the fact that the Post
Office has acquired some land in the centre
of the city, on which a Post Office will
       eventually

4.

eventually be built, though I gathered that, the Postal building programme being a large one, it will be some years before Wenchow is dealt with. When the Post Office ultimately vacates our two rooms, we could perhaps turn one into a Tidewaiters' Waiting Room, and add the other to the Customs Club alongside, so we can make good use of them. They are not suitable for quarters. I think the Post Office will certainly agree, in the meantime, to pay the increased rental, which is less than what they would have to pay elsewhere. I see no reason why we should continue to rent these premises at a pecuniary loss.

Coins.   Is it correct to assume that I.G. Circular No. 3312, N.C. No. 286 applies also to copper coins *exported* from this province? In the meantime I have withdrawn our notification allowing passengers to carry 5,000 copper cents (*Vide* Wenchow despatch No. 3662, N.C. No. 290 and S/O No. 249).

tion Work.   With reference to my despatch No. 3672 of to-day's date reporting how I propose

to

5.

to carry on examination of export cargo on the reclaimed foreshore lot, I had a visit on the 15th inst. from Mr. Shên Ming (沈銘), who said that the Superintendent fully concurred with my general plan of improving the facilities as regards dealing with export cargo, and would do what he could to persuade the C.M.S.N. Co. to cooperate, and he would also endeavour to effect the removal of the small house which obstructs the roadway and thereby interferes with the ingress and egress of cargo brought for examination.

Mr. C.A. de Bodisco, 3rd Assistant: B., seems to be acquainting himself thoroughly with General Office work, and I am helping him with advice as to his Chinese studies. He has settled down comfortably in his quarters, which have been renovated, and I am having an extra window made in his sitting room, as it is very dark owing to the lowness of the roof.

Watcher Lin T'ing-fang (林廷芳) has been ill with gastric ulcer for 12 days, but otherwise the health of the staff during this rather trying damp season (霉天) is very satisfactory.

satisfactory.

"qualified practitioners".
According to I.G. Circular No. 3089, only Chinese Medical practitioners who hold diplômas of graduation from medical colleges conducted on western lines are to be accepted by us as "duly qualified" for the purpose of requisitioning for prohibited drugs.

I see that the Chinese Government has now ordained that no doctors will be allowed to practice unless they qualify by special examination for a diplôma as Doctor of medicine (醫師). The local examinations were held here in the Police Headquarters on the 1st inst., but many doctors did not present themselves for examination, owing either to lack of money to pay the high entrance fees demanded, or to fear of possible disqualification and they continue to exercise the art of healing (?) with impunity.

Yours truly,

Ca S William P.

INSPECTORATE GENERAL OF CUSTOMS.

S/O.

PEKING, 3rd July 1922.

Dear Mr. Williams,

I have duly received your S/O letter No. 250 of the 16th June.

<u>Stamp Tax objected to by the Diplomatic Body: Consular Notification circulated in this connection.</u>

The notification appears to me to be a very silly one. For services rendered - telegraphs, post and railways - the Chinese Govt. has a perfect right to collect what charges it sees fit to impose in any manner it may find convenient.

Yours truly,

C.A.S. Williams, Esquire,
   WENCHOW.

CUSTOM HOUSE,

S/O No. 251.   Wenchow   1st July 1922.

Tank Installations.

Dear Sir Francis,

In my despatch No. 3674 I reported that the Chinese Authorities have at length accorded their approval of the Standard Oil Installation here. It seems curious that, on account of a legal quibble about a minute piece of adjoining ground, their approval should have been withheld for over three years, and I think there must have been other factors at work which do not appear officially. On the other hand the dislocation of the Provincial Government may have afforded an opportunity for the Superintendent to act more or less on his own responsibility.

It

FRANCIS AGLEN K. B. E.,
Inspector General of Customs,
  PEKING.

2.

It is extremely likely that the Asiatic Petroleum Company and the Texas Oil Company will both try to obtain permission to put up installations here in the near future, but it remains to be seen whether the officials will adopt a similarly obstructive policy in their case. Personally I think that, in the interests of trade, the Customs ought to have more say in the matter of the establishment of oil installations. In the case of the Standard Oil Company, the Commissioner of Customs was appealed to by the Company but was practically ignored by the officials.

You ask in your S/O of 19th June how a bankrupt government can pay for such things as armed motor vessels to check piracy in the manner suggested in my S/O No. 249. The solution of this problem is undoubtedly by retrenchment in other departments where unnecessary or less necessary expenses are incurred. I think it is quite within our province to make suggestions, as piracy has an adverse effect on trade, and

ipso

3.

ipso facto on our revenue receipts (vide Wenchow despatch No. 3604 of 1921 reporting that piracy along the Chekiang coast is a severe menace to the lorcha trade under the Chinese flag).

I admit the financial position of the country is somewhat precarious at present, but when the troops are disbanded, funds will be released for other purposes, and it might be possible to effect some saving in our own expenses as well, and thereby render some assistance in helping to raise funds for checking piracy.

The Native Customs Weiyüan do no work and should, in my opinion, be withdrawn. To my mind the issue of three-tenths of the net proceeds of fines and confiscations to the Superintendents, who all draw good salaries and have very little work to do, should be discontinued, as they do not assist in the making or deciding of the seizure cases. Funds secured by such savings as this would be more useful to go towards the financing of the efficient

checking

4.

checking of piracy.

tical situation.　　The situation here is quiet on the surface but there are undercurrents of unrest. Although Lu Yung-hsiang (盧永祥) has ceased to assume the title of Tuchün he has contituted himself 浙江軍務善後督辦 and still retains control over the troops, which hardly alters his position as military chief, in spite of the optimism of the Peking papers. He appears to be against the proposed dismissal of General Ho Fêng-lin (何豐林), Defence Commissioner of Shanghai in charge of the Arsenal, with whom he is on terms of friendship. Some time ago, on account of the decision of the Central Government to adopt a similar measure, hostilities very nearly ensued between Chekiang and Kiangsu.

　　On the 25th June the Superintendent and Taoyin sent their families away to Shanghai, from which it may be inferred that they are apprehensive of trouble arising with the local troops. I believe the Taoyin is non persona grata with the local T'uan Chang, who supports Lu Yung-hsiang, and I expect he will have to leave the port. The Superintendent

5.

Superintendent is evidently sitting on the fence and will probably go to Shanghai at the first sign of difficulty arising. Wenchow, however, has the reputation of being a quiet place, and I do not anticipate any rioting on the part of the military unless their pay is in arrears.

for famine relief.
On the 15th June the broker Chi Chi Hsin (吉記新) applied for the exportation of 450 bags of rice weighing piculs 661.50 to Hangchow via Shanghai for famine relief, under Provincial Governor's Huchao. As the period for passing famine rice free of duty expired at the end of May, permission to ship was refused, whereupon the Superintendent strongly urged me to allow the shipment in question, and I passed it on deposit of full and half duty under authority of I.G. Circular No. 2316. I see by the local paper that the Society for the Protection of Food Interests (民食維持會) protested to the Superintendent against this reduction of the food supplies.

It appears to me that the Superintendent, in thus going against the wishes of
the

ms College.

the people, is unduly interested in the exportation of rice.

  Some of the students in the Methodist College here have expressed the desire to enter for examination for the Customs College. I think it would be a good plan to have a form to be filled in by Candidates for the College giving full particulars and a list of questions to answer giving names, age, address, scholastic attainments, parents, references, etc. Then when applicants come forward, blank forms can be supplied to them. May I venture to suggest that this proposal be passed on to Mr. MacDonald in case it may be of any practical value.

         Yours truly,

         C. A. S. Williams.

INSPECTORATE GENERAL OF CUSTOMS.

S/O.　　　　　　　PEKING, 12th July 1922.

Dear Mr. Williams,

I have duly received your S/O letter No. 251 of the 1st July.

Marking of covers containing S/O letters.

Please mark covers 'S/O' in top left-hand corner.

Commr's views on retrenchment: the Native Customs Weiyüan do no work and should be withdrawn.

Of course they should but it is easier said than done: there is such a thing as 'face' in China !

Yours truly,

C.A.S.Williams,Esquire,
　　WENCHOW.

S/O No. 252.   Wenchow   15th July   22

ition of Likin and
ease of Customs

Dear Sir Francis,

With reference to my despatch No. 3679, N.C.No.293, reporting that the Superintendent wishes me to provide details for the drawing up of a scheme for the carrying out of the proposed abolition of Likin and corresponding increase of Customs duty, I have no doubt that the Ts'ai-chêng Pu has already approached you through the Ch'u in the matter.

I have written to the Hangchow and Ningpo Commissioners to enquire what their line of action is, as I should imagine the Superintendents at those ports are also attempting to "work" them as well.

Possibly

FRANCIS AGLEN K.B.E.,
Inspector General of Customs,
    PEKING.

2.

Possibly all that is required is a few suggestions, such as are given with great clarity in Mr. Wong's Memo. appended to the above-mentioned despatch.

I wonder when and where* the so-called Special Conference (特別會議) is to be convened for dealing with the scheme when it is duly cut and dried.

The Provincial Authorities seem to be in a terrible hurry to collect some information for the Ts'ai-chêng Pu, though they do not specify exactly what they want - perhaps because they do not know! I wrote a noncommittal letter to the Superintendent, saying that I was going carefully into the matter, but could not give him a reply without due consideration.

tic Petroleum any's prospective Installation at how.

I received a visit on the 11th instant from Commander G.F. Mulock, D.S.O., R.N. (retd), who is in charge of the Marine and Shipping Department of the Asiatic Petroleum Company at Shanghai.

He asked me for assistance in the matter of taking soundings in the vicinity

*I have just noticed in the Peking Daily News of the 8th inst. that the Conference is to be convened in Peking and "shall of formulate for the approval of the Powers concerned a detailed plan for the constitution of the Board of Reference".

3.

of a site on the north bank of the river down stream, 9 li from Wenchow City, outside the Harbour Limits, just above the Standard Oil Co.'s Installation, where his firm has acquired some land, with, he asserted, the permission of the local authorities, for the erection of an oil installation. He further stated that it was also the intention of the Company to install an oil receiving pontoon at that spot.

He requested me to make arrangements for a fresh survey of the river to be made, as he had heard that the channel is continually shifting, and he wished to compare the present position of the silt with the position in 1919 - when the last corrections to the Customs chart were made - with a view to deciding whether it would be advisable to engage in elaborate building on the Company's site or not.

He further asked for the loan of my private houseboat for a week or so for survey work, and for the Harbour Master to accompany him to assist in the process.

While

4.

While placing my houseboat entirely at his disposal, and showing him our charts, etc., I regretted being unable to spare the services of the Harbour Master, and told him that it was very unlikely that the Service would undertake a fresh survey of the river at present, as it would cost a considerable sum of money, and would be of no advantage, except for his particular needs, seeing that we take local soundings to keep ourselves acquainted with the channel, and supply pilots to ships if necessary.

He then proceeded in my houseboat, accompanied by the Chief Officer of the China Merchants S.S. "Haean", to carry out his survey operations; on the departure of the "Haean", he continued the work alone, or in company with the local agent of his firm, and is now exploring the various reaches of the river, and living in the boat. I have offered to put him up when his work is finished, until he is able to get a steamer from this port in about a week's time.

With

5.

cf.

With reference to my S/O of 16th ultimo, in which I stated that Watcher Lin T'ing-fang (林廷芳) was ill with gastric ulcer, this employé, after an illness of about three weeks, has now recovered. His father, T'ingch'ai Lin Yin-ch'iu (林银秋), whose death occurred on the 27th ultimo, as reported in my telegram and application for Service Benefit, just after he had applied - for the second time - for permission to retire (vide Wenchow despatch No. 3673) has left an exceptionally good record behind him. He acted as Pilot for many years, and latterly as trainer of another man for that duty, and he held the Sixth Rank of Military Merit. He was not allowed to retire under the terms of the Superannuation and Retirement Rules last year when he wished to do so, and it seems hard that he should have died in harness without reaping the reward of his services. Possibly you may see fit, in these circumstances, to issue a special post-mortem gratuity to his son.

The

6.

ang Telegraphic
istration severs
llegiance to the
o-t'ung Pu.

The 甌海潮日報 of the 10th instant, records that Chu Tsung-yüan (諸宗元), Superintendent of the Chekiang Telegraphic Administration (who I believe is apprehensive of his dismissal by the Central Government) has received orders from Lu Yung-hsiang (盧永祥), who now styles himself 浙江軍務善後督辦兼戒嚴總司令, to take charge of the Chekiang Telegraphic Administration independently from the Chiao-t'ung Pu from the 1st instant. The Administration of the province will be controlled by four Chiefs (局長) who will control the circuits of 錢塘, 會稽, 甌海, and 金華 respectively, and all requisitions for supplies, and administrative questions, are to be referred through the Chiefs, by the Clerks in charge of the various offices, to the Superintendent, who is vested with plenary powers.

In this connection it is interesting to note that Fêng Ssǔ (馮思) a native of Canton and Chief of the local Telegraph Office, appointed by the Chiao-t'ung Pu, left this port on the 3rd instant for Peking. Formerly every Office had its own Chief. The

ndary Dragon Boat
lval.

The people of this old-world town take every possible opportunity to indulge in festivities of all kinds, and consequently they did not fail to profit by the fortuitous occurrence of the intercalary 5th moon to engineer an extra Dragon Boat Festival on the 5th day.

One of the dragon boats entered the canal inside the city, which is against the local regulations, and the police held it up under a bridge known as Tao-ch'iao (道橋). This caused great excitement among the population, who crowded on the bridge, the parapet of which collapsed, precipitating a number of persons into the water, while the dragon boat also capsized. It is reported that many people were drowned or injured, seven bodies being recovered on the following day.

cultural prospects.

There is every expectation that an exceptionally good crop of rice will be harvested in a week or two, provided there are no typhoons in the meantime.

Yours truly,

C.A.R. Williams.

INSPECTORATE GENERAL OF CUSTOMS,

S/O.

PEKING, 28th July 1922.

Dear Mr. Williams,

I have duly received your S/O letter No. 252 of the 15th July.

<u>Abolition of Likin and increase of Customs duty: Supt. asks Commr. to provide details in re. Hangchow and Ningpo written to, to find out if similar requests are being made by the Supts. there.</u>

I haven't heard of this request being made elsewhere. You may make general suggestions but don't go into detail.

<u>Commr. asks if, owing to the special circumstances of the case, a post-mortem gratuity could not be issued to the son of T'ingch'ai Lin Yin-ch'iu.</u>

I don't think this will be possible.

Yours truly,

C.A.S. Williams, Esquire,
    WENCHOW.

S/O No. 253.   Wenchow 29th July 22

Dear Sir Francis,

amation and bunding oreshore for examina- of cargo.

With reference to my despatch No. 3672 forwarding proposals as to the utilisation of certain reclaimed and bunded foreshore for examination of cargo, the work of paving is well under way, and the China Merchants S.N. Co. have constructed a gate between this property and the Company's wharf, at their own expense, as I suggested.

ition of Likin.

The Hangchow Commissioner informs me that he is not likely to be approached on the subject of abolition of Likin as there is no Native Customs at that port.

The Ningpo Commissioner states that the Ningpo Superintendent considers that this question is outside the realm of practical politics at present.

Meanwhile

FRANCIS AGLEN K.B.E.,
Inspector General of Customs,
   PEKING.

Meanwhile the local Superintendent continues to press me to draw up a "pan fa" for him, as reported in my despatch No.3679, N.C. No.293.

nese Counterfeit s.

With reference to my despatch No. 3682 reporting a seizure of counterfeit Japanese 50-sen pieces, and asking how to dispose of them, I had a visit on the 25th instant from the Acting Superintendent, who said he had found that the culprit had made himself scarce, but that he had written asking the Juian Magistrate to investigate and report. He was not in favour of letting the Japanese Authorities know anything at all about the matter, for fear they might take the opportunity to send officials here to investigate and make things generally unpleasant. He suggested that the coins should be destroyed at once. I am holding them however until I receive your instructions

rtation of rice.

The present market value of Wenchow rice is $6.25 to $7.50 per shih of 150 catties

catties compared with the Shanghai rate of $11.70 to $14.00. A profit of three or four thousand dollars may therefore be made on an average shipment of 500 shih.

It is extremely likely that every effort is being made to move rice from Wenchow by any possible means.

I have had many requests to pass rice - ostensibly for famine relief - under expired Huchao issued by the Provincial Governor, and to oblige the Superintendent, I have passed several lots on deposit of full and half duty on condition that valid Huchao are to be obtained, but, as it is quite possible that these Huchao have been bought or procured in some illegal manner, I doubt very much whether valid Huchao will ever be produced, so I propose to bring the duty to account two months from date. Would it be advisable to continue this procedure, or should I pass rice declared for famine relief free under guarantee without taking any deposit?

In my despatch No. 3681 I reported a case of free release of military rice
under

4.

under special circumstances. I am anxious to avoid doing anything unconstitutional, but conditions are somewhat peculiar, and the Superintendent always tries to force my hand and seems to object to my taking duty deposits for any rice.

I received your telegram on the 25th instructing me to pass 50,000 shih of rice exported from Wenchow and 50,000 from Taichow "under guarantee Chekiang Governor Huchao" for western Chekiang, but so far no applicant has come forward.

Absence of Superintendent.

The Superintendent left by S.S. "Haean" on the 22nd for Shanghai, where he has recently built himself a house, leaving his Secretary Mr. Shên Ming (沈銘) in charge.

Sale of old newspapers.

I have recently sold for $29.00 a number of ancient newspapers, which took up a great deal of valuable archive space, and were of no further value for purposes of reference. They were bought by the local soapstone

soapstone dealers for wrapping up their wares. I carried the proceeds to account under A/c.D: Recoveries from A/c.A.

erty purchase.
  With reference to my despatch No. 3680 applying for permission to complete the purchase of a piece of land adjoining the Commissioner's garden, as originally arranged, but at a slightly increased price, I sincerely hope you will favourably consider this proposition. It will be a great relief to get rid of our unsavoury neighbour, and square off our property in a shipshape manner. This adjoining land has been properly levelled, and it is really most desirable to acquire it.

      Yours truly,

      C.A.S. Williams.

INSPECTORATE GENERAL OF CUSTOMS,

PEKING, 16th August 1922.

S/O.

Dear Mr. Williams,

I have duly received your S/O letter No. 253 of the 29th July.

Commr. asks whether it is advisable to continue the procedure of passing rice on deposit of full and half duty on condition that valid Huchao are obtained or should he pass rice 'declared' for famine relief under guarantee without taking deposit.

Carry out instructions: I think you would certainly be wise to cover any departure from them by deposit of duty.

Yours truly,

C. A. S. Williams, Esquire,
WENCHOW.

S/O No. 254.   Wenchow   12th August 22

Dear Sir Francis,

ese Shipping Strike.   Mr. T. C. Szee, the local agent for the China Merchants S. N. Co., came to see me on the 11th, and told me he had received a telegram from his Head Office at Shanghai informing him that all China Merchants vessels are to cease work and stop running until further notice - presumably on account of the Chinese seaman's strike for higher wages.

If this state of affairs continues, this port will be greatly affected, as a good deal of cargo is held up awaiting shipment, and we rely entirely on Chinese steamers for our communication with the outside world, as well as for the majority of our foreign food supplies. It is to be hoped that the Post Office may be able
to

FRANCIS AGLEN K. B. E.,
Inspector General of Customs,
    PEKING.

2.

to get a mail through via Ningpo occasionally on the small launches, if they continue running, though, owing to the prevalence of typhoons at this season, it may be difficult. We are having a typhoon at the present time, and a certain amount of damage has been done to Chinese property up river, judging by the wreckage floating down stream.

Mr. H. Garwood, Assistant Examiner B, has left on transfer to Ningpo. Mr. Lu Si Ho, 4th Class Tidewaiter B, who has been appointed to replace him, has not yet arrived, being possibly delayed either by the shipping strike or the typhoon.

We shall now be rather weak as regards Out-door Officers, being left with only Mr. G. E. Cammiade, recently promoted Assistant Examiner B, who is Eurasian, and has not had much practice in examination work, and the new raw Chinese Tidewaiter due to arrive. This combination is not ideal, and may not be popular with the public. I am afraid a good deal of extra work will be
thrown

3.

thrown on the shoulders of the Tidesurveyor. We shall, however, do our best with the material at our disposal.

erty Purchase.

With reference to your despatch No. 1109/90,595 authorising the conclusion of the purchase of the plot projecting into the Commissioner's garden, I shall attempt to justify this expenditure by laying out the garden and tennis court to the best advantage. The addition of the new piece is much appreciated. I might mention that there is a good well in this plot. This will be most useful, as the water in our present well is unpalatable, and we have to use a public well outside, which often runs nearly dry.

osed Revision of
ve Customs Tariff.

In the table of Native Customs tariff articles forwarded in my despatch No. 3684, N. C. No. 294, I have only included those goods, the duty rates of which are too low as compared with those of the Ningpo and Shanghai tariffs and also with half

Maritime

Maritime Customs rates. Those goods whose rates, though lower than the Ningpo tariff, are already equal to or above half Maritime Customs rates, are not given, as the Ministry of Finance has only approved of a tariff based on the 2½ % <u>ad</u> <u>valorem</u> system; the Ningpo Office, however, exceeds this limit in many cases, and the Shanghai tariff frequently falls below it.

It might be a good plan to amalgamate the Ningpo and Wenchow tariffs (there being no other Native Customs controlled by us in this province), and re-compile them into one volume, to be styled the "Chekiang Native Customs Tariff". This would be a step towards the unification of the Native Customs tariffs of China, if the other provinces would adopt the same policy.

In the meantime a local revision is proposed. Your attention is called to the notes in the remarks column of the above-mentioned table.

Magistrate

5.

ents of Chinese	Magistrate Chang Lien (張濂) left
bials.	for Hangchow on the 2nd, and it is rumoured that Taoyin Lin K'un-hsiang (林鵾翔) will be replaced by a new incumbent, Yü Ta-chün (余大鈞), in the near future. Superintendent Hu Wei-hsien (胡維賢) is still in Shanghai.

et of Rice.	There is strong opposition here to the wholesale exportation of rice, and a grave suspicion that it never reaches the famine districts, but is sold in Shanghai for the benefit of a limited clique. There is also a feeling that the profits (estimated at $28,000 for 20,000 shih) should be devoted to public interests. I am doing all I can to check private exploitation.

less stations on Chekiang Coast.	With reference to my S/O No. 249 of 3rd June in which I suggested that, in my opinion, wireless stations should be installed on the Chekiang Coast to communicate with vessels detailed for the capture of piratical craft, I notice that it is reported in the local newspaper 新甌潮日報 of the 6th instant that

6.

that the virtual Generalissimo Lu Yung-hsiang (盧永祥) has recently decided to establish wireless installations along the Chekiang Coast. He is also said, by the way, to be recruiting more soldiers.

A fire broke out beyond the city wall near the East Gate at 2.30 p.m. on the 6th in a lard-reducing establishment, and a number of the surrounding buildings were burnt down. The conflagration was extinguished by 5 p.m., about a dozen streams being brought to bear upon it from the hand-pumps provided by the neighbouring temples. It was an extraordinary sight from the upper verandah of my house, to which the fire was quite near, most of the streams being directed from the adjacent city wall, which was thronged with crowds of people.

osed demolition of wall.

The local District Assembly lately proposed that the city wall be pulled down and a road built in its place, but
considerable

considerable objection has been raised on the grounds that the local "fêng-shui" would be adversely affected thereby. Very probably, however, the wall itself will settle the controversy by falling down of its own accord, as it has not been repaired within the memory of man.

Yours truly,

C. A. S. Williams.

INSPECTORATE GENERAL OF CUSTOMS,

S/O.

PEKING, 7th September 1922.

Dear Mr. Williams,

I have duly received your S/O letter No. 254 of the 12th August.

Local revision of Native Customs Tariff proposed.

I doubt whether this is quite the best moment to start attempting to raise the N.C. Tariff in a Province practically independent of the Central Govt. If there is local opposition, there is no chance of getting it through. Better keep an eye on the ground !

Yours truly,

[signature]

C.A.S.Williams, Esquire,
    WENCHOW.

S/O No. 255.   Wenchow   26th August   22

Dear Sir Francis,

orological
itions.
       As reported in my last S/O, there has been some damage to Chinese property in this district owing to the recent typhoon, which prevailed from the 11th to the 13th, and was followed by a torrential downpour of rain for two days, resulting in a freshet up river, the banks overflowing in certain parts and washing away houses, furniture, etc., which could be seen as they swept down stream. The current of the river became dangerously strong, and the Tidesurveyor was unable to come over on the 14th from his quarters on Conquest Island. There was subsequently a considerable drop in the temperature which came as a welcome relief

after

FRANCIS AGLEN K.B.E.,
Inspector General of Customs,
   PEKING.

after a long spell of hot weather.

age caused by the
hoon.

The Elephant Rock Beacon opposite the Custom House broke down on the 13th after the heavy storm, being probably struck by floating timber. It was recovered later in bad condition, and is now under repair; the Coast Inspector has been asked to supply a new lamp for it. A portion of the stone bunding on the Island fell in, and I am having it repaired at the expense of the British Office of Works as it endangers the Consulate. On the 14th the Japanese hulk snapped her moorings and drifted down on top of the Ningpo steamer hulk. S.L."Yungching" and various lorchas also drifted away down river. Our two lower buoys moved out of position, and the gig moorings were lost. The buoys have since been recovered, though their moorings are damaged. Great changes have taken place in the channel necessitating the taking of a fresh lot of soundings. A small island across the river, at the

mouth

3.

mouth of the North Creek, has been washed away entirely. The China Merchants' pontoon commenced to founder on the 14th, and I allowed the Company to pump her out with our fire hose. The telegraph office issued a notice on the 15th stating that the lines were interrupted owing to the floods in the neighbourhood, but the service was in working order again a few days later.

...mer communication. Owing to the seamen's strike we have had no direct steamer from Shanghai since the 5th but it is rumoured that the China Merchants S.N.Co. are sending up their S.S. "Feiching" on the 29th, which may mean that the strike is over. The small vessels from Ningpo commenced to run again a few days ago, so we are getting our mails again.

...enue. Owing to the strike and the typhoon our revenue has fallen, and I have been unable to make any remittances to Shanghai. When normal conditions are resumed, however, I hope the deficiency will be made up, as considerable

considerable stocks of cargo have been accumulated for exportation at the first available opportunity.

elopment of property.　　With reference to our recent acquisition of land adjoining the Commissioner's compound, I am addressing an official application to you shortly for authority to attend to the matter of boundary walls, etc. If you will allow me to carry out the work as recommended, I shall take the greatest interest in developing this property as a whole to the best advantage.

　　　　　　　　　Yours truly,

　　　　　　　　　C. A. S. Williams.

INSPECTORATE GENERAL OF CUSTOMS,

S/O.   PEKING, 4th October 1922.

Dear Mr. Williams,

I have duly received your S/O letter No. 255 of the 26th August.

Commr's account of the damage caused by typhoon.

We seem to have come off fairly well on the whole.

Yours truly,

C.A.S. Williams, Esquire,
    WENCHOW.

S/O No. 256.   Wenchow 14th September 22

Dear Sir Francis,

ere Typhoon.   A typhoon of unprecedented violence struck this port on the 11th instant, and not a single house in the city is intact. Fortunately there was very little loss of life except on the river, and the staff are all safe. The wind blew fiercely from 3 p.m. to 1 a.m. and was accompanied by heavy rain.

With regard to Customs property, I am glad to say that the Custom House has come off fairly well without any serious

FRANCIS AGLEN K. B. E.,
Inspector General of Customs,
    PEKING.

serious damage, but the Commissioner's House and Compound are in a very bad state, and the attached snapshot shows the manner in which the roof was stripped of the galvanised iron sheets and boarding. The compound walls, which were twelve feet high, are almost entirely destroyed! My wife and family took refuge during the night in the billiard room - the only comparatively dry spot in the house. Mr. Assistant Bodisco's quarters suffered rather badly, and he has only one room he can use. As his kitchen is damaged he is having his meals with us.

Building materials are at a premium and workmen almost unobtainable. The Customs boatmen are patching up the roofs temporarily. I am submitting an official report embodying a statement of all the necessary repairs.

ds.

In continuation of my S/O No. 255 giving details of the damage caused by the recent storms, I have had further reports that several neighbouring districts have been so badly flooded that the people are homeless and

and destitute. Chin-yün (縉雲) and Li-shui (麗水), in the Ch'uchou prefecture, seem to have been most adversely affected, and subscriptions have been raised for relief purposes, to which the members of the staff have contributed; in handing over the funds obtained I suggested to the Superintendent that a part of the money raised should, in my opinion, be devoted to the care and cultivation of trees on the hillsides, as the freshets in the river would not be so violent if the hills were not denuded of timber. This suggestion is being transmitted to the Provincial Authorities.

munications.

Steamer communication with Shanghai has now been resumed, but the telegraph system is again interrupted.

cy.

I received a petition complaining that the Chinese Lorcha Chin Yuan Feng (金源豐) was pirated at Ta T'ou Shan (大頭山) off Shih-p'u (石浦) on the 3rd instant, and I transmitted it to the
Superintendent.

4.

Superintendent. The pirates made off with the arms and ammunition carried by the vessel (theoretically) for defence purposes, together with a bag of dates and the clothing of the crew, and they also held the Captain for ransom. Pirates can always obtain arms in this simple manner!

osion.   A disastrous occurrence took place on the 29th ultimo in a shop near the South Gate, when, after lighting a lamp, a match was carelessly thrown down near three barrels of gunpowder, which exploded and brought down the building on the heads of the unfortunate occupants. Thirteen persons were killed and many injured. It is said that this gunpowder was discarded stock purchased from the military authorities for the alleged purpose of the manufacture of fireworks - though no fireworks had ever been made by that particular shop, and there is a strong suspicion that the powder was actually intended for conveyance to the pirates by the junk people. A meeting was
held

held by the fire-cracker makers, who decided that, in future, gunpowder should not be stored in the City in such quantities as to endanger life and property.

Customs Tariff.   With reference to Wenchow despatch No. 3684 proposing a slight revision of the Native Customs tariff, we made a seizure the other day of some hemp skin, falsely declared as hemp. The latter has a higher value but pays a lower duty than the former, on account of the fact that the duty rates have been reversed in the tariff by mistake - as pointed out in the above despatch. The merchants here are always trying to take advantage of the anomalies in the Native Customs tariff. I have just received your S/O of 7th instant, in which you say that if there is local opposition to N.C. Tariff revision, there will be no chance of getting it through. Shall I sound the Superintendent in the matter, or would it be better to postpone the question for, say, three months, when

when the people will have settled down a bit after this terrible typhoon?

Yours truly,

Ca E Williams.

INSPECTORATE GENERAL OF CUSTOMS,

S/O.

PEKING, 21st October 1922.

Dear Mr Williams,

I have duly received your S/O letter No. 256 of the 14th September.

<u>Wenchow Despatch No. 3684 and Native Customs Tariff: owing to a mistake in the N.C. Tariff hemp, which has a higher value than hemp skin, pays less duty. Question of revision of the Tariff again mentioned.</u>

An obvious error of that kind should be corrected as soon as possible, but general revision had better be postponed for the present !

Yours truly,

C.A.S.Williams,Esquire,
    WENCHOW.

S/O No. 257.   Wenchow   28th September 22

Dear Sir Francis,

oon damages.

With reference to my despatch No. 3689, N. C. No. 298 requesting authority to carry out repairs to property damaged by the typhoon, my estimate of $1,900.00 is by no means excessive. It is impossible to describe the terrible state of ruin in this port; it has been aptly compared to the result of a concentrated air-raid and bombardment. Since writing my official report little has been done in the matter of repairs, firstly because the local workmen seem to have been practically paralyzed by the appalling catastrophe, and secondly on account of the difficulty of procuring

building

FRANCIS AGLEN K. B. E.,
Inspector General of Customs,
   P E K I N G .

2.

building material in sufficient quantities. Now, however, bricks and tiles have been imported, shipping facilities continued, and the people are recovering from the shock. There has been a subsidence of the Customs Boatmen's rented quarters on the island, which will have to be attended to, but I think I can manage to do this out of the margin allowed in my estimate for such contingencies. The Architect of H. B. M.'s Office of Works has agreed to the expending of $850.00 in the necessary repairs to the British Consulate and bund frontage rented by us for the Tidesurveyor. It is important that the collapsed bund frontage of the Examiner's House should be attended to as soon as possible. The attached photograph shows how
the bund
frontage has
fallen in.
If it is
not repaired
at once the
bank will be

all

3.

all washed away and the house endangered

I have just received your telegram sanctioning "judicious repairs" so I am proceeding with all emergency work. I hope you will agree that a stone boundary wall in the compound of the Commissioner's House is preferable to brick, especially as that part of the wall which is of stone withstood the typhoon so effectively. You may perhaps consider that the inner wall screening the Servants' Quarters from the garden might be of brick instead of stone, so I am not rebuilding the walls yet, and am at present confining my attention principally to making the houses weather-proof.

*ested purchase of for building *tant's Quarters.

With regard to the Assistant's Quarters, we seem to be continually patching them up. They provide very poor accommodation though the situation is good but very <u>exposed</u>, and the present occupant realises that he is better there than in a Chinese house in a crowded street. It would be distinctly advisable to buy a piece of

vacant

vacant land not far from the Commissioner's House and build quarters suitable either for a married or unmarried Assistant; shall I put the matter before you officially, or will you give me your semi-official approval to commence tentative negotiations, which necessitate the advancement of a few dollars bargain money before the owner will begin to consider the matter?

cations.

With reference to Statistical Secretary's Printed Note No. 492, in which my "Manual of Chinese Metaphor" is advertised for sale to Service Members at a reduced price, I hope this does not mean that the sales of this book have fallen off. I was under the impression that the proceeds of sale have already covered the initial cost of publication. I should be very interested to hear if the book has proved a financial success or not. I have just finished the manuscript of another book of a rather more ambitious nature. I should rather like to show it to you if it would interest you. It is an illustrated glossary of Chinese symbolism

5.

symbolism, which, according to the late Mr. Couling in his <u>Encyclopaedia Sinica</u>, p.537, "is a subject as yet imperfectly treated in any European tongue".

Dialect.

I have found it necessary to devote some attention to the local dialect, as it is so different from Mandarin, and I have to interview so many people who petition me on various matters which are much better settled by word of mouth.

ese Studies of
stant.

Mr. Assistant Bodisco is making rapid progress in Chinese, and I predict brilliant success for him in the future. I am going to examine him - at his own request - every three months - but I shall be careful to see that he does not overdo things.

ves.

I am going through the archives and putting them into good order, and I am also personally working at the card-indexing of the 45 years correspondence of this

6.

this Office.

Yours truly,

C. A. S. Williams.

INSPECTORATE GENERAL OF CUSTOMS,

S/O.

PEKING, 28th October, 1922.

Dear Mr Williams,

I have duly received your S/O letter No. 257 of the 28th September.

Suggested purchase of land on which to build Assistants' Quarters.

Report officially: I seem always to be buying land at Wenchow !

Commr. mentions that he would be very interested to hear if his "Manual of Chinese Metaphor" has proved a financial success or not.

I will enquire and let you know.

Manuscript of another book finished and Commr. would like the I.G. to see it.

Many thanks but I fear I have no leisure to read such an MS. at present.

Yours truly,

C.A.S. Williams, Esquire,
   WENCHOW.

CUSTOM HOUSE,

S/O No. 258.   Wenchow, 13th October 1922.

Dear Sir Francis,

ion of Reporting
sition of Property.   There are two pieces of property
which we have recently acquired at this
port, viz: the Lin property, now incorporated
with the Commissioner's garden (Wenchow
despatch No. 3690 of 19th September 1922),
and the foreshore lot, the reclamation and
bunding of which at a cost of $6,942.56
was sanctioned by I.G. despatch No.1018/83,913
of 1921. The latter construction work has
just been completed, and consists of a well
paved enclosure with two gates, and proves
most useful for examination work. I am not
quite sure as to how to report these two
properties, as I do not quite know whether
                                                          the

FRANCIS AGLEN K. B. E.,
Inspector General of Customs,
    PEKING.

2.

the new property forms, mentioned in I.G. Circular No. 3240, have been completed at the Inspectorate or not, and, whether I should apply to the Statistical Department for them, or wait until they are supplied to this Office direct. I would venture to ask if it is your intention to issue further Circular instructions in this respect. With reference to the reclaimed foreshore lot, as the cost of reclamation and paving was passed by the Shui-wu Ch'u, will it be necessary for me to address an official despatch to you accompanied by a Chinese version notifying the completion of the work, in case you may wish to transmit it to the Ch'u ?

cy for typhoon rs.

I am anxiously awaiting your official sanction for the detailed repair work recommended in my despatch No. 3689. The building of walls of the rough stone of the locality is distinctly advisable, as they are most durable. A wall of this style, built round the temple previously

occupied

occupied by the Commissioner, is still in excellent condition and quite unimpaired by typhoons. I hesitate to build up the fallen walls until I receive your decision as to the nature of construction, i.e. stone or brick.

er typhoon.

Since the typhoon of the 11th ult. reported in my despatch No. 3689 there was another typhoon on the 28th ult., followed by heavy rain. A part of the south wall of the city fell down, and a man was killed. Some junks were wrecked, and houses up river washed away by a freshet, which also caused damage to the paddy fields. There was, however, no further destruction of Customs property.

f of Distress.

On the 4th inst. I received a visit from the Magistrate, Taoyin, and Superintendent, who asked me to give my support in the formation of a local branch office of the Sino-Foreign Society for Relief of Distress (華洋義賑溫處支會) for the purpose of devising means to assist persons

impoverished

4.

impoverished on account of the recent floods and typhoons. According to the local press the Head Office of the Society in Shanghai has decided to remit $200,000 for relief in Chekiang, $100,000 being for Ningpo, Taichow, Shaohsing, and Wenchow, but the Superintendent was unwilling to commit himself on this point when I asked him whether it was a fact or not.

  I attended the first meeting of the Society on the 9th inst., and was elected to officiate with the Taoyin on a local Committee consisting of representatives of the principle Chinese and Foreign residents.

r and Lushih st increase of pay.
  On the 9th inst., I was approached by a deputation consisting of the Writer and all the Lushih on the Staff of this Office, who stated that owing to the increased cost of living of recent years, they found their pay insufficient for their needs, and therefore requested me to make representations to you on the subject of some reorganisation of the pay

5.

pay of Writers and Lushih. I gather that the Writers and Lushih in other ports are also raising the same question, as although they are entitled to promotion every three years, instead of every five as formerly (Circular No. 2986 of 1919), I believe they feel that their pay has not been raised in the same relative degree as that of other grades of Service employes. The cost of the necessaries of life in this port has been gradually increasing, though rice has recently been fairly cheap. The effects of the floods and typhoons, however, will react very considerably on local market prices for some time. If this matter is being taken up with you by Commissioners at other ports, I presume it will not be necessary for me to raise it officially myself. Possibly the revision of the tariff will release sufficient gunds to enable you to effect some improvement in the pay of the Writers and Lushih, and I would ask whether you can consider any such proposal to increase their pay. A comparative statement of market prices of local necessaries, in 1919 and 1922

as

as submitted to me by the Writer and Lushih Staff is appended.

Yours truly,

[signature]

APPEND.

Comparative statement of market prices of local necessaries in 1919 and 1922.

Name of Article.			1919. $	1922. $
Rice	per	catty	0.0355	0.0588
House rent	"	month	7 - 8	10
Clothing, silk	"	coat	13 - 14	20
" cotton	"	"	3.00	4.00
Firewood	"	catty	0.0025	0.005
Fish	"	"	0.16	0.30
Pork	"	"	0.125	0.222
Eggs	"	piece	0.01	0.0143
Salt	"	catty	0.025	0.05
Vegetable oil	"	"	0.1111	0.1538
Vegetables				increase double.

		民國八年 西1919	民國十一年 西1922
食米		每元 二十八斤	每元 十七八斤
房租		每月七八元	每月 十元
衣料	綢	每件 十三四元	每件 二十元
	布	五件 三元餘	四元餘
柴		每元 四百斤	每元 二百餘斤
黑肉		每斤 壹角玖分	每斤 三角
肉		每元 八斤	每元 四斤半
虫宝		每角 十個	每角 七個
血		每角 四斤	每角 二斤
蔬菜類		每斤加倍	
木油		每元 九斤	每元 六斤半

以上所開各物以及雇用僕媼均係日常所必需者至於子女教育親友酬應等費臨時所出者更不知凡幾為此斂气

鑒查俯賜轉祈

總稅務司鴻慈格外一視同仁從優加給薪水藉免捉襟露肘曷勝感禱之至謹及

CUSTOM HOUSE,

S/O No. 259.

Wenchow, 28th October 1922

Dear Sir Francis,

ess of repairs
operty damaged
phoon.

  With reference to my despatch No. 3689 of the 19th of last month requesting authority to carry out repairs to property damaged by the typhoon, there was great difficulty at first in obtaining workmen and building materials, but good progress is now being made. The Custom House, Examination Shed, and Tidewaiters' Quarters are now in order. The Assistant's Quarters are rendered fit for occupation, though the compound wall has not yet been rebuilt. The roof of the Commissioner's House has been repaired and some of the rooms are being colour-washed, and I hope to be able to make

arrangements

FRANCIS AGLEN K.B.E.,
 Inspector General of Customs,
  PEKING.

arrangements for rebuilding the garden walls as soon as possible, as it is very inadvisable for the house to remain unprotected and open to public view. May I venture to request you to reply to the proposals regarding repairs given in the above-mentioned despatch so that this very necessary work can be carried on.

Relief Work.

The local Committee for Famine Relief has now decided to restrict its operations solely to the following places Yung-chia (永嘉), Jui-an (瑞安), Ping-yang (平陽), Yo-tsing (樂清), Yu-huan (玉環) and Tai-shun (泰順), and as Vice President I find it my duty to depute members of local firms and missions to make investigations in these places, after which I shall have to report in detail for issue of relief by the Ningpo Committee. I have been offered an allowance of $80. a month for secretarial expenses, but I declined to accept it, and trust I am right in so doing.

There

tation of rice. There were several shipments of rice to Hangchow during July and August, declared for famine relief, covered by Superintendent's Chuanchao and expired Huchao issued by the Provincial Authorities. In response to urgent requests by the Superintendent I passed these shipments, but, in each case, I obtained a written declaration from the shipper to the effect that if a valid Huchao issued by the Provincial Authorities was not procured and presented within two months, the full duty taken on deposit would be forfeited and brought to account. This time limit is now about to expire and the Chamber of Commerce has requested me to return the deposits. Should I hold them to their bargain, or return the deposits as requested?

y. Piratical attacks on Chinese craft are becoming more numerous off the Chekiang coast than ever before, owing principally to the impoverished conditions resulting from the floods and typhoons. The saying goes that
what

what has not been destroyed by the weather has been stolen by the pirates! A **very** miserable outlook for the winter!

    Yours truly,

      Ca. S. Williams

INSPECTORATE GENERAL OF CUSTOMS,

PEKING, 13 November 1922.

Dear Mr. Williams,

I have duly received your S/O. letters Nos. 258 and 259 of the 13th and 28th of October. Repairs to property damaged by typhoon : I.G. Authority requested.

Telegram authorising this expenditure was sent on the 27th of September last.

Yours truly,

A.S. Williams, Esquire.
    WENCHOW.

CUSTOM HOUSE,

S/O No. 260.   Wenchow 11th November 1922.

ng interests
ted by piracy.

Dear Sir Francis,

        Although the pirates which infest the islands of the Chekiang coast generally restrict their operations to native craft pure and simple, they are now inclined to extend their activities in other directions, seeing that the measures taken by Maritime Police are so utterly inadequate to cope with their increasing numbers. The following vessels have been recently pirated; and I have received petitions from the owners to report their respective cases to the local authorities:-

Lorcha Chin Yüan K'ang (金源康) on the 24th Sept.
Junk Chin T'ai Fêng (金泰豐)　　"　" 5th October
Lorcha Chin Yuan Fa (金源發)　　"　" 26th　"
　　" Chên Hsiang (臻祥)　　　"　" 2nd November

        Besides

FRANCIS AGLEN K. B. E.,
Inspector General of Customs,
　　P E K I N G .

2.

Besides the above there have been many other instances not directly brought to my notice, and a couple of days ago the lowdah of a junk acting as Lights Tender for the Santuao Customs reported that his vessel was attacked by pirates on the 3rd instant, and suffered a loss of $90, Customs monies intended for paying salaries of Light Keepers, and one man wounded. I reported this case to the local Superintendent and the Santuao Commissioner - vide copy of my letter to the latter.

ppended.

ective magnetic
vations at Wenchow.

I expect Mr. Bülow-Ravens, Surveyor, with his party of Chinese Observers, to arrive on the 20th to obtain the magnetic observations asked for by the Japanese Hydrographic Department from the Chinese Government, and have offered to put him up. I have asked the Superintendent to inform the local authorities that the observations are being taken on behalf of the Chinese Government, and requested that the Surveyors should

3.

should be afforded the necessary facilities to carry out their work.

on repairs.

I am afraid I have been labouring under a slight misunderstanding as regards your authority for repairs to property damaged by the typhoon of 11th September, and in my last S/O I asked you to give me your official sanction for the repairs as detailed in my despatch No. 3689, not knowing that they had already been sanctioned. The fact is that owing to an error in transmission of your telegram of 27th September sanctioning the repairs I was under the impression that you were not prepared to sanction the whole but only a part of the repairs; however on receipt of your confirmation of the September telegrams, and verification of the same, I found out the mistake, and am now carrying out all the necessary repairs as applied for and sanctioned. I hope to have everything finished in about two months.

An

taxes.

An additional 10% on steamer passages between Shanghai and Wenchow is to be collected by the C.M.S.N. Co. for one year for famine relief, and 3 cents per unit of electric light a month levied for educational purposes.

rd table.

The billiard table in the Commissioner's House has now been fully re-conditioned, and is a most useful source of recreation - especially during the rainy seasons of the year.

on Hills for
ctive summer
nce.

I have procured ten mou of land on the hills across the river for $160, in case you may decide to build a summer residence for the Wenchow Commissioner there at some future time as suggested in your despatch No. 1094/89,795. It is a magnificent site and there is ample room for a good garden and tennis court, but the land will require a certain amount of levelling before building can be commenced.

APPEND.

Yours truly,

APPEND.

Wenchow, 9th November 1922.

Dear Hartshorn,

I wired to you to-day:- "Junk Su Hsin Ch'un or Ma Yung Shêng serving as Santuao Lights Tender attacked and robbed by pirates writing".

A junk came in and reported at the Native Customs to-day carrying a pass book issued by your office authorising the vessel owned by Ma Yung Shêng (馬永生) to act as Santuao Customs Lights Tender. The laodah Su Hsin Ch'un (苏新春) also produced two Chinese paysheets said to be issued by your office and some torn up pieces of a canvas bag said to be the property of your office. He stated that, while proceeding to pay the salaries of the Lights Staff on behalf of your office, his vessel was attacked by pirates who wounded one man and made off with Customs money amounting to $90.00, etc.

I am reporting the occurrence to the local authorities and am having the wounded man attended to by the Customs doctor.

As the pirates took everything they could find on board, I advanced $5.00 to the Laodah for food, and I told him to return to Santuao, but at present he is not too anxious to venture on the return trip.

These

6.

These pirates are becoming a great nuisance, and I think it is quite time something was done, in the interests of revenue and trade, to check their activities on the Chekiang Coast.

Yours sincerely,

(Signed) C.A.S. Williams.

TRUE COPY:

INSPECTORATE GENERAL OF CUSTOMS,

S/O.   PEKING, 6 December 1922

Dear Mr. Williams,

I have duly received your S/O lette No. 260 of the 11th of November.

Increase of Piracy.

I am trying to get the Ministry of Navy to take up the Coast Guard question seriously. The state of things everywhere is a scandal and disgrace.

Yours truly,

C.A.S. Williams, Esquire,
   WENCHOW.

CUSTOM HOUSE,

S/O NO. 261.　　　　Wenchow, 23rd November 1922.

Dear Sir Francis,

ns interests
ted by piracy.

In continuation of my remarks in regard to the prevalence of piracy off the Chekiang Coast, to the detriment of trade, and even affecting vessels detailed as Lights Tenders by the Customs, I advanced $15. for food, etc. to the Lowdah of the pirated junk acting as Lights Tender for the Santuao Customs, and the vessel has now left for Santuao. The Lorcha "Chên Hsiang" (臻祥), which I mentioned in my last S/O as having been pirated on the 2nd instant, was pirated again on the 8th instant. I

hope

FRANCIS AGLEN K. B. E.,
Inspector General of Customs,
　　PEKING.

hope the Santuao Lights Tender will not also be subjected to another attack.

tic observations **nchow.**

Mr. Bülow-Ravens, Surveyor, with his party of four Chinese Observers, arrived today to obtain the magnetic observations asked for by the Japanese Hydrographic Department from the Chinese Government.

ation for re- **isation of pay by** **r and Lushih.**

In acknowledging receipt of my S/O No. 258 of 13th ult., you did not refer to the matter of the pay of Writer and Lushih brought forward in that S/O. When I go to Shanghai I will ask Mr. Lyall if any similar representations have been made by his Writers and Lushih.

ents of Officials.

Superintendent Hu Wei-hsien (胡惟賢), left this port on the 3rd instant. I understand he is going to Singapore, where he was formerly Consul, and other places, to raise funds for Chekiang famine relief, and will return in four months time. During his temporary absence Mr. Ou-Yang Pao-fu (歐陽保福)

3.

(欧阳保福) will superintend the current work.

Taoyin Lin K'un-hsiang (林鹍翔) left for Shanghai on the 16th instant, and is not expected to return.

Called information re to navigation called by Chiao-t'ung Pu.

On the 12th October I received a despatch from the Superintendent calling for details of channels, lights, buoys, etc. in this district, and suggestions for their improvement. This information was being sought, at the instance of the Ministry of Communications, in order to provide material for discussion at the forthcoming 13th International Navigation Conference to be held in London in July next. As reported in my Return of Non-urgent Chinese Correspondence I sent a brief reply referring to the Statistical Department's published list of Lighthouses, etc. and said that the changes in the channel were duly observed and notified. This reply, however, was not considered sufficiently informative, and on the 15th instant, I received another despatch calling for most minute details, i.e. latitude and

4.

and longitude, construction, style and power of light, cost of upkeep, maps, etc.- I therefore sent him a rough sketch map showing the position of the various aids to navigation, and all the details required - with the exception of the cost of upkeep, which, I believe, you would not wish me to touch upon. I venture to ask what attitude I should adopt in case of any further enquiries.

On the 10th instant a few small boxes of opium were seized by a number of soldiers and police from a shop styled Ch'ên Chao-ho (陳朝和) owned by a native of Formosa.

with suspicion on.

A fire broke out outside the West Gate at 3 a.m. on the 11th instant and about 20 shops were burnt down. On the 21st there was another fire outside the East Gate and about 30 houses burnt. No lives were lost but it is rumoured that these fires were caused by incendiaries for purposes of of theft.

Owing to the most improvident and wholesale export of rice from this port during the summer, and the damages caused by the typhoon, it has now been found necessary to import rice to make up the shortage, and 3,800 piculs were carried by S.S. "Feiching" arriving today.

for Commissioner's
        With reference to my despatch No. 3,698 of 8th instant applying for a <u>Kalmac carpet</u> for the Commissioner's Office, I notice that the Engineer-in-Chief recommends a <u>Cord carpet</u> as being cheaper and more durable, and I concur in this opinion.

Yours truly,

CA Williams.

INSPECTORATE GENERAL OF CUSTOMS,

PEKING, 23 December 1922

Dear Mr. Williams,

I have duly received your S/O letter No. 261 of the 23rd of November.

<u>Detailed information re Aids to Navigation called for by Chiao-t'ung Pu.</u>

I, of course, got the same questionnaire and have dealt with it here. I replied that the subjects were far too technical for Harbour Masters in the ports to be able to submit any views of value on them, and that such questions should be referred to the Government's Conservancy engineers. The questions dealing with Aids to Navigation would be dealt with by Coast Inspector and Engineer-in-Chief.

In future cases submit the question officially and ask for instructions.

Yours truly

A.S. Williams, Esquire.
  WENCHOW.

S/O NO. 262.

CUSTOM HOUSE,

Wenchow, 9th December 1922.

Dear Sir Francis,

...sion of magnetic
...ations at Wenchow.
      Mr. Bülow-Ravens, Surveyor, and his party of four Chinese Observers, completed their magnetic observations in this port and returned to Shanghai on the 27th of last month. The original observation stone had been moved during some structural alterations in the Methodist Mission Compound. A new stone was therefore laid down. As there is no suitable hotel here, Mr. Bülow-Ravens was my guest during his visit.

Relief work.
      I have been asked by the local Committee to assist in the collection of subscriptions for Famine Relief in the six districts in the neighbourhood of Wenchow, but

SIR FRANCIS AGLEN K. B. E.,
  Inspector General of Customs,
    PEKING.

2.

but this proposition seems to me to be rather in the nature of attempting to get blood out of a stone. However I may be able to raise a little money among the principal residents and firms of Wenchow. It is also proposed to engage distressed persons for purposes of construction of a road which has been commenced from here towards the provincial capital.

The sea-robbers continue their depredations with unabated violence. The Maritime Police Gunboat "Yung An" had an engagement with five pirate ships, which were repulsed with heavy losses. Unfortunately the Gunboat, while in pursuit of the pirates struck a rock and sank. The crew were saved by three junks which were being attacked by the pirates. On the 5th instant the Lorcha "Chin Hua" (金華) was pirated at Shinp'u (石浦) and most of her cargo seized, including some kerosene oil, which, it is said, was being imported from Shanghai by the Asiatic Petroleum Co.

There

3.

There have been two fires recently, one on the 26th of last month outside the South Gate, where about 20 houses were burnt down, and another inside the city near the Yunch'ing Gate (永清門) on the 6th instant where seven houses were burnt.

*ctive sea-plane
*n from Wenchow to

I heard privately in Shanghai that Sir Keith Smith intends to make a sea-plane flight from Wenchow to Japan in the early spring, and he will require to be supplied with the following information:-

"PARTICULARS REQUIRED

Wenchow

Approx. size of landing space. Whether
    approaches are open or over buildings,
    wireless masts etc.
Prevailing wind and speed of current.
Exact spot where petrol and oil will be
    located.

ARRANGEMENTS FOR LANDING

Smudge fire to give off plenty of smoke for
    wind direction.

Motor

4.

  Motor boat to take aircraft in tow to
    mooring buoy.
  No other boat to approach aircraft until
    propellor has stopped.
  Clear area required to land in, about 600
    yds. square.
  Chart of harbours with full particulars
    marked on it to be delivered to us
    at previous landing ground.
  In this case Hongkong."
  This information was given to me semi-officially by Commander G.F. Mulock, Head of the Marine Department, Asiatic Petroleum Co., Shanghai; the A.P.C. have been approached in the matter, but as there is nothing definite as yet the Company will wait before laying down stock for Sir Keith.

housing problem. I am making enquiries as to the possibility of acquiring some land on which to build Assistant's Quarters, and will report on the matter in due course. I believe the British Government is making efforts to sell the British Consulate on the island;

island; this building is at present rented by us and used as Tidesurveyor's quarters. We offered to buy it for $7,500.00, but this offer was not considered high enough, and, indeed, I am not surprised. I think we ought to offer $13,000.00 for the Consulate and Constable's House; the latter would be useful for the Examiner, as the present Examiner's Quarters are exceedingly poor and I think we should relinquish them. If the Consulate is sold we should be unable to buy land and build for less than $15,000.00 to $25,000.00.

Yours truly,

C.A.S. Williams.

CUSTOM HOUSE,

S/O No. 263.

Wenchow, 23rd December 1922.

Dear Sir Francis,

housing.

  I have gone very carefully into the question of the housing of the Staff at this port, and am now putting forward definite proposals to you officially. My idea is for the Service to possess three blocks of property:- (a) Custom House and Tidewaiters' Quarters on the river front (already acquired); (b) Residences of (1) Commissioner, and (2) Married or unmarried Assistant, in the town (the former now acquired; the purchase of the latter proposed); (c) Quarters for (1) Tidesurveyor, and (2) Examiner, on the island (the former now rented; purchase of both proposed).

With

FRANCIS AGLEN K. B. E.,
 Inspector General of Customs,
  P E K I N G.

2.

With reference to our former offer of $7,500.00 for the British Consulate on the island for use as Tidesurveyor's Quarters, I enclose copy of a recent letter from Mr. V. L. Savage, H. B. M's Consul for Hangchow, Ningpo, and Wenchow, from which you will see that the present would appear to be a most suitable time for us to renew our offer of purchase of this property, including - in addition - the Constable's House, which is solid and well built and most suitable for Examiner's Quarters.

With regard to the ten mou of land I have obtained for the Service on the adjacent hills for a prospective summer bungalow, I think it would be advisable to level it and surround it with a wall. All I have done at present is to put in boundary stones, but it is possible that the rains may affect the ground - previously looked after by the farmers - if it is not cut out at the back and banked up at the front. The expenditure of a few

hundred

hundred dollars now may save money later on, and then building could be commenced at any time you may wish.

n(au)guration of Wenchow (S)teamship Company.

Some of the local gentry and merchants have combined to form a new concern known as the Wenchow Steamship Company (溫州輪船公司). The first vessel of this shipping firm, the S.S. "Shin Lee" (升利), arrived here on the 7th instant laden with general cargo and cleared on the 9th with goods of local production.

(Move)ments of Chinese (Of)ficials.

Mr. Chang Lien (張濂), the local Magistrate, left on the 19th by S.S. "Yung Chuan" for Chiang Yin (江陰), and is expected to return in about a month. We are still without a Taoyin, as the new incumbent Yü Ta-chün (余大鈞) has not yet arrived.

cy.

The Wenchow Junk Guild has forwarded a petition to the Chiao-t'ung Pu requesting that some more effective means be devised

devised for the suppression of piracy along the coast from Fukien to Kiangsu. The Guild complained in their petition that the Maritime Police Staff has been reduced, and the disbanded men have become pirates!

Repairs and construction in Commissioner's compound.

The typhoon repairs to fallen walls, etc., in the Compound of the Commissioner's House, are now nearly finished, but, when the dividing wall between the old compound and the newly acquired portion was removed, the ground was found to be at different heights and it was necessary to level it and to strengthen the stone-faced base of the hill side. On this account it may be possible that the original estimate may be slightly exceeded, but I hope not. It has been a difficult piece of work, and it was impossible to foresee everything which was necessary to be done. The property will soon be in excellent order, and is not likely to suffer any serious damage from further typhoons.

Yours truly,

ENCLOSURE.

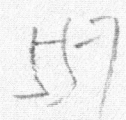

COPY OF LETTER FROM MR. V.L. SAVAGE, H.B.M'S CONSUL FOR HANGCHOW, NINGPO AND WENCHOW, TO COMMISSIONER OF CUSTOMS, WENCHOW.

          British Consulate,
           Ningpo,
           11th December 1922.

Dear Mr. Williams,

  There is evidently some adverse decree of fate against my going to Wenchow.

  Now, I have caught a bad cold, which has brought about laryngitis. I have been strenuously endeavouring to cure it, so as to go to Wenchow at the appointed time; but my efforts have been only partly successful.

  I feel that you, and Mrs. Williams, would scarcely thank me for turning up in my present condition, in which, by frequent bouts of coughing and sneezing, I should be very likely to spread the infection.

  On the other hand, this is not the best of times to be travelling about when one has throat trouble etc. The cold winds from the north are sure to blow every few days, and one may get caught in conditions which make it difficult to protect oneself adequately against them, particularly when travelling by the small coasting steamers.

             However,

2.

However, there is really no urgency about Wenchow, and I think it will be best if I leave the trip until March or April.

Between ourselves, I have been given a hint that the Government might be willing to part with the Consulate property at a great sacrifice. They want to get rid of superfluous property, and the costs of upkeep it entails. I understand the Customs formerly offered $7,000.00 for the Consulate property at Wenchow. If the amount were raised to Hk.Tls.7,000.- or say $10,000.- I believe the Office of Works would be ready to sell at that figure. Hitherto, I have been given to understand that they would not take much less than $17,000 or $18,000, but I have heard otherwise lately.

I do hope that my numerous changes of plans, however involuntary on my part, have not caused you and Mrs. Williams any inconvenience. If they have, I wish to express my great regret and hope you will accept my humble apologies.

In the hope of reaching Wenchow some day, and finding you and yours well and flourishing when I do, I remain, with all good wishes for Xmas and the new year.

Sincerely yours,

(Signed) V.L. Savage.

TRUE COPY:

1923 年

CUSTOM HOUSE,

S/O No. 264.   Wenchow, 6th January 1923.

Dear Sir Francis,

Revenue.

With reference to my despatches Nos. 3715 and 3716, N. C. No. 302, I am glad to draw your attention to the fact that record revenue collections have been secured by both the Maritime and Native Customs establishments in this port during the past year.

Native Customs Property.

I am beginning to consider the matter of the most practical utilisation of the various Native Customs buildings at this port and its sub-stations.

The Native Customs Head Office, to my mind, is badly situated and far too large

SIR FRANCIS AGLEN K. B. E.,
    Inspector General of Customs,
        PEKING.

2.

large for our purposes, and in the near future it is my intention to make an official proposal for transmission to the Shui-wu Ch'u, if you so wish, for the sale of the N. C. Head Office property and the acquirement of a site on the river front for building a more suitable office, where better control can be exercised over the shipping. This transaction should not entail any extra expense and might even result in a financial profit.

The Ningtsun N. C. building is also too large, and in a very bad state of repair. I propose to have it properly repaired and reduced in size. Some improvements may also be made to other N. C. property.

I should like to know, however, before raising the question of improvements and suitable disposal of N.C. Office accommodation, whether it is likely that the Native Customs is a Service which the Government intends to maintain for some time to come or not, as, if not, it will be

hardly

hardly worth while to bring forward any suggestions.

Postal Tariff.

The Chekiang provincial officials, following the procedure adopted in Szechuan, Fengtien, Honan, and Kuangtung, issued instructions through the various Taoyin, to the Postal and Telegraph Administrations, to discontinue the increased rates on letters and telegrams from the 7th December, and to revert to the original charges collected previous to the 1st November. The local Telegraph Office complied with these orders at the stipulated time, but the Post Office did not do so until the 1st instant. On the 3rd instant, deputies of the Magistrate and Police proceeded to the Post Office to ascertain whether the instructions of the provincial authorities were being carried out or not.

Deaths by drowning.

On the 1st instant, some Chinese passengers, disembarking in sampans from S.S. "Shin Lee", were drowned, owing to the capsizing

4.

capsizing of the sampans during a gale of wind.

Fire.   On the 4th instant, at 6.30 a.m., a fire broke out in the centre of the city and about 40 houses were burnt down.

Yours truly,

C.A.S. Williams

INSPECTORATE GENERAL OF CUSTOMS,

S/O

PEKING, 8 January 1923.

Dear Mr. Williams,

I have duly received your S/O letter No. 262 of the 9th of December.

<u>Proposed purchase of British Consulate and Constable's House.</u>

Perhaps the Consulate offer requires re-consideration, but, if you want this, you must officialise. I can't deal with expenditure questions semi-officially !

Yours truly,

C. A. S. Williams, Esquire.
 WENCHOW.

INSPECTORATE GENERAL OF CUSTOMS,

S/O

PEKING, 16 January 19 23.

Dear Mr. Williams,

I have duly received your S/O letter No. 263 of the 23rd of December.

<u>Purchase of British Consulate</u>.

I am prepared to give Hk.Tls.7000 for the whole property but <u>vide</u> the remarks of my despatch No. 1136/92598.

Yours truly,

A. S. Williams, Esquire.
WENCHOW.

CUSTOM HOUSE,

S/O No. 265.   Wenchow, 20th January 1923.

Dear Sir Francis,

Movements of Officials.

Taoyin Lin Kun-hsiang (林鵾翔), and his successor Shên Chih-chien (沈致堅) arrived by S.S. "Hsinfung" on the 12th. Mr. Shên, a native of Hupeh, took over charge on the following day, and tells me that he was at one time Superintendent of Customs at Shanghai when Mr. Harris was Commissioner there. I found him very affable during his and my return visits.

Competition of shipping firms.

The China Merchants S.N. Company, with the object of competing with other companies for the Ningpo trade, has invited certain

SIR FRANCIS AGLEN K.B.E.,
　　Inspector General of Customs,
　　　　PEKING.

certain Ningpo merchants to share in the running expenses and profits of S.S. "Kwangchi", which will now ply between Ningpo and Wenchow via Haimen. The question of the examination of her Haimen cargo by the Native Customs, in such a way as not to give her any advantages over the other companies, will be somewhat difficult to arrange, and I may have to put this matter to you officially, though I hope to be able to settle it locally without troubling you. Competition of this kind, in the interests of the revenue, should certainly be fostered by us. There are signs that the trade of the port is improving, and I shall do all I can to assist the process.

Assistant's Quarters.	I note that, according to your despatch No. 1135/92,558, you are not disposed to buy land here for building Assistant's Quarters. If we are eventually able to negotiate the purchase of the Consular property on the island, on which I shall shortly be addressing you again officially,

officially, it may be possible to provide the Assistant with more suitable quarters on the island. The attached photograph of the present Assistant's Quarters (rented), taken shortly after the typhoon of 11th September, will serve to illustrate the flimsy and ranshackle nature of the construction of this building.

Summons of N.C. Weigher for opium smoking.

In Wenchow despatch No. 3579 of 1921 it was reported that Lin Yin-li, Weigher in the Native Customs at this port, was falsely accused of smoking opium and summoned for investigation by the police and afterwards released. Mr. Lin received another summons last month, and when I heard of this, I informed the Superintendent of the previous instance when the accusation was shown

shown to be unfounded, and asked that, if the police found it necessary to arrest any of my staff, they should first apply to me.

Kidnapping and traffic in children.

There has been strong susppicion recently that S.S. "Kimboh Maru", a Japanese vessel registered in Formosa and plying between Wenchow and Amoy, has been engaged during her last two trips in kidnapping and traffic in children, and Mr. Lu Si-ho, 4th Class (Chinese) Tidewaiter brought 2 women and three children ashore with him from this vessel yesterday. The Superintendent hearing of this asked me to send these women and children to him for transmission to the police for investigation, and to have the vessel searched for further cases. Mr. Lu stated that the children asked to be brought ashore and so he took them into his boat. I told the Harbourmaster to hand them over to the Chinese Captain who came ashore, but the Police took them in charge. In the meantime the ship left the port.

I am sorry that we became implicated in

in this affair, and I told Mr. Lu not to bring any persons ashore again. The Chinese authorities are afraid to make arrests on a Japanese ship and would like us to do this for them, but I see no reason why we should, and venture to ask if I am correct in this assumption.

Fire.   A fire broke out not far from the Commissioner's House the night before last and 12 houses were burnt.

Yours truly,

C. S. Williams

CUSTOM HOUSE,

S/O No. 266.   Wenchow, 3rd February 1923

Dear Sir Francis,

Revenue. A substantial revenue increase of Hk. Tls. 5,790.975 was secured during the month of January. This is due, not, as might be supposed, to the Tariff revision, but to general improvement in the local export trade. A brisk demand for Wenchow products has recently sprung up in Manilla and Japan, and there are distinct indications that this district is being well developed.

Examination of I.W.S.N. Cargo. With reference to my despatch No. 3,718, N.C. No. 304 re examination of I.W.S.N. cargo, although Mr. Alabaster reported that the new procedure of forcing the steamer companies to move

SIR FRANCIS AGLEN, K. B. E.,
    Inspector General of Customs,
        PEKING.

their cargo to the Maritime or Native Customs for examination, as instituted by Mr. Tanant, was "working satisfactorily", the shipping agents inform me that they have never been satisfied, as it causes them great expense in cargo boat hire, and also loss of valuable time, and they say they will pay anything for examination at the wharf where the steamer is lying. I think Mr. Tanant's policy was rather obstructional and very detrimental to trade, though it was strictly in accordance with the regulations. In my opinion we ought to assist and not hinder trade. We could quite easily satisfy all complaints and still maintain the principle that Maritime Customs goods should be examined by the Maritime Customs (though not necessarily at the Maritime Custom House) and N.C. goods by the N.C. (though not necessarily at the Native Customs). Our staff, is, however, rather scanty, as I pointed out when a Chinese Tidewaiter was sent here in place of a foreign Examiner transferred to Ningpo, and it is not easy for us to be continually sending men here and there for examination of various cargoes (vide my S/O No. 254 of 12th August, 1922, on

the

subject of staff shortage).

Staff.
  Mr. K'o Yu-p'ing, 2nd Clerk, C, has been ill for a few days, but I am glad to say he is well again.

  With reference to my last S/o and my Return of Non-urgent Chinese Correspondence for January, Mr. Lin Yin-li, Native Customs Weigher, was summoned on a charge of opium smoking on the 1st inst. I understand he was accused of smoking opium in a shop. The informer, however, had no witnesses, and, in my private opinion, the case was concocted merely for the purpose of extorting money from Mr. Lin. I have heard nothing more about the matter.

  The secretarial and accounts work in this office is now really more than one man can tackle singlehanded, and though I assist in it as far as possible, I really think it is necessary to have another man to work under the Secretary and Accountant. Would an application for a Candidate Clerk be considered?

      Yours truly,

      C.A.S. Williams.

INSPECTORATE GENERAL OF CUSTOMS,

S/O

PEKING, 9 February 1923.

Dear Mr. Williams,

I have duly received your S/O letter No. 264 of the 6th of January.

A/Commr. enquires whether it is likely that the Native Customs Service will be maintained.

I am afraid my opinion on such questions is not worth much ; but even if Likin goes, Coast Native Customs Establishments will probably remain and may even grow in importance !

Yours truly,

C. A. S. Williams, Esquire.
    WENCHOW.

INSPECTORATE GENERAL OF CUSTOMS,

PEKING, 15 February 1923.

S/O

Dear Mr. Williams,

I have duly received your S/O letter No. 265 of the 20th of January.

<u>Kidnapping and traffic in children.</u>

If the children were really being kidnapped, it was perfectly right for the Tidewaiter to bring them ashore. Any women and children who appeal in this way are certainly to be assisted !

Yours truly.

C. A. S. Williams, Esquire.
    WENCHOW.

INSPECTORATE GENERAL OF CUSTOMS,

S/O

PEKING, 22 February 1923.

Dear Mr. Williams,

I have duly received your S/O letter No.266 of the 3rd instant.

Revenue increase due to local export trade.

If we can get increased revenue from exports side by side with revised tariff increase, we ought to do well this year!

Secretarial and Accounts work : application for supplementary Candidate Clerk.

Candidate Clerks are no longer appointed to the Service. What hours does your Secretary and Accountant keep?

Yours truly,

C. A. S. Williams, Esquire.
   WENCHOW.

CUSTOM HOUSE,

Wenchow, 24th Feb., 19

S/O No. 267.

Dear Sir Francis,

China New Year.

On account of the temporary interruption of steamer communication with the outside world for some days during the New Year festivities, I was unable to despatch the usual letter to you before today. On the eve of the new year it is the local custom to light large bonfires all along the streets, a procedure which I have not observed in any other port; I left the office rather late, and it was raining at the time, so I was carried home in my chair literally "through fire and water!" The Police made an attempt to prohibit the firing of large crackers on account of the danger caused by sparks falling on the surrounding buildings, but the fire-cracker shops

protested

SIR FRANCIS AGLEN, K. B. E.,
Inspector General of Customs,
PEKING.

protested so vehemently that the prohibition was not enforced.

Movements of Officials.

Mr. Hu Wei-hsien (胡惟贤), Wenchow Customs Superintendent, who was deputed by the Provincial Authorities to proceed to Singapore, where he was formerly Consul, to collect funds for famine relief in Chekiang, has now arrived at Shanghai, and is expected to return here at the end of the month. I understand he has raised about $ 60,000.

Bank Failure.

A Shanghai bank styled Chên Ch'ang-yü has recently failed, and owing to the fact that most of the local banks dealt exclusively with this concern, the local trade has received a severe setback. Fortunately the Bank of China and the Ningpo Bank (四明银行) advanced $ 40,000 to the Wenchow banks, and thus assisted them to tide over their difficulties.

Development of Property.

I hope soon to be able to submit an estimate for enclosing the new hill property with a rough stone wall. The work in the recently extended portion of my compound is going on well, and

and I expect to be able to turf the tennis court in a few days time. I have started a small orchard containing apples, pears, peaches, apricots, plums, oranges, pumeloes, and grapes, and I am planting shade trees round the walls, together with various flowering shrubs, etc. Owing to the violent typhoon of September, the garden was almost totally destroyed, so there is a good deal to be done.

Staff.	I shall be very sorry to lose Mr. H. J. Christophersen, Tidesurveyor, B, when he goes on home leave this spring. He has done very good work here, and, as mentioned by some Wenchow correspondent writing to the North China Daily News on the 17th inst., he has considerable energy and initiative. He has a particularly good knowledge of this river, and I venture to hope that his successor will arrive here at least by the 1st April, so that Mr. Christophersen will have time to make him *au courant* with local conditions.

Yours truly,

Ca. Williams.

CUSTOM HOUSE,

S/O No. 868.   Wenchow 10th March, 19

Dear Sir Francis,

Revenue.

A revenue increase of Hk. Tls. 1,469.176 was secured during the month of February. Had it not been for the bank failure reported in my last S/O letter, the increase would have been larger. Our revenue depends almost entirely on exports, as nearly all imports arrive duty-paid under E.C., and thus the Tariff revision will not affect this port to any great extent.

Fraudulent Dealing in Rice.

It is my firm impression that a large proportion of the rice consigned to Hangchow - ostensibly for famine relief - in the early part of last summer, was diverted at Shanghai and unloaded on the market at a very profitable rate. I am corresponding with Hangchow on this question, as it appears to me that a matter of about Hk. Tls. 40,000 is due to us if we enforce the bonds. Query: will the Provincial Authorities support the rice-ring or not ?

Time

SIR FRANCIS AGLEN, K. B. E.,
    Inspector General of Customs,
        P E K I N G.

Time will show.

Staff: question of appointment of extra Clerk.

With reference to my S/O letter No. 265 asking if the appointment of an extra Clerk, to assist in the Secretarial and Accounts work, could be considered, and your reply of 22nd ult., enquiring what hours my Secretary and Accountant keeps, it all depends on the extent of the current work. During the first month of each quarter, he frequently remains in the office until six or seven o'clock, but at other times he does not necessarily stay so long. He is always in the office before nine. If he had a junior Clerk to do the clerical routine work, he could devote more attention to investigation of special local questions and accounts matters, and there would also be someone to carry on the routine work if he should be absent from the office on account of sickness, etc. Moreover the new system of rendering daily returns to Shanghai is about to be introduced very shortly, and when secretarial work is slack, the new Clerk could assist in the General Office if necessary. A junior Clerk would adequately meet the case.

Manual of Chinese Metaphor.

I have reported to you officially that the Académie des Inscriptions et Belles Lettres have awarded me the

Prix

Prix Stanislas Julien for my "Manual of Chinese Metaphor." As this book was published by the Service, I am very glad it has been noticed in this way. This distinction was awarded to Giles for his "Chinese-English Dictionary" and Couling for his "Encyclopaedia Sinica", but I believe I am the first member of the Service who has been fortunate enough to qualify for it.

Yours truly,

C. A. S. Williams.

[A.—42]

S/O

INSPECTORATE GENERAL OF CUSTOMS,

PEKING, 12 March 1923.

Dear Sir,

I am directed by the Inspector General to inform you that your S/O letter No. 267, dated 24 February, has been duly received.

Yours truly,

B. Foster Hall
a/asst Private Secretary.

C.A.S. Williams, Esq.

Wenchow

CUSTOM HOUSE,

S/O No. 269.   Wenchow, 24th March 1923

Dear Sir Francis,

hekiang Provincial axation.

A proclamation was put up here a few days ago signed by the Chief Civil and Military Provincial Authorities notifying the inauguration of a 20% tax on Cigars and Cigarettes, and it is reported that Mr. Chang I-p'ing (張益平), local Sub-manager of the Bank of China, will resign from his post and take up the appointment of Chief of the Wenchow Branch Office for the collection of this tax. I append a copy and translation of the notification in question. With reference to Article 5 in the rules for the collection of this tax as given in the Bulletin* of the Chinese Government Bureau of Economic Information (taken in by the Service),

the

SIR FRANCIS AGLEN, K. B. E.,
    Inspector General of Customs,
        PEKING.

*17th March 1923.

2.

the Revenue Inspector apparently has to have access to the "Customs Certificate and the Bill of Lading". I presume that no Customs documents are to be shown to the tax officers without your authority, and I hope there will be no interference with our examination work. I hear from Mr. Savage, H.B.M.'s Consul for Hangchow, Ningpo, and Wenchow, that there is considerable opposition on the part of the dealers to the levy of this tax but that if they do not begin to pay it by the end of the month, severe measures will be taken by the Chinese authorities. I understand Messrs Liggett Myers have closed down locally on account of the tax. I wonder how the matter will affect the proposed arrangements for the Customs Surtax.

raudulent dealing
n rice.

With reference to my last S/O. No. 268 of 10th instant, I find it difficult to trace the movements of all the rice consigned to Hangchow last summer. The Shanghai Office says that certain untraceable lots, according to the statement of the importers, were sent

on

on by train to Hangchow, but this seems to me very unlikely as the freight by rail is so much higher than that by steamer, and, in any case if sent by rail the movements should have been reported to the Shanghai Office at the time, and failure to report seems to me to entail loss of privileges. I am still waiting for further details.

Official Archives.

I shall be well occupied for some considerable time in card-indexing and arrangement of despatches and letters, and superintending the proper binding of the archives from 1877. It will certainly be a great advantage to have all the correspondence readily accessible and in good order. A good deal will also have to be done to the Office library, which is in a sad state.

Yours truly,

C.A.S. Williams

Append

APPEND.

PROCLAMATION FOR THE COLLECTION OF A SPECIAL TAX ON CIGARETTES AND CIGARS ISSUED BY THE CIVIL GOVERNOR AND TUPAN DATED 25TH FEBRUARY 1923.

Chinese version.

浙江省軍務善後督辦署佈告五號

浙江省長公署佈告一號

為佈告事照得捲菸一項係屬奢侈物品浙省輸入歲有增加銷耗民財為數甚鉅查各國稅法對於捲菸徵稅特重要應辦理要政如修築有道等項需款甚亟浙省現在應做成規就本省輸入捲菸進行徵稅以挹地方之財與地方之利捃刊此項稅章程完全出自吸戶取之有道令出惟行為此一體知悉凡買賣吸食日期均應遵章納稅此佈

行章程

浙江省境內人民瞬吸捲菸為紙捲菸及雪茄紙菸

徵收捲菸特稅暫行章程公佈後本省境內商民等一律遵照其除將問買賣吸食捲菸諸項應自本佈告道日期九條佈告均應自本佈告日起遵章完納

1. 允許吸食捲菸特稅前項特稅以特稅印花徵收之

2. 捲菸特稅之價值或包或盒計算捲菸之指罐或盒

3. A 輸入捲菸請領印花單以執備用標準用印花之手續應由販賣商店按照貼印花於卸貨時須報由稽徵員逐箱檢查實貼

B 員掣取請領印花單將須頻處所後須查照驗革向稽徵員所發

C 箱原批捲菸批發時須將請領印花單如貨交付如折原箱捲菸卸應購備印花分按承購人

D 零賣店或商人對於未備印花之捲菸不得承辦
E 凡捲菸一經開箱或開原封時（封係指箱內之總盒或包）須將印花並特逐件粘貼件係指最小之容器
F 粘貼印花時應在印花上加蓋與營業特許牌照
G 粘貼印花而墊欵繳稅得照印花票面扣提相
各號相符之騎縫圖章

分承辦貼用印花而不足稅率
當文酬金其規則另定之
遺漏或不足稅率
規則另定之
6. 違犯本章程各項規定應處以相當之罰金其罰金
又凡有外省入境之旅客隨身所帶捲菸以五十枚為
限加逾此數須於下車起岸時交候稽征員查驗補
貼印花不得隱匿
8. 舉發違犯本章程各項規定而為負責之見證者
以罰金之半數與之
9. 偽造印花或曾經貼用印花改造再貼者照刑律偽
造有價証券論罪

中華民國十二年二月二十五日

浙江省軍務善後督辦處盧永祥
省長公署張載陽

6.

Translation.

"Roll-tobacco" is a luxury which comes into Chekiang in increasing quantities year by year. It is a great waste of the people's money. The tariff duty rate on "Roll-tobacco" in foreign countries is extremely high: a good plan is to stop smoking by means of heavy taxation. Money is urgently needed for necessary work in Chekiang at present – i.e. construction of the provincial road, etc., which must be carried out at once – and the precedent existing in foreign countries should be followed now: the special tax on "Roll-tobacco" will be put into force provisionally. It will be advantageous to the locality if local money is raised. It is right to collect this tax because it is imposed on the smoker. Orders are now issued and should be obeyed. Nine provisional regulations are now printed and promulgated for the information of the public. All those dealing in "Roll-tobacco" should obey the rules and pay the tax: infringement of the regulations entails a fine. Orders have been issued to the tax office to announce the date of commencing collection, and the regulations are herewith promulgated:

Chekiang Provisional "Roll-tobacco" Tax Regulations.

1. All people in Chekiang smoking "Roll-tobacco" should pay

7.

pay Special Tax of 20 % ad val (the word "Roll-tobacco" means Cigarettes and Cigars).

2. Special Revenue Stamps will be used in collecting the "Roll-tobacco" Tax.

3. Revenue Stamps will be affixed in accordance with the value of "Roll-tobacco" in smallest containers for sale ("smallest containers" means tins, packages, boxes).

4. Merchants shall affix Revenue Stamps according to the following rules.

(a) When the imported "Roll-tobacco" is discharged from a ship it should be reported to the Examiner and an examination certificate will be pasted on each box. Concealment is not allowed.

(b) When the "Roll-tobacco" is brought to the shop or godown on importation, Revenue Stamps should be purchased from the examiner in accordance with the examination certificate and kept ready for use.

(c) When the "Roll-tobacco" is sold in original boxes, the Revenue Stamps shall be handed to the purchaser together with the cargo. If the box is opened and tobacco is sold in small lots, Revenue Stamps should be purchased and given to the purchaser.

(d) Shops or merchants should not buy the "Roll-tobacco" without being provided with Revenue Stamps.

(e) As soon as the boxes or packages (in the box) are opened, the Revenue Stamps are to be affixed to the

the packages (smallest containers).

(f) When the Revenue Stamps are affixed, they should be cancelled with the seal of the shop on the specially authorised trading certificate.

(g) Revenue Stamps are not allowed to be omitted or affixed to a lower value on the packages.

5. Those who use Revenue Stamps and pay the tax in advance, are allowed to receive commission according to the face value: the rate of commission is specified in a special tariff.

6. Infringement of these regulations and other articles entails a fine. The amount of the fines is stated in special rules.

7. Passengers from other provinces entering Chekiang are allowed to carry 50 pieces each. If more the excess is to be presented to the examiner for examination and Revenue Stamps are to be affixed on landing: concealment is not allowed.

8. Informants who report contravention of these regulations and are responsible as witnesses will receive half of the fines.

9. Making spurious Revenue Stamps and using old ones (by removing the cancellation marks) will be punished according the law governing the crime of forging valuable documents.

TRUE TRANSLATION:

INSPECTORATE GENERAL OF CUSTOMS,

S/O PEKING, 5 April 1923.

Dear Mr. Williams,

I have duly received your S/O letter No.269 of the 24th of March.

Provincial Taxation of cigars and cigarettes.

This tax is a nuisance and will put the clock back. Be very reserved in your attitude towards these doings !

Yours truly,

C. A. S. Williams, Esquire.
WENCHOW.

CUSTOM HOUSE,

S/O No. 270.   Wenchow   7th April, 1923.

Dear Sir Francis,

Revenue. We collected nearly ten thousand taels in duty last month – an increase of Hk.Tls. 3,737.326 over March 1922 – while the revenue for the first quarter of the year, Hk.Tls. 26,621.242, shows an increase of Hk.Tls. 12,416.242 over the corresponding quarter last year. At this rate we should go well over the hundred thousand tael mark by the end of the year, and the status of Wenchow as a duty-collecting office will be considerably raised.

Cigarette Tax Stamps. With reference to my telegram of today's date requesting authority to pass free of duty and examination 4 cases of cigarette stamps for the local provincial tax office, I may mention that the stamps were brought up on S.S. "Feiching" by the compradore, and were not passed through the Shanghai Customs

SIR FRANCIS AGLEN, K.B.E.,
    Inspector General of Customs,
        P E K I N G.

Customs. I understand there will be further arrivals of these revenue stamps, which I believe are being printed by the Commercial Press, Shanghai.

Local Demonstration.	A demonstration was organised here on the 5th inst. in favour of the retrocession of Dairen and Port Arthur and the abrogation of the Twenty-one Demands. A procession with bands and flags, headed by the Members of the Chamber of Commerce, and including students of both sexes, and boy scouts, perambulated the town distributing propagandive leaflets. Some representatives of the movement interviewed me in my office and requested me to oppose all infringements of China's rights; I told them I was always ready to advance the interests of China in any possible way, whereupon they all cheered, waved their flags, and continued on their peregrinations. I was, however, rather surprised to notice in the local Chinese paper on the following day that, in the account of the demonstration, it was wrongly stated that "the deputation requested the Commissioner to write to his Minister and advocate justice, which he agreed to to do!"

Piracies.		As will be seen from my Return of Non-urgent Chinese Correspondence for last month, piratical assaults on Chinese craft continue as usual - much to the detriment of local trade.

Fire.		On the 4th inst. there was a fire outside the West Gate and five houses were burned down.

Staff.		The Staff are all well. I went to bed with a mild attack of influenza during the Easter holidays and am all right again now, though suffering rather from weakness of the eyes, brought on I think by overstrain. Mr. Coxall, the newly appointed 2nd Class Tidewaiter, seems to be a very nice young fellow, and is getting on well with his work in the Native Customs.

Yours truly,

C.A.S. Williams

INSPECTORATE GENERAL OF CUSTOMS,

S/O

PEKING, 12 April 19 23.

Dear Mr. Williams,

I have duly received your S/O letter No.268 of the 10th of March.

<u>Appointment of extra Clerk requested.</u>

A man is being sent this Spring.

<u>Commissioner awarded Prix Stanislas Julien for "Manual of Chinese Metaphor".</u>

Congratulations on this well-deserved honour !

Yours truly,

C. A. S. Williams, Esquire.
   WENCHOW.

CUSTOM HOUSE,

S/O No. 271 (Special).　　　Wenchow, 12th April, 1923.

Dear Sir Francis,

With reference to S/O Circular No. 37 calling for a special report on local effects should the proposed abolition of Coast Duty be carried out, I can safely say that the reduction in the volume of documents to be prepared at this Port would not be so large as to justify a reduction of the Indoor Staff, Foreign or Native.

The proportion in which Coast Trade Duties contribute towards the Maritime Customs Revenue of Wenchow is very small (from 4 to 5%), and the abolition would reduce the work of the two men (one Clerk and one Lushih) engaged in assessment only to a very slight extent.

The abolition of Coast Trade Duty would not diminish the work of the Examiner, and therefore it would

SIR FRANCIS AGLEN, K.B.E.,
Inspector General of Customs,
　　　PEKING.

would not be possible to effect any economies in the Outdoor Staff, Foreign or Native.

It is possible that the abolition may result in the diversion of certain goods from the Native Customs to the Maritime Customs, but I am not prepared to make any definite statement on this point.

Yours truly,

C.a.S. Williams.

CUSTOM HOUSE,

S/O NO. 272.   Wenchow, 21st April 1923.

Dear Mr. Bowra,

Relief Rice under expired Huchao.

With regard to my despatch No. 3732 reporting on Weiyüan Yeh Ch'u-ch'ün's shipment of rice on deposit of duty, the Huchao presented being expired, in my S/O No. 253 of 29th July 1922 I mentioned that my suspicions had been aroused in the matter of exportation of so-called relief rice under false pretences, and that I had passed several lots covered by expired Huchao on deposit of full and half duty pending production of valid Huchao. I.G. S/O of 16th August 1922 in reply stated "Carry out instructions, I think you would certainly be wise to cover any departure from them by deposit

C. A. V. BOWRA, ESQUIRE,
    Officiating Inspector General, ad interim,
        P E K I N G .

2.

deposit of duty". In each case I obtained a written promise from the applicant to forfeit the duty if the valid Huchao was not procured within two months. None were produced, so the full duty was brought to account and the half duty (to which we are not entitled but was only taken as an extra inducement to hasten the settlement) was refunded. Yeh Ch'u-ch'ün was treated in exactly the same way. If I treated him differently the others would have complained. The fact is he tried to "work" the Governor to force me to refund the duty, and I feel pretty sure that the rice was not used for famine relief at all, but was sold at Shanghai (as reported in my despatch No. 3728). The Governor's eyes will be opened to the rascality of his Weiyüan when the Ch'ü sends him my report forwarded to you in my despatch No. 3732. I think Yeh is afraid of being found out. This case has no connection with the case reported in despatches Nos. 3681 and 3697 (as suggested in I.G. despatch No. 1155/94,017), which was

a

3.

a matter of military rice, and is settled.

Raw Cotton: prohibition of export abroad.
  Some time ago the Superintendent, at the instance of the Ch'u, asked me to sign a joint notification prohibiting the export abroad of Raw Cotton. I have not done so as I have received no instructions from you in the matter. I suppose there are objections from the Diplomatic Body.

Cigarette Tax.
  The Superintendent has not yet issued a Government Stores Certificate for the Provincial Cigarette Tax Stamps imported recently, so the Duty still remains on deposit. Does the Central Government recognise this Tax? The Tax Office commenced to function on the 11th instant. I understand that when a case of cigarette is opened, stamps have to be bought to cover the contents. As fully one third of the cigarettes go bad at this damp season of the year, it means that one third of the tax will fall on the dealer instead of, as intended, on the consumer.

I

4.

amine Relief Work.

    I have been interesting myself as far as I can in Famine Relief Work, and raised subscriptions for this object amounting to $800 odd. I also wrote to Mr. Carey, Co-Chairman of the Chinese Foreign **Famine** Relief Committee in Ningpo, and asked him if he could arrange for a larger proportion of famine funds to be remitted here, with the result that a special grant of $15,000 was made to Wenchow.

llitary activities.

    On the 8th instant 80 northern soldiers, who had retreated from Fukien **via** Lung-ch'üan (龍泉), arrived here, and proceeded to Shanghai on the 19th instant. On the 16th one **ying** of the local troops proceeded to Lung-ch'üan, and on the 19th one **ying** left for Chiang-shan Hsien (江山縣) **via** Ch'uchow (處州). We have only one **ying** left, which will also be despatched to Chiang-shan, when a fresh detachment **arrives** from Hangchow to relieve it.

tercourse with ficials.

    I am maintaining very friendly

relations

relations with the local officials, and invited the Taoyin, Magistrate, and Superintendent to lunch on the 9th instant.

Boycott of Japanese Goods.

On the 10th instant a boycott of Japanese goods was started. Some students broke the lock and seals of a red box and came into the Custom House Compound, and interfered with the examination of cargo, so I sent a mild letter of protest to the Superintendent asking him to request the students not to interfere with our work in future.

District Assembly.

The Yungchia District Assembly opened its session this year on the 1st instant.

Yours truly,

C. A. W. Williams.

INSPECTORATE GENERAL OF CUSTOMS,

S/O.

PEKING, 27 April, 19 23.

Dear Williams,

A despatch is being sent you transferring Mr. Wong Haiu Geng to Santuao. He is being replaced by Mr. Chü Kam Po from Ningpo. Although transferred from 1st May Mr. Wong - presuming he can get fairly good connections - need not be in any great hurry, as he is replacing Mr. Tai Tin-tsoi, going on leave from 1st June.

Yours truly,

G. C. F. Holland.

[A.—42]

S/O

INSPECTORATE GENERAL OF CUSTOMS,

PEKING, 1 May 1923.

Dear Sir,

I am directed by the Inspector General to inform you that your S/O letters No. 270 & 271, 272 dated 7th and 12th Apr., and 21st April has been duly received.

Yours truly,

B. Foster Hall
a/asst Private Secretary.

C.A.S. Williams Esq.

Wenchow.

CUSTOM HOUSE,

S/O NO. 273.   Wenchow, 5th May 1923.

Dear Mr. Bowra,

evenue.

  The Revenue for last **month showed** an increase of Hk.Tls. 3,923.230 as compared with last April.

hortage of Outdoor taff.

  I made a definite application to you in my despatch No. 3737, N.C. No. 310, for a Foreign Tidewaiter and a Chinese Watcher. Mr. Garwood, Assistant Examiner **B**, was transferred to Ningpo in August last and replaced by Mr. Lu Si Huo (盧詩和), 4th Class (Chinese) Tidewaiter **B** - a young fellow of practically no experience - thus weakening our already small staff. Since that time there has been a gradual increase of tonnage at this port, which is now very difficult for us to deal with. I tried, however,

A.V. Bowra, Esquire,
 Officiating Inspector General, ad interim,
  PEKING.

2.

however, to carry on as well as I could, because I thought, as promised in I.G. despatch No. 1145/93,098, N.C.No.168, of 9th February 1923 that further staff arrangements would be made. As there were no spring appointments to this port except the new Tidesurveyor, I thought I had better lay the matter before you.

Movements of Officials.

The permanent incumbent of the Superintendency, Mr. Hoo Wei Yen (胡惟賢), returned here on the 25th of last month from Singapore, where he had collected $40,000.00 for famine relief in this province. Magistrate Chang Lien (張濂) has vacated his post for the time being to attend to his late father's obsequies, his place being temporarily held by Chang P'êng-i (張鵬羽), detached from the Taoyin's Yamen. The latter took over charge on the 30th ult., and I have exchanged calls with him. He is a native of Hupeh.

Military activities.

One ying of Chekiang troops arrived here on the 2nd inst., and one ying of Northern

3.

Northern men left here today.

Chinese Examination of B.A.T. Agent.

Mr. C.A. Wolf, local Agent of the British-American Tobacco Co., wished to sit for an Examination in mandarin colloquial set by the Shanghai British Chamber of Commerce, and I was asked to supervise and subject him to an oral test, as there is nobody else here who knows mandarin. I thought there would be no objection on your part, so I conducted the examination on the 2nd instant and the candidate passed a very creditable examination, which entitles him to a bonus of $25. a month from his firm.

Relief Rice under fired Huchao.

In continuation of my remarks in my last S/O anent the Yeh Ch'u-ch'ün rice fraud, I append an extract from the local paper "Sin Ngau Chau" (新甌潮) of 30th April, from which you will see that public opinion is distinctly opposed to Yeh Ch'u-ch'ün's manipulations of rice last year. Yeh's name is not actually mentioned, but he is the person implied. My action in taking up the case

case is approved of.

     Yours truly,
      C.A.S. Williams.
    APPEND.

Extract from Local Newspaper "Sin Ngau Chau" (新甌潮) of 30th April 1923.

> 米稅有追繳之消息
> 樂清奸商易叔英去歲與某省議員等漏米漁利借照影射當時地方輿論大譁羣起反對茲開此案舊事重提省議會某議員提起質問省長發交杭監督查復查得該奸商等在吾溫辦去公米均未到省另處售賣借照漁利已可概見阮未運辦到省應不能免稅放運著補繳稅銀共三萬元現奉海關飭追一時聞者莫不拍手稱善後之漏未劣紳當以此為殷鑒也

TRUE COPY:
  [signature]

[A.—42]

INSPECTORATE GENERAL OF CUSTOMS,

S/O

PEKING, *19 May* 1923.

Dear Sir,

I am directed by the Inspector General to inform you that your S/O letter No. *273*, dated *5 May*, has been duly received.

Yours truly,

B. Foster Hall
a/asst. Private Secretary.

C.A.S. Williams Esq.

Wenchow.

CUSTOM HOUSE,

S/O NO. 274.   Wenchow, 19th May, 1923.

Dear Mr. Bowra,

Timber Rafts.

As reported in my despatch No. 3739 I have instituted a new system of raft measurement. This matter probably would not have come to my notice had it not been for the fact that the recent changes in the Out-door Staff have had the effect of a new broom which sweeps clean. Not that the former staff were in any way to blame, but a new man is often quicker to notice irregularities which have developed into a practice. Mr. Coxall, 2nd Class Tidewaiter, is very energetic in his examination work at the Native Customs, and as a result the fines and confiscations have considerably increased. It was owing to the large discrepancies he found in timber rafts, that led me to take the matter up. The Chinese Examiners

A.V. BOWRA, ESQUIRE,
  Officiating Inspector General, ad interim,
    P E K I N G.

2.

Examiners and Watchers in the N.C. are a poor lot, and do not work any more than they can possibly help; so they have to be kept up to the mark.

rospective A.P.C. Oil nstallation.

A good deal of my time has been taken up during the past few months over the question of the Asiatic Petroleum Co's arrangements for obtaining a site for an oil installation. The idea is to put up two large tanks and godowns just outside the Harbour Limits and the Company continually asks us to supply them with soundings of the channel, etc., and wants me to give my formal approval of the site and to obtain the sanction of the Chinese authorities for the installation. They intend to build first and take the risk of being turned down by the Chinese authorities afterwards. The site appears to me to be suitable as far as the Customs is concerned, but no license can be issued until the sanction of the Chinese is obtained. I suggested they should apply for this sanction through the Ningpo Consul, but they say they anticipate better

better results be dealing through me. I am not sure whether I ought to act for them in this capacity however, though Mr. Tanant did so in the case of the Standard Oil Company. It would hardly be fair to refuse one firm what was accorded to another. What the Company wants at the present time is for me to assure them that, as far as the Customs is concerned, there is no objection to the proposed installation site. May I give them qualified approval subject to the consent of the Chinese authorities? This will enable the Company to commence arrangements for land purchase, etc.

There was a serious fire last night in two fish shops next door to the Custom House, but fortunately no damage was caused to the latter as there was no wind. I took the opportunity to request the Superintendent to arrange with the local authorities that when the burnt-out shops are rebuilt they shall be set back further away from the Custom House, as the street is very

very narrow at that part.

Visit of Salt Cruiser.

The Salt Revenue Cruiser "Kungsheng" visited the port yesterday with several foreign Inspectors on board who had come from Peking, Foochow and Ningpo. They did not appear to be anxious to give me any information as to why they had come, but I think it must have been in connection with some difference of opinion over the amount of the taxation of Fukien Salt so largely imported into Chekiang for fish preserving purposes.

Liangt'ou Dues on I.S.N. Vessels.

Ningpo informs me that you authorise the discontinuation of the levy of Liangt'ou Dues on Inland Waters Steamers, so I am following suit here (<u>vide</u> I.G. despatch No. 1661/94,027 to Ningpo).

Yours truly,

C. A. Williams.

INSPECTORATE GENERAL OF CUSTOMS,

S/O

PEKING, 1 June 1923.

Dear Mr. Williams,

I have duly received your S/O letter No. 274 of the 19th of May.

Timber Rafts.

This is a useful matter to take up but I am afraid you overlooked the fact that there is a Customs publication on the subject of Timber Rafts.

Prospective A.P.C. Installation; may Commissioner approve site subject to consent of Chinese Authorities ?

No, better not ! If the A.P.C. intend to build **first** and get official sanction **later**, your qualified approval might be made use of in defence of their action.

Moreover, the Santuao Commissioner is having difficulty with the A.P.C. with regard to Tank Installation matters. You had better, therefore, stick to the usual and proper procedure. (N.B. Art.1 of the A.P.C. Tank Regulations at Ichang in Regulations, Customs : Harbour - Misc. No.25, p.17). Was not the Standard Oil Company's Installation established without the

C. A. S. Williams, Esquire.

WENCHOW.

the permission of the local Authorities ? (vide Wenchow despatch No.3674).

Liangt'ou Dues on I.W.S.N. Vessels: Commr. follows Ningpo.

You should report officially any action in such a matter.

Yours truly,

CUSTOM HOUSE,

S/O NO. 275.   Wenchow, 2nd June 1923

Dear Mr. Bowra,

rease of trade, and k of godown accommoda- n.

The import and export trade is now double as compared with last year, and I am trying to get the China Merchants S.N. Co. to enlarge their godowns as we have considerable difficulty in examining cargo, which is often piled up in the Customs compound, and even along the streets! I shall probably have to address you officially on this matter.

I do not anticipate any objection on the part of steamer agents to pay the demurrage charge of $1.00 a day as compensation for loss of the boatman's time when waiting

C.A.V. BOWRA, ESQUIRE,
  Officiating Inspector General, ad interim,
    PEKING.

2.

waiting at the mouth of the river to pilot a vessel which is late in arrival (vide my despatch No. 3743).

ange of route of rchas.

The Superintendent proposes to change the route of 27 lorchas plying between here and Shanghai and allow them to run to certain inland places for 3 months without getting authority from the Chiao-t'ung Pu. Is there any objection to this? It might develop into a practice, and I fancy it may result in some loss of revenue.

ingt'ou Dues.

Passenger boats running from here to Yo-ts'ing (Kuant'ou), which is not under our jurisdiction, are beginning to carry cargo, so I am levying Liangt'ou Dues on them. Strictly speaking passenger boats are exempt, but it seems to me that if they carry cargo to any great extent, they change their status. There is some objection on their part to the levy, but I hope to be able to arrange matters satisfactorily.

anese Boycott.

No Japanese goods are arriving now, and

3.

and the Germans and Americans seem to have seized the opportunity to enter into the sundry goods trade. I have had no further trouble with the students who have not interfered further with our examination work.

aff.

The Staff are all well. The Tidesurveyor held an examination on the 30th ult., for selection of a local Chinese Watcher as authorised by your despatch No. 1664. Mr. Lau Kieng Hing, 2nd Clerk: A, has gone on 4 months leave, so I have put the new man Mr. Ling Chan Ngau, 3rd Clerk: C, into the General Office for the time being. We shall, however, be glad when Mr. Lau returns. Mr. K'o Yu-p'ing, 2nd Clerk: C, is very pleased at your decision to date his seniority for superannuation and retirement purposes from the time he joined the Native Customs (as per your despatch No. 1165); I have, as before, recorded in the Service List the date of his first appointment as from the time he joined the Maritime Customs. Is this correct?

I

4.

ce.

I append a copy of an extract from the Sin Ngau Chau (新甌潮) from which you will see that the local people have telegraphed to the Hangchow Authorities to investigate the matter of relief rice consigned to Hangchow last year, and sold en route.

Yours truly,

C.A.S. Williams.

Append

APPEND.

Extract from local Newspapers "Sin Ngau Chau"
(新 甌 報) of 25th May 1923.

電請嚴懲售賣賑米

永嘉公民范繼文等昨日電致杭州軍民兩長浙江督辦盧省長張省議會鈞鑒去歲甌籍紳紳向省署籲請護照名為運賑浙西實則恃符包漏此種情弊閣之省議員曹維翰君所提關於甌米出運護照事項簡問書頗為詳確毋庸再贅惟此案至今尚無貫徹目的正滋疑惑甌關稅務司准杭關來文查得去年八九月間時在甌屬風災之後商人盧榮發源茂順記等號先後保自溫州裝由飛鯨海晏等輪出口運杭賑米一萬三千五百七十七擔並未到達指運地點諒在半途貪圖厚利違章售賣函請監督令縣派警提保罰辦等因在卷伏查此項護照係趙

悦羣王志澄等首名請領當然負完全責任在若輩以代議士資
格不惠與利革弊竟復幸災樂禍藉官廳之護照為滿海之行為
圖飽私囊貽慨民生萬懇立予重懲並將曹議員前次質問之案
切實澈查嚴重處分庶為藉照漁利者戒永嘉公民范繼文朱文
釗余覲型金亮胡方樞邵一望董超王章陳慕植謝徐濂李崧鄭
景珊熊怡祖施拯張宗栻等同叩

TRUE COPY:

INSPECTORATE GENERAL OF CUSTOMS,

S/O

PEKING, 12 June 1923.

Dear Mr. Williams,

I have duly received your S/O letter No.275 of the 2nd instant.

Increase of trade and lack of godown accommodation.

This is rather remarkable. What is the reason for this sudden growth in the trade of Wenchow?

Liangt'ou Dues. Commissioner assumes that passenger boats change status if they carry cargo.

If any instructions are required, the matter should be reported with full particulars by despatch.

Mr. K'o Yu-p'ing: Commissioner records ce List the date of his first appointment as from time he joined the Maritime Customs. Is this correct?

Yes!

Yours truly,

C. A. S. Williams, Esquire.
WENCHOW.

S/O NO. 276.

CUSTOM HOUSE,

Wenchow, 16th June 1923.

Dear Mr. Bowra,

property matters.

With reference to your telegram of the 7th instant, informing me that an architect was proceeding here and you authorise the purchase of the H. B. M.'s Consulate and Constable's House if these buildings are structurally sound, Mr. W.J. Leahy, architect, duly arrived here on the 14th instant, and is now engaged in examining the properties in question. The Engineer-in-Chief suggests that any other property questions might also be brought to Mr. Leahy's notice, so I intend to give him my views as to the best disposition of all our property in this port. He will be
here

C.A.V. BOWRA, ESQUIRE,
    Officiating Inspector General, ad interim.
        PEKING.

2.

here for a fortnight, and I am putting him up as there is no proper accommodation for him elsewhere.

Much could be done to improve our examination facilities. Now that trade is increased our examination arrangements are quite inadequate. It is my hope to be able to secure for the Service the foreshore rights in front of the Custom House, and we could then have a proper jetty and Examination Shed and link up our property along the bund. On the other hand the Native Customs Head Office is far too large and badly situated away from the river bank. Tomorrow (Sunday) I am taking Mr. Leahy up the hill to survey the Customs Bungalow site, which is in a bad state and requires attention as it is being washed out in many parts by the rains. It really needs levelling and enclosing, but, according to the instructions of I.G. despatch No.1151/93,724, this work is not to be done until experience has established the necessity. In the meantime I have built a small bungalow of my own on an adjoining plot, where my family are

3.

are going to spend the summer. The Methodist Mission has asked for the first refusal of this bungalow if I should be transferred from this port, but I doubt whether they will really buy it, in which case the Service might possibly acquire it. In any case the Customs property will make a fine garden and tennis court, and its cost was practically nil. My bungalow is all stone with a flat reinforced cement roof, and is therefore typhoon-proof.

ngt'ou Dues on senger Boats.

On going further into the question of Liangt'ou Dues on Passenger Boats (vide my despatch No. 3746), I find that the revenue obtainable under this heading will not be very high, and if opposition continues, you may perhaps decide that it is not worth while levying on these vessels.

ge of route of chas.

The Superintendent has now withdrawn his proposal to change the route of 27 lorchas plying between here and Shanghai (vide my last S/O No. 275).

I

binet crisis.   I hope there will be no rioting in Peking on account of the resignation of the Chinese Cabinet at this critical time.

Yours truly,

Ca S Williams.

INSPECTORATE GENERAL OF CUSTOMS,

S/O

PEKING, 23 June 1923.

Dear Mr. Williams,

I have duly received your S/O letter No.276 of the 16th instant.

Wenchow building plans. Commissioner's private bungalow.

For reference and to complete the property archives a full report on Service property at Wenchow will be useful, but I am afraid that, with the many pressing demands on Service funds elsewhere, any proposals to incur expenditure will have to await future consideration.

As regards your hill bungalow, the acquisition of a bungalow for your port, either by building or purchase, is not at present contemplated and any arrangements for its sale, either now or in future, should be made without any idea that the Service may be a prospective purchaser.

Yours truly,

A. S. Williams, Esquire.
WENCHOW.

CUSTOM HOUSE,

S/O NO. 277. Wenchow, 30th June 1923

Dear Mr. Bowra,

Preliminaries to purchase of Consul's and Constable's Houses.

      Mr. Leahy, Architect, reported the Consul's and Constable's Houses as structurally sound, but found that a few minor repairs would be advisable, either now or in the future. He estimated the total cost of these repairs at $550 for the Consul's House and $500 for the Constable's, though certain essential repairs will only amount to $200 and $400 respectively. I wrote to the Divisional Architect, H.B.M. Office of Works, Shanghai, and asked if all these repairs could be effected or the cost deducted from the price of the houses. When I receive his reply I will report on the whole

C.A.V. BOWRA, ESQUIRE,
  Officiating Inspector General, ad interim.
    PEKING.

whole matter.

ter supply.

In my despatch No. 3749, N.C. No. 315, forwarding Mr. Leahy's report on our property at this port, and making certain recommendations, I omitted to mention the matter of the water supply at Wenchow. The facilities in this respect are poor, as we depend on public wells, which do not always contain good water, and occasionally run dry, and we import water from the North River about 2 miles away at a cost to the Service of $67.80 per annum for the Out-door Staff on Conquest Island and $22.56 for the Tidewaiter on the mainland. The Catholic Mission has an excellent artesian well, and the Sisters of St. Vincent de Paul are now having another one made. I asked Mr. Leahy to make enquiries at Shanghai about the cost of boring artesian wells, and he said he would do so, and, as far as he knew, a fee of $50 is required for prospecting, and $500 if water is struck. I do not know whether it is in order to apply for

authority

authority for such expenditure, as an artesian well could only be put down in the Commissioner's compound, and would not benefit other members of the staff, though it might perhaps be possible to supply the staff with water from such a well, and thus save $90. a year to the Service. By the way, I bored an ordinary well quite successfully in the compound of my bungalow on the hills.

elopment of Custom se and communications.

With reference to Schemes A, B, and C, for development and improvement of the Maritime Customs Offices and environs as detailed in my despatch No. 3749, N.C.315, if you are in favour of my taking the matter up with the Superintendent, I propose to ask the Works Department to make me some duplicate blue prints of the plans, which the Superintendent can transmit to the Provincial Authorities, District Assembly, Chamber of Commerce, Magistrate, and Taoyin, in order to facilitate investigation and discussion. I feel that, even if we do not derive all the

4.

the benefits we anticipate, we shall at least pave the way to future improvements, and probably secure some advantages. My relations with the officials are very cordial at present, so it would be a good time to start negotiations.

toms Out-door Staff galow at Mokanshan.

Mr. Coxall, 2nd Class Tidewaiter, who was transferred here from Shanghai in April, reports that, when on the Shanghai Staff, he was promised leave to go to the Customs Out-door Staff Bungalow at Mokanshan, and asks if there is any objection to his going there from here. Is this Bungalow provided entirely for the Shanghai Staff, or are members of the Staff of other ports entitled to go there?

ff.

The Staff are all well, though the weather is now very hot and oppressive. My family are all installed in our new bungalow on the hills, and my wife intends to invite Mrs. Ayden, the Tidesurveyor's wife, to stay with her there for three weeks. I shall

shall go up for the week-ends.

Yours truly,

C.A.E. Williams

INSPECTORATE GENERAL OF CUSTOMS,

S/O

PEKING, 10 July 1923.

Dear Mr. Williams,

I have duly received your S/O letter No. 277 of the 30th of June.

Development of Custom House and communications.

This will be dealt with by despatch.

Out-ports and O.D.S. bungalow at Mokanshan.

They are entitled to go if there is room. The Shanghai Commissioner should be applied to.

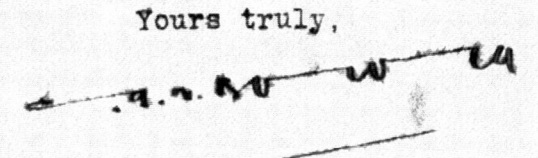

Yours truly,

A. S. Williams, Esquire.
WENCHOW.

CUSTOM HOUSE,

S/O NO. 278.　　　　　　　　　　Wenchow, 14th July 1923

Dear Mr. Bowra,

ilding Plans.　　　　　In your S/O of 23rd ult. you remark that any proposals to incur expenditure for building must await future consideration. I hope, however, that you will have no objection to the formulation of a building programme which can be carried out gradually as funds permit. There is no doubt that much should be done for the improvement of Customs, shipping, and mercantile facilities at this port. The bund and communications in the neighbourhood of the Custom House, and steamer wharves, and the approaches through the crowded fish market to the main gate of the city, present a decayed and ill-developed appearance not calculated to impress

any

C.A.V. BOWRA, ESQUIRE,
　　Officiating Inspector General, ad interim,
　　　　PEKING.

any person desirous of trading to and from this port; while the lack of accommodation for cargo actually impedes both trade and traffic.

It has occurred to me that, if the wherewithal is lacking to ameliorate these unsatisfactory conditions, we might seek other means to secure the necessary funds. For example the Enclosure for Examination of cargo (styled Customs Yard in the plans of Schemes A, B, and C in my despatch No. 3749), will be of little value to us if we acquire the foreshore rights in front of the Custom House, and if we sold it to the China Merchants S.N. Co., it would form a most valuable addition to that Company's property, which it adjoins, and moreover it would then be possible for the Company to extend their godowns which would be a great advantage to us, and to the merchants, on account of the distressing lack of cargo accommodation. Some funds might be obtained from the provincial treasury for alterations to roads, etc. As far

3.

far as the Native Customs is concerned, as I said in my despatch No. 3749, it is quite possible that the sale of the Head Office will provide us with all the money we require for building more suitable premises on the bund. At the same time one cannot expect to carry out extensive building operations without a certain amount of outlay.

hives and card-dexing.

I forgot to mention in my despatch No. 3751 that I have already started the card-indexing of the correspondence with Ports and the Public from the new series of numbering started by Mr. Acheson in 1914. I am putting the date on the left hand side on cards unprovided with date headings. I have looked through this correspondence as far as it exists before this date, and there is really nothing of great interest which is likely to be required for reference in modern times, as all the more important questions have arisen later. I have indexed to 1919 so far.

The

4.

The archives are in process of binding and a more workmanlike present aspect; the next Commissioner will find correspondence, orders, notifications, Service and miscellaneous publications, etc., etc., all properly arranged and suitably indexed.

I have presented to the Commissioner's Library a copy of my "Anglo-Chinese Glossary for Customs and Commercial Use."

aff.

I thought it would be advisable to give some short leave to Mr. Coxall, 2nd Class Tidewaiter. He had been working extremely hard, and had been promised leave before he was transferred from Shanghai. At the same time the public were complaining that he was rather too assiduous in the matter of searching and confiscation; this, of course, is a fault on the right side, and I do not like to check him too much or he will feel discouraged.

Mr. Bodisco, 3rd Assistant B, is well, and working up for his Chinese Examination. I make him knock off at the week-ends,

5.

week-ends, which he spends with us in the hills.

Mr. Ryden, the new Tidesurveyor, is very industrious and has just completed a survey of the Native Customs stations, which he visited in my private houseboat. He thinks the N.C. Staff could be reduced with advantage, and is strongly in favour of the provision of a motor-boat for inspection and preventive work, the N.C. houseboat being slow and unhandy. He believes the revenue is not as high as it might be with the aid of a motor-boat.

vements of Officials.
On the 31st ultimo Magistrate Chang Lien (張濂) returned to his post.

The Superintendent went to Shanghai on the 4th instant, leaving his Secretary, Mr. Shên Ming, in charge; he told me he would come back if any very important questions cropped up. He bought a house in Shanghai last year.

On the 6th instant General Hao Hsü-tung (郝旭東) arrived to take charge of of the local forces.

              Yours truly,

              C a E Williams

INSPECTORATE GENERAL OF CUSTOMS,

S/O

PEKING, 28 July 1923.

Dear Mr. Williams,

I have duly received your S/O letter No.278 of the 14th instant.

<u>Building proposals</u>.

Service funds are limited and building operations can only be sanctioned when clearly necessary and when funds are available.

<u>Proposed reduction in N.C.Staff</u>.

Reduction of N.C.Staff is desirable, but this proposal should be made officially when it has been thoroughly gone into.

Yours truly,

A. S. Williams, Esquire.
   WENCHOW.

CUSTOM HOUSE.

S/O NO. 279.   Wenchow, 28th July 1923.

Dear Mr. Bowra,

asting operations.

With reference to Coast Inspector's Despatch No. 3139 re dynamite and detonators for blasting out the hull of S.S. "Hanyang Maru" sunk in the Wenchow Harbour, these explosive materials duly came forward, and the hull of the vessel has been blasted out as required.

inese Employés
used of accepting
bes and extorting
ey.

In my Return of Non-urgent Chinese Correspondence for this month you will find details of a case in which certain Native Customs Watchers and Boatmen are accused of releasing a seizure of opium on receipt of bribes of various sums. There is also mention of a Maritime Customs Tidewaiter
extorting

C.A.V. BOWRA, ESQUIRE,
    Officiating Inspector General, ad interim.
        PEKING.

extorting money. I did not think it worth while to report these cases by despatch, as I am convinced that they are false accusations, an opinion in which the Superintendent concurs.

In sifting the evidence of the first of these cases, however, I came to the conclusion that our control over native shipping is not as good as it might be, and I intend to study this question and report to you thereon in due course.

ss-stitch Work.

I shall be writing officially on the matter of duty-treatment of local cross-stitch work. I believe a Wenchow firm is attempting to obtain privileged treatment from Peking.

e Harvest.

An excellent rice crop is now being harvested, and it is to be hoped that the stormy weather will not interfere with the process.

Yours truly,

A. E. Williams

CUSTOM HOUSE,

S/O NO. 280.   Wenchow, 13th August 1923.

Dear Mr. Bowra,

Typhoon.

On the 7th instant a typhoon, almost as severe as the one of last September, and longer in duration, struck this port and took a heavy toll of damage to property ashore and afloat. After blowing for about 24 hours the typhoon passed inland, and, just as we were congratulating ourselves on its departure, another one arrived on the 10th to rage with even fiercer intensity for two days more!

Profiting by the former experience of last year I had taken measures to safeguard Customs buildings as far as possible. Owing to the typhoon bars I had

prepared

A. V. BOWRA, ESQUIRE,
  Officiating Inspector General, ad interim.
    PEKING.

prepared in readiness, all serious damage to
windows was avoided, and the new stone wall
round the compound of my quarters resisted
the storm safely, which would not have been
the case had it been rebuilt of brick as
before, seeing that the brick wall of the
Methodist College collapsed again. The
Assistant's quarters, as usual, were badly
damaged - much in the same way as last
year; a photo of these quarters was sent
you after last year's typhoon in my S/O
No. 256 of 14th September 1922. It would
be an economy to provide a more substantial
house for the Assistant. The roof of my
quarters, which rests on hollow brick pillars,
was lifted up and down by the wind, and
will require to be fixed on securely again
or a subsequent storm will certainly break
it up; as the iron roofing was carefully
attended to last year, it remained intact
though shaken loose here and there. My
family were in my hill bungalow, where no
damage was done except to a few windows.
The Methodist Mission hill bungalow was
badly

badly broken up and several rooms were rendered useless. The rice in the immediate neighbourhood had fortunately just been harvested, but further up river, where the temperature is lower, it was not quite ready to reap and must have been all destroyed. A strong freshet is coming down the river and much of the surrounding country is badly flooded.

Measures for flood control.

On the 5th instant Mr. A. C. Akehurst, formerly Commander of R.S. "Likin", and now attached to the Whangpoo Conservancy, arrived here, accompanied by Mr. Rhodin, a forestry expert, and an interpreter, being engaged by the International Famine Relief Committee to make a tour of inspection of this province with a view to devising means for flood control, for which a (rather inadequate) sum of $25,000 is available. They intend to proceed up river by houseboat shortly, and I have borrowed a steam-launch from the Standard Oil Company to tow them as far as Ch'uchow. In the meantime they are

are being feasted by the officials and gentry. Their instructions are to consult the Taoyin and myself as to their intinerary and _modus operandi_. I have had several interviews with them, and expressed my views as to what is required in the way of flood control along this river and on the coast. Owing to the typhoon and subsequent floods they certainly have a unique opportunity of seeing the country in its worst possible condition!

Prospective purchase of Consular Property.

With reference to your telegram of 2nd instant, instructing me to await further orders with regard to the purchase of the Consular property as the title is not clear, you will have noted that in my despatch No. 3750 I reported that one of the conditions I made with H. B. M.'s Divisional Architect was that a clear title should be shown to the land, and I was informed that the title-deeds were being handed to you for inspection. I therefore concluded that the title would be made clear to you. On receipt

5.

receipt of your telegram I reiterated this condition and asked for full information as to how the land is held. As far as our present Conquest Island property is concerned, we pay a nominal ground rent, as, for instance, ?2 a month for one plot, and I have been given to understand that the British Government originally paid a nominal rental for the ground in question, though I was under the impression that the payment of this ground rent was allowed to lapse and the land became the property of the British Government by right of possession. As soon as I receive the Architect's explanation of the matter I intend to request the Superintendent to effect the free transfer of the land as the Service is about to purchase the buildings. As you know I successfully negotiated the free transfer of 10 **mou** of land in the hills to the Service, but of course the Island is regarded as sacred, and the principle is not to **sell** ground to outsiders, but if we argue that we are, as it were, a

Department

6.

Department of the Chinese Government, no doubt the transfer can be arranged, failing which of course the only thing is to pay a merely nominal ground-rent as in the case of our other island property. In the meantime I will not take any definite step until I have the orders referred to in your telegram, and I shall report to you and await your reply before actually handing over the purchase-money for the buildings.

organisation of venue Matters.

On the 24th of last month I received a despatch from the Superintendent transmitting the Ts'ai-chêng Pu's instructions for preparation of certain elaborate statistics required for the purpose of reorganising revenue matters, and illustrating the history and work of this office, shipping, method of duty collection, receipts and expenditure, regulations, staff, Native Customs control, map of district, etc., etc. These details are required within two months, and I find myself entirely at a loss as to how to comply with such a large order in so brief a

a time with the staff at my disposal.
Given a financial expert, a cartographer,
and a staff of clerks, it could be done !
I have sent you a copy of this despatch in
my July Summary of Non-Urgent Chinese
Correspondence, but I presume you have
already received a similar communication.

aff.
The staff, in spite of the
unhealthy state of the weather, are all well.
The Native Customs Lushih and
Examination Staff have petitioned for increase
of pay, and I append copies of their
petitions. The Lushih request that the
treatment laid down in I.G. Circular No.
3406 for non-linguist members of the Chinese
Indoor Staff in the Maritime Customs be
extended to them. The scale of pay for
the Native Customs was revised in October
1920 according to the instructions of I.G.
despatches Nos. 946/79,348 and 968/80,725.
The Weigher detached from the Maritime
Customs had his pay increased according to
I.G. Circular No. 3054.

I

oposed absence.	I have just received your despatch No. 1182/95,399 in which you disapprove of the arrangements I proposed for carrying on the work during my absence from Office for 27 days from 20th instant to 15th proximo. Will you have any objection to my officially reporting absent in the usual way for a few days in September? Mr. C.A. de Bodisco 3rd Assistant B, is capable of superintending the current routine-work of the office during this brief time.

Yours truly,

C.A.L. Williams

APPEND.

Copy of petition from Native Customs Lushih requesting increase of pay.

呈為呈請體恤下情恩准增薪與洋關一律待遇事竊錄事等供職甌海常關迄今八載薪水多者不過念餘兩少者十餘兩已艱數用際茲米珠薪桂生活程度逐漸增高月得薪水除儲蓄外所餘有限誠不足以瞻家眶勉從公復憂內顧此次洋關華文內班均蒙

恩准增薪仰見我

總憲俯念下情培植屬員之至意惟常關人員亦係我

總憲所統轄未蒙

恩及不無獨抱向隅之嘆且常關薪水本較薄於洋關即而公事實有倍於洋關即以甌海一隅而論洋關錄事三人常關僅有二人至於進出口之船隻洋關每星期不過十餘次而常關則日有數十起之多 錄事等每日於上午

七八時進關下午至早非到五六點鐘不能下關事情之繁簡於茲可見事既繁而薪又薄勞力憂薪困難實感不得已瀝情呈懇

稅務司乞為據情轉請

總憲懇照洋關華文內班一體待遇准予加薪俾錄事等內無兼顧之分憂外可致身以從事則戴

德無涯矣此呈

稅務司戴

中華民國十二年七月　　日

甌海常關華文內班錄事　段台南
　　　　　　　　　　　楊寶琛

Copy of petition from Native Customs Examiners and Weigher requesting increase of pay.

呈為呈請物力艱難勞費支絀僉祈一視同仁量加薪俸事竊司事等在關任務有年歲收加增幸無隕越惟近來生活程度較之五六年前百物騰貴困難百倍薪俸所入實難敷衍正擬集議請求體恤乃

總稅務司適有特准新關錄事加薪之請仰見仁心普照俯念時艱矣伏思新常關均是屬員內外班同是盡職新關華員之俸給素較常關為優常關外班之公務又較內班為勞優者既准予加給勞者當不令向隅一人之費已屬不敷數口之家將何以堪不已僉詞呈請

伏乞

稅務司轉詳

總稅務司體恤困難俯如所請使內外人員各無事蓄

之虞同盡從公之責則感

德靡涯矣此呈

稅務司威

瓯海常關華文外班司事陳煒

袁彬 陳可品 楊超 杜志強

郭桓 吳寶琛 王鼎 劉駿圖

枰手 林銀梨

中華民國十二年七月　　日

TRUE COPIES:

A.—42]

INSPECTORATE GENERAL OF CUSTOMS.

PEKING, 18/8 1923.

Dear Sir,

I am directed by the Inspector General inform you that your S/O letter No. 279, ted 28 July, has been duly eived.

Yours truly,

B. Foster Hall
a/asst. Private Secretary.

C. A. S. Williams Esq
Wenchow.

INSPECTORATE GENERAL OF CUSTOMS,

S/O

PEKING, 27 August 19 23.

Dear Mr. Williams,

I have duly received your S/O letter No.280 of the 13th instant.

Superintendent requests compilation of Customs handbook on behalf of Ministry of Finance.

If the Superintendent presses you, say that you cannot act without the I.G.'s instructions.

Commissioner's proposed absence in September.

No objection.

Yours truly,

A. S. Williams, Esquire.
    WENCHOW.

CUSTOM HOUSE,

S/O No. 281. Wenchow, 27th August 1923

Dear Mr. Bowra,

lorchas.

With reference to my despatch No. 3758 reporting on the proposal of the Wenchow Shipping Guild to allow all the Wenchow lorchas to run inland, I have really kept you fully informed of this matter as far as I have been able to do so (vide my S/O Nos. 275 and 276 and Summary of Non-Urgent Chinese Correspondence for June), and it was greatly to my surprise that the Superintendent, after distinctly informing me in writing that, owing to the various objections I raised, the request for the

lorchas

C. A. V. BOWRA, ESQUIRE,
   Officiating Inspector General, ad interim.
     PEKING.

2.

lorchas to ply inland had been definitely refused, he should have sent on the Guild's petition with his recommendations.

No doubt the Superintendent would collect fees for issuing temporary registers and the duty on the goods carried would all be collected by his extra 50-li stations, and, as I believe this duty collection is farmed to the highest bidders, the Superintendent would benefit considerably. It is significant that the Superintendent said nothing to the Chiao-t'ung Pu about his proposal to issue 27 registers himself, though, strictly speaking, they should be issued by the Ministry, on payment of the usual fees - to the Ministry.

Assistant's Quarters.

With reference to my despatches Nos. 3757 (N.C.No.317) and 3759, I regret very much to have to apply to you, not only for typhoon repairs to the Assistant's Quarters amounting to $389.00, but also for repairs of $361.00 due to the depredations of white ants. This makes a rather formidable total of

3.

of $750.00, which is a lot of money to pay for quarters rented on a quarterly lease. The landlord will do nothing, and would not object to our vacating the premises, rather than his having to spend any money on them.

Although you have ruled that the status of the port does not justify the purchase of land and construction of more substantial Assistant's Quarters, yet perhaps you would be inclined to consider the advisability, for reasons of economy, of purchasing a house outright. I have an opportunity, which may not be open to me for long, of acquiring a good semi-foreign house on the bund, with foreshore rights, and a good garden containing a small go-down, for $5,000.00. The house and garden would be useful for an Assistant. The house would require some alteration, and the godown would have to be taken down. If you wish, I will go into the matter and report officially. I do not think that it is financially advantageous to continue to pay large sums in repair to a house in such an exposed position, as well as rent, when an eventual
saving

4.

saving would be certainly effected by the purchase of more substantial quarters at a reasonable price.

sses of Boatman-
lot on account
Typhoon.

On the 9th instant, Boatman Hu Yen-ch'in was deputed by the Tidesurveyor to go by sampan to the entrance of the river to pilot a Japanese vessel into port. He was caught en route by the typhoon and barely escaped with his life, losing personal effects to the value of about $30.00. It is a pity we have no motor-launch for use on these occasions as well as for general preventive work. If I report officially, would you be inclined to consider refund of the boatman's losses, seeing that he suffered them while obeying the Tidesurveyor's orders ?

ty Treatment of
cks locally knitted
foreign wool.

The 7th Day Adventists are starting an Industrial School, the students of which will knit socks to be sold in America to pay for their education. They will study in the mornings and knit in the afternoons. Mr. Gregory of the Mission asked me to

enquire

5.

enquire if there would be any possibility of obtaining any refund or special valuation on export of the socks, seeing that they will be knitted of American duty-paid yarn. Should I raise this question with you officially, or tell Mr. Gregory to raise it through his Consul ?

Yours truly,

C. S. Williams.

CUSTOM HOUSE.

S/O No. 282.　　　　　　　　　　Wenchow, 8th September, 1923

rding and Patrol
ies

Dear Mr. Bowra,

　　　　With reference to my despatch No. 3755, N. C. No. 316:

　　　　requesting authority to purchase a sampan for $30. and engage a Boatman at Hk.Tls. 6. a month in order to continue an experimental system of boarding and patrol work in the Native Customs:

and your despatch No. 1186/95,644, N.C.No.179 in reply:

　　　　saying that seeing that the new system has proved to be of value it may be continued, but there should be no increase of staff or expenditure unless warranted by an increase

C. A. V. BOWRA, ESQUIRE,
　　Officiating Inspector General, ad interim.
　　　　PEKING.

2.

increase of revenue:

I should explain that for the first month's working a sampan was lent to the Native Customs by the Maritime Customs and a sampan-man engaged @ $8. I issued instructions to the Native Customs that in future vessels are to be boarded for preventive purposes not only by the Foreign Officer, but also by boarding parties consisting of one or more Watchers and one or more Boatmen, whose duty will be to search vessels for smuggled goods, check the cargo with the manifest, verify the documents carried, and make a daily report in Chinese to the Assistant-in-Charge, who with the Foreign Officer, will be responsible for the organisation of the work.

At the end of the first month it was found that the revenue had benefited to the extent of Hk.Tls. £46.00, being the amount realised by fines and confiscations derived entirely as a result of the new system, and quite apart from the ordinary seizure cases made by the Foreign Officer.

As

3.

As the full amount of the fines and confiscations is paid into the Native Customs Account as revenue, I take it that your proviso is covered, i.e. as there is thus an increase of revenue, the increase of staff (Hk.Tls. 6 a month) and expenditure (one payment of $30.) is fully justified.

Moreover, the new system draws our net tighter, and gives us more effective control over junks failing to enter, and loading and discharging without permit, etc. I can assure you that it is my object to increase the revenue to the fullest extent, and any expenditure made for this purpose will only be suggested after careful consideration.

atches not replied
I would respectfully call your attention to the fact that the requests contained in my despatches Nos. 3703, 3733 and 3749, have not yet been replied to.

M. Consular Property.
With regard to our prospective purchase of H.B.M. Consular property and in continuation

4.

continuation of my remarks on this subject in my S/O No. 280, I received a letter from H.B.M.'s Divisional Architect informing me that the annual ground rent of the property (excluding the so-called "Temple Site" owned by the British Government) is $72.00. This rent is paid on the 5th September to the Wenchow Taoyin. I have asked the Superintendent to arrange for the waiving of this ground-rent, seeing that the property is to be acquired by us, but I have had no reply as yet; perhaps you would prefer to take up the matter of exemption from ground rent with the Shui-wu Ch'u. If so, I think it would go through quicker; you will find a copy of my letter to the Superintendent in my Summary of Non-urgent Chinese Correspondence for last month. Of course this is really only a nominal rent, and you may not wish to trouble about it.

t absence from Office. I have left everything up to date in my Office and Mr. Bodisco, 3rd Assistant, B. will have no difficulty in supervising

the

5.

the current work during my week's absence.

Inferior Kwangtung Currency.

The somewhat complicated method of settlement of cases of seizures of inferior Kwangtung subsidiary silver coins seems, I venture to say, to be rather unsatisfactory. It appears to me that, if the Chinese Government wants to recall any particular kind of currency, it ought to be done, as in other countries, by the banks. We have made a number of seizures here, and much time is engaged in counting, melting, assessing, and division, which is hardly Customs work, and, in any case, could be easily attended to by the Superintendent, who has more time at his disposal. Sometimes there are only a few coins, sometimes a shipment is concealed in different parts of a vessel, and occasionally the banks, as in the recent case, are the chief offenders. In this case (reported to you by telegram on the 4th instant) the coins were found concealed on S.S. "Pingyang" in a disused privy, which had been converted into a paint locker, and the Superintendent

immediately

immediately asked me to inflict a small fine and release them. It is to be noticed that the local market is flooded with these Kwangtung coins. I believe the Ch'u instructed the Superintendent to issue a notification to the public about the prohibition of shipment, but I fancy he did not do so as the province is more or less independent. In the Ch'u's despatch to you (Circular No. 3370) there was no mention of a notification, but of course the smugglers know about it, and the Chamber of Commerce informed me that, on a previous occasion in Shanghai, a shipment of coins was detained by the Customs, but released on the plea of ignorance of the new rule. Thus, by giving way at one port, as alleged, another port immediately claims to follow the same precedent. The excuse of ignorance of the rules has been used in Wenchow so often that it has become exceedingly threadbare!

Yours truly,

C. A. S. Williams

INSPECTORATE GENERAL OF CUSTOMS,

S/O

PEKING, 12 September 1923.

Dear Mr. Williams,

I have duly received your S/O letter No.281 of the 27th of August.

<u>Proposed purchase of Quarters for Assistant.</u>

You may bring up the question officially, giving full details of alterations etc. required.

<u>Boatman-pilot's losses during typhoon: proposed claim.</u>

No ! We cannot open a door for claims of this sort. It would be too dangerous !

<u>Missionaries ask Customs for special treatment of knitted socks on export to America.</u>

No ! It is not our business to obtain privileges for foreigners. The question should be raised through the Consul.

Yours truly,

A. S. Williams, Esquire.
    WENCHOW.

INSPECTORATE GENERAL OF CUSTOMS,

S/O

PEKING, 21 September 1923.

Dear Mr. Williams,

I have duly received your S/O letter No.282 of the 8th instant.

Despatches not replied to.

3703 has been filed ; 3733 will be answered in due course ; and 3749 has been already replied to.

H.B.M.Consular Property : payment of ground-rent. Should exemption be applied for ?

I think perhaps it will be best to pay this small sum.

Yours truly,

S. Williams, Esquire.
WENCHOW.

CUSTOM HOUSE.

S/O NO. 283.   Wenchow, 24th Sept. 1923.

Dear Mr. Bowra,

urn with family Wenchow.

After my week's holiday, I returned from the hills on the 15th instant, with my wife and family, who have derived considerable benefit in health from the mountain air they have enjoyed all the Summer. If my bungalow had not been ready in time, I was thinking of sending the governess and children to Japan, which would have cost me $1,000 - and also considerable anxiety!

egular movement Munitions of War.

On the 12th instant the Superintendent requested the passing of 489 rifles, 29 boxes ammunition, 896 packages uniforms, 426 packages luggage, and 1,424 packages furniture

C. A. V. BOWRA, ESQUIRE,
    Officiating Inspector General, ad interim.
        PEKING.

2.

furniture for export to Hangchow for military use, under Chekiang Tupan's Huchao and Superintendent's Government Stores Certificate. A telegram was sent to you asking for your instructions in this matter, but you have not given me any reply. The Superintendent told me he had wired to the Shui-wu Ch'u, but the Chekiang Military Authorities insist on the movement of these munitions of war, and will not be governed by the Luchün Pu's instructions. I informed him that, under ordinary conditions, the Luchün Pu's instructions were necessary, but, of course, in the circumstances, I could only bow to force majeure, and report to you, and I suggested that the shipments be made in lots not exceeding 500 packages of each kind. Seeing that a treaty of amity has been concluded between Chekiang and Kiangsu, no doubt the provincial authorities are acting on the adage, "Si vis pacem para bellum". A shipment of 206 rifles, 29 cases ammunition, 223 packages uniforms, 349 packages personal effects, and 594 packages furniture,

3.

furniture, is being made to Ningpo by S.S. "Kwangchi" today for transhipment to Hangchow. The Chinese Gunboat "Hsin Pao Shun" arrived today and is standing by. I trust that you will approve of my action in this matter.

Commissioner's Quarters. My quarters have been thoroughly repaired, and are most comfortable now that the carpets and curtains have arrived. The drawing-room furniture you have kindly sanctioned will be much appreciated. The garden is in excellent condition, and I have just made a new tennis-court, which is far better than the old one.

Assistant's Quarters. With reference to my S/O No. 281 and your reply of 12th instant, I will do as you say, i.e. report officially on the proposed purchase of more substantial Assistants' Quarters, but I notice that, in your despatch No. 1189/95,836 of 14th inst., you authorise the thorough repair of the present Assistants' Quarters. Pending
preparation

4.

preparation of a full report, I am not carrying out the repairs in extenso. As the question involves many technical points, I would strongly recommend that Mr. W.J. Leahy, Architect, Works Department, be deputed here to go into the pros and cons, as he has been here before and knows the local conditions. I am anxious to arrange matters in the most practical and economic manner.

ξested appointment Mason.

I am thinking of applying to you for authority to appoint a mason permanently on the Staff. Every year there are typhoon repairs to be carried out, and the last two years have been exceptionally bad. It would be a saving to have our own mason.

ive Customs anisation.

My house-boat is under repair, and when it is ready I intend to make an extended tour of inspection of the Native Customs Sub-stations, preparatory to the submission of a detailed report on Native Customs organisation, and proposals for improvement of its efficiency in this district.

district.

Yours truly,

C.A.S. Williams.

INSPECTORATE GENERAL OF CUSTOMS,

S/O

PEKING, 4 October 19 23

Dear Mr. Williams,

I have duly received your S/O letter No.283 of the 24th of September.

<u>Commissioner suggests that an architect be sent to Wenchow to advise on repairs to Assistants' quarters</u>.

Cannot you and the Tidesurveyor arrive at a practical decision about repairs to a Chinese building ? It seems a waste of time and of travelling and other expenses for an architect to be deputed for this work. As regards the appointment of a mason, the I. G. is averse to increasing staff, but if a mason is wanted, official application must of course come forward. One of the boatmen should be a mason by trade.

Yours truly,

A. S. Williams, Esquire.
WENCHOW.

CUSTOM HOUSE,

S/O No. 284.   Wenchow, 4th October 1923.

Dear Mr. Bowra,

-enue.   The Maritime Customs revenue still continues to increase, and I am about to turn my attention more particularly to the Native Customs, which I think can be made to bring more grist to the mill.

-ss-stitch work.   With reference to my despatch No. 3753 of 2nd August reporting the payment of duty under protest on 5 postal parcels of local cross-stitch work, and proposing to charge ad valorem duty in future on this article according to the valuation of the Shanghai Customs Appraiser, the merchant concerned

C. A. V. Bowra, Esquire,
   Officiating Inspector General, ad interim.
      PEKING.

concerned has requested an early settlement of this matter as he wishes to make further contracts with foreign firms.

nese Out-door Staff

I think the reasons for the recent petitions for increase of pay handed in by the Native Out-door Staff of the Maritime and Native Customs (<u>vide</u> my despatches Nos. 3764 and 3766: N.C. 322) are (1) apparently a general movement on the part of T'ing-ch'ai throughout the Service for more pay, (2) some increase in the cost of living in this port - usually regarded as one of the cheapest ports in China - due to the disastrous typhoons of the last two years, which have reacted somewhat unfavourably on the grain supply.

. Lushih and
mination Staff.

I sent you copies of petitions for increase of pay from the Native Customs Lushih and Examiners in my S/O. No. 280 of 13th August, and, in order to officialize the matter, I included them with the Native subordinate Out-door Staff petitions in my
despatch

despatch No. 3766: N. C. 322, so that the whole question of N. C. Staff pay can be treated as a whole.

Transfer of Assistant.

I shall be sorry to lose Mr. C.A. de Bodisco, 3rd Assistant, B, whom you have transferred to Peking to study Chinese, but I am sure it will be a good thing for him as he shows considerable promise in the language. I should also like to remark that during his time here, he has given satisfaction in all respects. His successor, Mr. I.B. Brown, 4th Assistant, B, on probation, will have to be temporarily housed in a vacant room in the Tidewaiters' Quarters while the Assistants' Quarters are being attended to.

Dilapidation of Assistants' Quarters.

In my despatch No. 3768 of 2nd instant, you will find a full description of the difficulties encountered in the efficient repair of the Assistants' Quarters. It is rather fortunate however that, at this juncture, the landlord proves most amenable in the matter of a long lease; he

4.

he is a new man, the former landlord having died a few weeks ago, and now is the time to strike while the iron is hot.

I have put forward, quite impartially, several proposals for partial or thorough repair, rebuilding, or purchase of the house referred to in my S/O. No. 281 and your S/O. of 12th ultimo in reply. On the whole I should judge that the most practical arrangement would be to lease the old quarters for as long as possible at $100.00 a year, pull them down, and build a good bungalow on the site for $3,000.00. The landlord has no objection whatever!

Would it be possible for you to instruct the Engineer-in-Chief by telegram to send an Architect here to report on the technicalities of this question. Mr. J. W. Leahy, Architect, Works Department, has been here before and knows the local conditions. The matter is urgent.

rior Kwangtung ency.

With reference to my S/O. No. 282 and despatch No. 3789, N.C. No. 321, reporting the

5.

the seizure of a large number of inferior Kwangtung silver coins, and the protest of the Chamber of Commerce, I think there are also some of the gentry and merchants implicated in this case; although the only names appearing are two bankers. The Superintendent's proposal seems to be the best way out of it, but of course the coins will not, as he suggests, be "returned" to the place of origin and melted"; this is only a juggling with words to save the face of the Pi-chin Chü. I suppose we shall simply have to give the coins back again. The best way would be to give them all back and claim 2/10ths of the value as a reward. Then of course they will be put on the market again and probably smuggled out on the next opportunity. I am holding up another case - also reported in the same despatch - which I think ought to be settled in the same way. I should like to enquire if seizures of these Kwangtung coins are made in other southern ports where they are also in

common

common use.

chow Literary iety.

On the 28th ultimo a Chinese Literary Society was formed by the foreign residents of this port, which has for its object the preparation of dictionaries and text-books on the Wenchow dialect, readings and lectures on idiom, phonetic script, local manners and customs, etc., etc. The first lecture will be given on "tone combinations". I have joined the society, but I find I am unable to devote so much attention to Chinese now as formerly, as my eyes do not appear to be so strong as they were, and continual research work is rather a strain on them.

ival of Chinese ugees from Japan.

On the 29th ultimo about 800 Chinese refugees from Japan arrived on the S.S. "Feiching". The Magistrate advanced funds to supply them with travelling expenses to their homes in the surrounding districts. Subscriptions will be raised locally to cover these expenses.

Yours truly,

C. A. S. Williams

CUSTOM HOUSE,

S/O No. 285.   Wenchow, 18th October 1923.

Dear Mr. Bowra,

enue.

The following table of Maritime and Native Customs Revenue Receipts for the period of January to September, this year, will interest you:-

1. - MARITIME CUSTOMS.

	1923. Hk.Tls.	1922. Hk.Tls.
March Quarter	24,621.240	13,623.761
June "	31,571.495	22,609.235
September "	20,102.135	12,266.131
Total January to September	76,294.870	48,499.127

Increase to date: Hk.Tls. 27,795.743.

2.

C. A. V. BOWRA, ESQUIRE,
    Officiating Inspector General, ad interim.
        PEKING.

2. - NATIVE CUSTOMS.

(a) Intra 50-li.

	1923. Hk.Tls.	1922. Hk.Tls.
March Quarter	10,857.755	12,634.405
June "	21,570.009	19,782.942
September "	13,775.478	8,897.735
Total January to September	46,203.242	41,315.082

Increase to date: Hk.Tls.4,888.16.

(b) Superintendent's extra 50-li.

(Net, i.e. excluding expenditure)

	1923. $	1922. $
January	1,304.476	1,505.442
February	1,123.175	1,187.096
March	1,524.689	1,543.999
April	1,438.120	1,723.159
May	1,580.382	2,053.389
June	1,653.710	2,040.129
July	1,021.148	1,139.140
August	711.527	894.308
September	879.684	911.396
Total January to September	11,236.911	12,998.058

Decrease to date: $1,761.147.

You will note that there is a large

3.

large increase in Maritime Customs duty and every expectation for a total of well over Hk.Tls. 100,000.00 for the whole year.

The Native Customs intra 50-li duty is higher than usual but the Superintendent's extra 50-li duty shows a decrease. The Superintendent tells me that his decrease is due to the typhoons in August, when the revenue began to fall off, but no doubt this excuse was well exploited by the persons to whom the duty was probably farmed. Moreover August and September seem to be always bad months for the extra 50-li revenue.

rovement of Customs inistration.

With reference to my S/O No. 280 informing you that the Superintendent requested the compilation of various elaborate statistics for the preparation of a handbook of Customs procedure, so that, with its aid, the Ts'ai-chêng Pu may devise means for general improvement of Customs administration, and your reply of 27th August, instructing me, if the Superintendent presses,

4.

presses, to say that I cannot act without your instructions, I received a further request for these statistics and replied as you instructed. In this connection I see by the Shanghai Shun Pao that Mr. Wong Haiu Sing (黃厚誠), 2nd (Chinese) Assistant: A, detached to the Shui-wu Ch'u, and formerly Dean of the Customs College when I was there, has been deputed to the various ports to obtain the information required; if he should apply to me, I think it would be a good plan to give him a memorandum embodying my views as to certain possible improvements in this district, and if you approve, I will submit you a copy first. On the other hand I would ask you to kindly let me know if I am not to supply him with any information.

um seizure.

On the 15th instant, 140 catties of native opium was seized from double linings of crew's bunks on S.S. "Yungning". I fined the Yungning S.N. Company Hk.Tls. 150, which they paid without demur. Specimens of the labels

labels attached to the packages of opium will be sent to the International Anti-opium Association in accordance with Circular instructions. According to Circular instructions this opium cannot be burnt until after the end of the quarter. It is a pity it cannot be burnt at once, as we have no really safe place to keep it, and, on a former occasion, our small godown was broken into and opium stolen.

Anti-Japanese Boycott.

I had hoped, in the interests of trade and revenue, and out of sympathy with the recent Japanese Earthquake, that the Anti-Japanese Boycott would die a natural death, and the local piece goods merchants were evidently of the same opinion, as they lately imported Japanese piece goods to the value of $100,000.00, but unfortunately the students have forbidden them to take delivery, being anxious to burn all these so-called "inferior" goods. The Custom House compound has been crowded with students during the last few days, and they are a serious

impediment

6.

impediment to the efficient examination of cargo, so I wrote to the Superintendent referring to the last case of interference with examination work (<u>vide</u> my S/O No. 272 of 21st April) and asked again for his good offices in arranging that the students should not enter the Customs compound unless they have Customs business. A policeman was immediately put on point duty at the Custom House, but he does not seem to pay much attention to the students.

kiang Revenue Stamps.   I hear that revenue stamps are being printed by the provincial authorities, but I have not seen any yet on documents handled by this Office.

cial Permit Fee A/cs.   I notice that the voucher in A/c.D, Schedule F: Vr.a, recording receipts of Special Permit Fees, is still divided into two headings, i.e. for <u>subsidised</u> and <u>unsubsidised</u> vessels. These headings do not seem to be necessary any more now that the Post Office is separated from the Customs, and steamer
companies

companies do not any longer receive any part of the Permit Fees, but are paid to carry mails by contract with the C.P.O.

rchase of Consulate.

The purchase of H.B.M. Consular property at this port is still held up as I have had no reply yet to my request for waiving of the ground rent of $72.00 per annum.

ase of premises to P.O.

I think after all it is rather unsatisfactory that we have no lease of the premises rented to the Post Office, and I am now negotiating with the object of drawing up a lease. I will report to you later on this matter.

aff.

Mr. I. S. Brown, 4th Assistant, B (on probation), arrived yesterday. In the absence of your reply to my despatch No. 3768 of 2nd instant, asking for instructions as to (1) repair, (2) rebuilding, or (3) purchase of Assistant's Quarters, I am putting Mr. Brown up myself, as I do not think

8.

think it would be right to house him in the Tidewaiters' Quarters with the Tidewaiter. I may be able to place him temporarily on the island until quarters are available for him, but I should like to have your reply to the above despatch before deciding the matter.

Mr. Brown says he saw Mr. Leahy, Works Department Architect, in Shanghai, and the latter said that he found it difficult to comment on my despatch above mentioned without seeing the two houses, i.e. the old house and the new house. In your S/O of 4th instant, you ask if I and the Tidesurveyor cannot arrive at a practical decision about repairs to a Chinese building, and you consider it a waste of time and expense for an architect to be deputed for this work. I think however, that the time and expense would be justified, as it is a question of the advisability of either rebuilding or abandoning the house, which can best be reported on by an expert, a good deal of service money being involved.

I

9.

I must say I shall be glad when the Wenchow housing problem is laid to rest, and I am doing my best for this object. Good quarters, in a small port like this, are essential to the well-being of the staff, who have little to do after office-hours but to take an interest in their houses and gardens. I cannot wish for better quarters myself, and I should like to see the rest of the staff comfortably housed as well.

lera.

There is an epidemic of cholera in the city and there have been a number of fatalities. Many people have had preventive injections at the Blyth Hospital. At one time I thought of issuing a notification to the neighbouring ports to the effect that Wenchow is cholera-infected, but as there have been no deaths during the last few days I decided that it would not be necessary.

erintendent.

The Superintendent, Mr. Hu Wei-hsien (胡惟贤), returned yesterday, & kindly presented

10.

presented my wife with some tea and biscuits. He had been living in his Shanghai house since the 4th July. I expect to see him to-morrow, and I have asked him to lunch on Monday.

itical situation.

Chekiang still remains independent. The local Superintendent has received a telegram from General Lu Yung-hsiang saying that the provincial authorities will not recognise Tsao Kun as President as he has been illegally elected by methods of bribery.

Yours truly,

C.A.E. Williams

P.S.

istant's Quarters.

With reference to the Engineer-in-Chief's comments on Wenchow Despatch No. 3768/I.G., various Commissioners have pointed out the inadvisability of the Assistant living on the Island. Besides difficulty of access to the Assistant in an emergency, the

11.

the cost of the sampan-hire is also an objection. Moreover the site of the present Assistant's Quarters is the best.

The Examiners' Quarters cost us very little and cannot be said to be good housing. I intend later on to negotiate for the lease of this building to outsiders, and to house the Examiner in the Constable's House, when the purchase of the latter is concluded.

I recommend rebuilding the old Assistant's Quarters as proposed by the Engineer-in-Chief.

INSPECTORATE GENERAL OF CUSTOMS,

S/O

PEKING, 31 October 1923.

Dear Mr. Williams,

I have duly received your S/O letter No.285 of the 18th instant.

Revenue increase.

This is very satisfactory and looks as if, in the end, Wenchow might justify its existence as a Treaty Port.

Shui-wu Ch'u mission to ports to obtain Customs information.

I am not sure that this appointment will materialise. As usual, financial difficulties arise. Where is the money for the mission to come from?

Consulate Ground-rent question.

This question was answered in my S/O letter of the 21st of September last, when I said "I think perhaps it will be best to pay this small sum."

Special Permit Fee A/C.: superfluous Voucher sub-heading.

This subdivision is, of course, unnecessary

A. S. Williams, Esquire.
WENCHOW.

unnecessary and can be discontinued.

Assistants' Quarters.

  Similar difficulties and drawbacks exist in many ports. At the present time the strictest economy must be exercised in all directions and I regret that I am unable to go beyond the instructions of my despatch in reply to Wenchow No.3768.

       Yours truly,

CUSTOM HOUSE,

S/O NO. 286.   Wenchow, 2nd November 1923.

Dear Mr. Bowra,

velopment of Custom
ise and Communications.

        Various factors, such as (1) the desire on the part of the Ts'ai-chêng Pu for general improvement of revenue administrations, and the Ministry's instructions through the Shui-wu Ch'u for obtaining suggestions to this end, (2) the increase of the local export trade, (3) the lack of examination facilities at this port, (4) the inconvenient position of the N. C. Head Office and the necessity for having a more suitable position on the river front, (5) the advantage of having a private jetty and proper examination shed at both the Maritime and Native Customs, (6) the

narrowness

A. V. BOWRA, ESQUIRE,
  Officiating Inspector General, ad interim.
       PEKING.

narrowness of the streets and inconvenience of the communications in the neighbourhood of our offices; have all been subjects of discussion at various times with the local officials, and on the 22nd ultimo, a meeting was convened by the Superintendent at the China Merchants S.N. Co.'s Office for consideration of ways and means. I have raised these points with you both officially and semi-officially, and you appear to be in favour of some improvements in our facilities, but you stress the difficulty of supplying funds. The question of funds was raised by the meeting and I instructed my Secretary, Mr. K'o Yu-ping, 2nd Clerk, B, who represented me, to say that funds must be raised locally as far as possible. I sent Mr. K'o to represent me as I wished personally to remain in the background at the outset, in accordance with the views expressed in your despatch No. 1187/95,670.

It appears that the best way to obtain funds is by the creation of a
Board

Board of Works to administer a collection of Wharfage Dues levied under the Ningpo system by this Office, if you approve of the arrangement.

Then again, as I have pointed out previously, by the sale of the N.C. Head Office (which is too large and inconveniently placed) and the Enclosure for Examination of Bulky Cargo (which is too small and rather a white elephant), we can obtain further funds, also subject to your approval. The balance, if any, can be met by a grant from the Revenue applied for by the Superintendent.

The meeting approved of cutting through the city wall and thus widening the main street in the neighbourhood of the Custom House.

On the day after the meeting I invited the Taoyin, the Superintendent and his Secretary Mr. Shên Ming (沈銘), Mr. Lü Wên-ch'i (呂文起) - Chief of the Gentry - and Mr. Shih Chao-hsin (施肇信) - Manager of the China Merchants S.N. Co., to tiffin,

tiffin, and the conversation naturally led to the meeting of the day before. They all seemed anxious to advance the interests of the port, and I believe they are really beginning to think they have thought it all out themselves!

I should be greatly interested if you would be so good as to give me any advice or indications you think necessary for pushing the matter on, and I should particularly like to know your views on the Wharfage Dues question.

-Japanese Boycott.　　On the 22nd ultimo 47 packages of Japanese piece goods, value $20,000, were seized by the local students, and set on fire in the compound of the Tenth Middle School, in revenge for the alleged shooting of Chinese in mistake for Corean looters in Japan. The balance of the piece goods (<u>vide</u> my last S/O) are being returned to Shanghai. The control of the boycott was well in hand by the local military officer in charge, but unfortunately, at this

juncture,

juncture, a more senior officer arrived, who took the view that the boycott of Japanese goods was a matter not for him but for the civil authorities, who, of course, are quite powerless to cope with the situation.

**ux of Chinese
gees from Japan.**

During the last two months over 5,000 Chinese refugees have arrived from Japan, and most of them have gone to their family homes in the surrounding districts.

**ing of Agency for
ui Bussan Kaisha.**

On the 31st ultimo, I received a visit from Mr. G. Hirano, who has been sent here to open an agency for the Mitsui Bussan Kaisha for exportation of charcoal, kittysols, etc., direct to Japan on that Company's steamers. He brought with him letters of introduction from Mr. J.H. Macoun, Commissioner, and Mr. L. K. Little, 2nd Assistant, A of the Amoy Customs, who spoke very well of him, and his work on the Kulangsu Municipal Council. He seemed a pleasant individual, and I suggested that possibly he might care to rent the old

Examiner's

6.

Examiner's Quarters on the Island from us when the Examiner moves into the Constable's House, on the purchase of the latter being concluded.

acies.

With the approach of the winter, the piracies on the Chekiang Coast, become, as usual, more numerous.

rding of vessels soldiers and police.

In my Summary of Non-urgent Chinese Correspondence for last month you will find that on two occasions I have had to protest to the Superintendent against the boarding by soldiers and police of vessels in harbour engaged in working cargo, and to ask that, in future, such boarding shall only take place in company with a Customs Officer. In the case of the Portuguese M/V "Kimboh" a protest was entered with me by the Chinese Captain. This vessel was formerly under the Japanese flag and was occasionally employed for kidnapping children (vide my S/O No. 265 of 20th January), but in this instance it was a question of

detaining

7.

detaining a passenger who had not paid his fare. In the case of the Junk "Chin Shun Fa", the hatches were suddenly sealed by order of the local court on account of some financial liabilities on the part of the owner.

en Coins.

I hear that silver subsidiary coins minted in Fukien are being seized by the Shanghai and Ningpo Customs, but I do not know of any instructions to seize any varieties but those minted in Kwangtung, and I should be glad to know if Fukien Coins should also be confiscated.

r-launch for
entive Work and
ltage.

Several of my predecessors have semi-officially advocated the provision of a motor-launch at this port.

Mr. J. Acheson, in his S/O letter No. 9 of 26th August, 1914, reported that it was necessary for Native Customs inspection work as the river is tidal; again in his S/O No. 50 of 7th August, 1916, he remarked that it would prevent junks loading cargo

8.

cargo down river; in his following S/O he mentioned that it would benefit the revenue and recover its initial outlay in three or four years; in his next S/O he again prophesied increase of revenue by means of a motor-launch.

 Mr. C. E. Tanant, in his S/O. No. 204 of 29th September, 1920, stated that a launch or motor-boat will eventually be required, and in his S/O No. 214 of 5th February 1921, he expatiated on the difficulty of inspection of the channel without a suitable boat, and explained that to go to and return from the bar at the month of the river requires $1\frac{1}{2}$ days by native boat.

 In my S/O No. 278 of 14th July, 1923, I mentioned that the provision of a motor-boat for inspection and preventive work is advisable, as the N. C. houseboat is slow and unhandy; in my S/O No. 281 of 27th August, 1923, I observed that a motor-launch would be most useful for pilotage, which is undertaken by Customs employés at Wenchow.

9.

Wenchow.

No doubt the matter has not been raised officially on account of the expense, but trade is now double its former value, and I feel assured that it will be money well invested, which will pay interest by good results in the future.

I have asked the Tidesurveyor to go carefully into the matter of the expediency of provision of a suitable motor-launch, and he recommends a sailing-boat with auxiliary motor, and that the cost be debited to Maritime Customs, Native Customs, and Pilotage A/cs.

The matter is now being placed before you officially for the first time.

era Epidemic.

The Medical Officer considers that as the weather is turning colder, the cholera epidemic will gradually disappear, but he reserves his opinion for a couple of days as to whether a quarantine notification is necessary.

10.

145

  I am glad to say that none of the Staff have been taken ill with cholera, but unfortunately N.C. Watcher Ch'ên Sên (陳森) died of heart failure on the 19th ultimo, and N. C. Examiner Ch'ên Wei (陳煒) died of typhoid on the 1st instant. I do not propose to replace these employés, whose salaries are Hk.Tls. 18. and 24. respectively. The Native Customs is slightly overstaffed.

        Yours truly,

        C.A.E. Williams

INSPECTORATE GENERAL OF CUSTOMS,

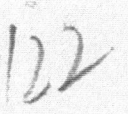

PEKING, *12 Novembre* 1923.

r Sir,

I am directed by the Inspector General ɔrm you that your S/O letter No. *284* *4 October*, has been duly e bd.

Yours truly,

B. Foster Hall
a/asst. Private Secretary.

C. A. S. Williams Esq,

Wenchow.

CUSTOM HOUSE,

S/O. No. 287.   Wenchow, 17th November, 23

Dear Sir Francis,

...era Epidemic.   With reference to my S/O. Letters Nos. 285 and 286, according to the Medical Officer, the cholera epidemic is now over, but, with reference to your Circular No. 3452 of the 31st ultimo instructing that Commissioners are to inform Commissioners at other ports of the outbreak of such epidemics, I was under the impression that the actual declaration of cholera infection should be approved by the Superintendent of Customs and Senior Consul.- Harbour Notifications are frequently issued by various ports

declaring

SIR FRANCIS AGLEN, K.B.E.,
    Inspector General of Customs,
        PEKING.

declaring that "Notice is hereby given that the Superintendent of Customs and the Doyen of the Consular Body have declared the port of.........to be infected." During the early part of this month, when cholera cases averaged at least three new cases a day (constituting an epidemic according to Circular No. 1717), I telegraphed to H.B.M. Consul at Ningpo - who controls Wenchow - asking if he had any objection to this port being declared cholera-infected, and he replied that he had no objection. I then wrote to the Superintendent proposing to inform the Commissioners at Shanghai, Ningpo, Amoy and Foochow, and asking if he would similarly inform Superintendents at those ports, but he asked me verbally to postpone the declaration for one week on account of the inconvenience to trade. At the end of the week the epidemic was over. I should be glad to know if my action is approved or whether, in future, I should notify the port Commissioners at once without referring to the Superintendent and Consul. Your Circular

3.

Circular No. 3452 was received here on the 14th instant, when the cholera epidemic was at an end. It seems to me to be necessary, in any case, to inform the Superintendent, Consul, and local steamer companies beforehand, but the point is whether I should wait until the Superintendent notifies his approval. There is generally cholera here every year towards the end of the summer.

ments of Officials.

On the 3rd instant, Mr. Chang Lien (张濂), Magistrate of this district, died of heart failure, after an attack of cholera On the 10th Mr. Ch'ên Hsü-tung (陈旭东), Chief of Police, took over temporary charge of the Magistracy, and the T'ungchüan (Likin) Weiyüan Mr. Hsü Lin-hsiang (徐麟祥) is now appointed Acting Magistrate. Mr. Li Chia-chên (厉家稹), formerly Chief of Police, is appointed T'ungchüan Weiyüan.

tion of Lorcha
ocal Court.

The position of the Police and legal authorities vis-à-vis the Customs ought to

4.

to be more clearly defined by the Chinese Government. Many cases occur when certain action is taken without informing the Customs, thus causing considerable interference with our work. I drew attention to this state of affairs in my last S/O. letter, and in my Summary of Non-urgent Chinese Correspondence for this month you will note the case of the arbitrary detention of the lorcha "Chin Yüan Hsing" by the local court. Beyond protesting to the Superintendent, however, these seems to be little to be done, but we ought not to be continually ignored in this flagrant manner.

Mr. I. S. Brown, 4th Assistant, B (on probation) is getting on quite well with his work, and I have given him a schedule of Chinese study, etc., to be carried through by the end of January, when I have to report on him.

I should like to draw your attention to the fact that Mr. K'o Yu-p'ing (柯呦苹), 2nd Clerk, B, has been
extremely

extremely well reported on by previous Commissioners, and, in my opinion, the fact that he served for seven years in the Native Customs, before joining the Maritime Customs, should be taken into consideration, not only for purposes of Superannuation (as already sanctioned) but also in his Service career, more especially as he is decidedly a cut above the ordinary clerk. In my last Confidential Report I recommended Mr. K'o to be made an Assistant. He certainly deserves encouragement, and I think he is at present a little discouraged with his slow progress in spite of his diligence and length of service.

Another very useful employé on the Staff of this Office is Mr. Huang P'ing-chên (黄聘珍), Lushih. He is very good at drawing plans, and knows some English.

Yours truly,

C. A. Williams

INSPECTORATE GENERAL OF CUSTOMS,

S/O

PEKING, 26 November 1923

Dear Mr. Williams,

I have duly received your S/O letter No.286 of the 2nd instant.

Development of Custom House and Communications : proposals for raising funds for same.

This is the first I have heard of this development and I have had no time yet to study the question. The principle that funds for local development must be found locally is the one to follow. Would it not be as well to ascertain what funds could be raised. Wharfage Dues will require international consent if levied on foreign goods !

Proposed non-replacement of deceased N.C. Watcher and Examiner.

That is right : keep down unnecessary Staff.

Yours truly,

S. Williams, Esquire.
WENCHOW.

CUSTOM HOUSE,

S/O. No. 288.   Wenchow, 1st December 1923.

Dear Sir Francis,

...ntees for inland ...ers.

    I hope my proposal to allow discharge of imports from Ningpo into a guaranteed godown by certain inland steamers, as submitted in my despatch No. 3777, N.C. No. 324, will meet with your approval, as it is to our advantage, as well as for the benefit of the public and companies concerned.

...rd Transit ...dure.

    With reference to my despatch No. 3781 reporting the objection to restriction of Wenchow Outward Transit Rules to 31 articles on the lines of the Chinkiang Rules it

FRANCIS AGLEN, K. B. E.,
Inspector General of Customs,
    PEKING.

2.

it is to be noted that the 31 articles of the Wenchow Rules do not entirely agree with the 31 articles of the Chinkiang Rules, and, reading between the lines of previous official correspondence, it seems to me that the Chinese authorities were not in favour of putting anything in the list which would be likely to be brought from the interior except Tobacco Leaf, which the Japanese were interested in at the time, and the fact is that, with the exception of some movements of Tobacco Leaf in the past, nobody has had occasion to avail themselves of any of the other 31 articles. Likin has thus been protected to the fullest extent, which was the evident desire of the Chinese authorities, and Tobacco Leaf was merely included as a sop to Cerberus, i.e. the Japanese trader. It is manifestly unfair, however, to favour the Japanese to the exclusion of other merchants, merely in order to keep up the Likin receipts, which are notoriously extortionate in this province, and highly detrimental to trade.

In

3.

In my opinion the list should be cancelled altogether, but I am afraid the Chinese authorities are disinclined to do anything to reduce the revenue of the Likin, or T'ungchüan (call it what you will), which they control themselves and can manipulate to their own advantage without foreign intervention.

ses leased to Office.

With reference to my despatch No. 3779, I feel sure it will be a good thing to know exactly how we stand in the matter of the lease and repairs to the premises rented to the Chinese Post Office. I was very much afraid that the wooden floors would not stand all the heavy usage to which they are put. Large mail-bags and baskets are dumped down, and numbers of letter carriers and sorters are continually running here and there in the rooms concerned, so concrete floors seem to me to be the best solution, and even if the Post Office eventually move to other premises at some future time, the concrete floored

4.

floored rooms will be useful for storage purposes as they are not suitable for living rooms. The Customs Library is at present in an adjoining room, and I will allow the Postmaster to use it while the concrete floors are being made: I can put the books in a vacant room upstairs for the time being. It will be an advantage to have a proper lease, as proposed, when all interior repairs can be carried out by the tenant in future.

ary Rice.

The Superintendent has notified me that 1,000 piculs of rice consigned to Hangchow for military use are to be passed free of duty under Chekiang Tupan's Huchao and the Superintendent's Government Stores Certificate. I am wiring for your formal consent to this procedure, as no Lu Chün Pu authority will be obtained, the province being more or less independent as usual. At the same time I asked the Superintendent to wire to the Shui-wu Ch'u for instructions.

In

ntion of vessels
ocal authorities.

In continuation of my S/O. Letters Nos. 286 and 287 commenting on the detention of certain Chinese sailing vessels by the local court pending trial of cases of disputed financial liabilities of the owners, the Superintendent has applied to me for all the papers of the vessels concerned for transmission to the court for inspection and verification of actual ownership, etc., and I have complied with his request as I felt I could hardly refuse to assist the aims of justice, though I had some misgivings as to whether I was fully justified in relinquishing my control of the documents, thus delivering the shipping owners into the hands of the enemy, i.e. the local court, which can then exact from them their uttermost farthing!

ents of Officials.

Mr. Hsia Chi-yü (夏啟瑜) was appointed T'ungchüan Weiyüan in place of Mr. Li Chia-chên (厲家楨) on the 26th ultimo. Brigadier General P'an Kuo-kan (潘國綱) arrived on the 29th by S.S. "Paohua" to inspect

6.

inspect the local forces.

etition between 1 Steamer Companies.
There has recently been some cutting of freight and passenger rates as a result of the competition for the carrying trade of the local steamer companies but they have now reached a definite agreement to resume their ordinary rates. The rates for passenger tickets from Wenchow are as follows:-

	Cabin. $	Deck. $
Wenchow to Shanghai	6-25.	5.00
" " Ningpo	4.50	2.60
" " Tinghai	4.00	2.40
" " Shihpu	3.00	2.00
" " Taichow	2.30	1.00
" " Hanmen	1.10	0.80

On the 26th ultimo there was a fire near the South Gate at 6 p.m., and a banking establishment was burnt down. On the 28th at 9.p.m., a fire broke out in the compound of the Chamber of Commerce; one house was burnt and a woman next door died

7.

died of fright; the archives of the Chamber of Commerce also perished in the flames, but there was a strong smell of kerosene oil in the neighbourhood of the fire, which rather leads to the supposition that some inconvenient accounts and other records were destroyed on purpose.

itation of
gn Settlement.

The local press has a rumour that, owing to the increase of trade, the limits of the foreign settlement will be definitely laid down, in case an influx of foreigners occurs.

ers and Police
aged to search
uggled rice.

The Taoyin has just received a despatch from the Provincial Authorities offering official posts and pecuniary rewards to petty officials, soldiers and police, who are instrumental in the detection of rice clandestinely shipped from Wenchow. The sale of this rice is expected to be very profitable. A copy of the despatch to the Taoyin, as published in the local press, is appended. We made a seizure of rice

ourselves

ourselves the other day, however, which elicited quite a storm of protest, as the local authorities wanted to handle the case themselves.

14. Consular Property.	I am anxious to have your decision in the matter of the conclusion of the purchase of H.B.M.'s Consular Property for Staff Quarters, but I have profited by the delay in repairing the typhoon damages to the bund and sea-wall at a cost of $230.00 and servants quarters @ $61.80, which is being paid by the British Government.

ue.	The Maritime Customs Revenue to date is Hk.Tls. 92,467.226, so by the end of the year we shall certainly exceed Hk.Tls. 100,000.00 for the first time.

Yours truly,

Ca. E. William.

Append

APPEND.

录浙江公报中华民国十二年十月三十日

浙江省军务善后督办处暨省长公署指令第一○四七○号

令瓯海道尹

呈一件据呈报重申漏米出海禁令录送章程由

禁令录送章程由

十月二十六日

呈准查禁漏米章程八条缮摺

恭呈钧鉴

瓯海道道尹沈效坚谨将

如呈备案仰即知照附件存此令

计开

一水陆营警能破获漏米五万石以上者於提充公米价五成给赏外该管员弁另予记功一次十万石以上者记大功一次县知事自行破获者亦如之

一縣知事能將破獲漏米之案究出奸販刁牙或包庇之劣紳地棍一併懲辦者每案記功一次三次改記大功

一水陸營警於該管區域內有漏米之案或經過該管區域不能破獲被他處發覺者每案記過一次三次改記大過或有故縱情事者立即呈請撤懲縣知事亦如之

一劣紳地棍有敢包庇漏米者一經查獲將米充公外另按充公米價之數加倍處罰

一米行奸商有包辦漏米者一經查有實據即調銷牙帖停止營業並酌量處罰

一船戶敢裝載漏米者一經查獲無論己船租船沒收充公

一人民知有漏米准其赴就近警區或縣公署指明報告因而查獲者俟標賣後於提賞五成內酌量從優分給充賣倘係挾嫌誣訐或空

11.

言擅報亦須依法懲處

一 出海商船大船每船准帶食米一千斤中船七百斤小船四百斤違此規定者即以漏海論

TRUE COPY:

INSPECTORATE GENERAL OF CUSTOMS,

S/O

PEKING, 7 December 1923

Dear Mr. Williams,

I have duly received your S/O letter No.287 of the 17th of November.

Cholera epidemic : method of declaration of Port infection.

A port does not **declare itself** "infected". Port A, on learning that there is an epidemic at Port B, declares Port B to be **infected** and institutes quarantine against all vessels arriving from Port B. If there is an epidemic at Port B, it is for the Commissioner to inform Port A and other ports, and these latter can take what action seems best, i.e. declare B infected or **not** as seems best to their **own** interests.

In informing other Commissioners of an epidemic such as the one you describe, you should let them know that, in all probability, it will be all over in - say - 10 days, if such is the experience of the Port. It will be best, I think, to write to the

Commissioners

S. Williams, Esquire.
WENCHOW.

Commissioners officially when you have occasion to notify an epidemic and let the Superintendent know that you have done so. If he wishes to be consulted first, he will let you know. But, as you will only be giving information to other ports and *not* declaring your own port "infected", the Superintendent will probably not raise any difficulty in your carrying out the instructions of Circular No.3452.

  You should, when the opportunity occurs, have this rule added to the Regulations.

          Yours truly,

INSPECTORATE GENERAL OF CUSTOMS,

S/O

PEKING, 13 December 1923

Dear Mr. Williams,

With regard to the query in your S/O letter No.286 of the 2nd of November, concerning the alleged confiscation of Fukien coins by the Shanghai and Ningpo Customs, your information is not correct as you will see from the enclosed replies to S/O enquiries addressed to the above Commissioners. Fukien coins are not to be confiscated as such.

Yours truly,

[signature]

S. Williams, Esquire.
    WENCHOW.

APPEND.

Shanghai Commissioner to Inspector General.

30th November 1923

Dear Sir Francis Aglen,

In reply to your S/O of 27th November

November, 1923:

  This office does not detain Fukien Coins, duly manifested.

  Two seizures were made this last quarter of Silver Coins ex the "Feiching" from Wenchow, which were found on the steamer, unmanifested. These upon examination proved to be a mixture of Kwangtung Prohibited coins and Fukien and old Dragon Mould Coins. The Kwangtung Prohibited Coins were smelted, 2/10 being confiscated and resold to owner, while the Fukien and Dragon Mould coins were released.

        Yours truly,

        (signed) L. A. Lyall.

<u>Ningpo Commissioner to Inspector General.</u>

        Decr. 5th, 1923

Dear Sir Francis Aglen,

  This is in reply to your letter of the 27th November, asking whether this Office is seizing <u>silver subsidiary coins minted in Fukien</u>. The answer is in the negative. On one occasion only we have come across any

any Fukien 20-cent pieces, when a few were found amongst a lot of the Kwangtung inferior variety : they were returned to the owner. Whenever we make seizures of this kind, every coin is carefully examined, and the good separated from the bad.

       Yours faithfully,

      (signed) Fred. W. Carey.

CUSTOM HOUSE,

S/O No. 289.   Wenchow, 15th December 1923.

Dear Sir Francis,

...sed Motor Launch
...enchow Customs.

      With reference to my despatches Nos. 3775 and 3782 proposing provision of a motor launch for this port, I am strongly in favour of the supply of some sort of a motor launch, even if it is smaller than the type suggested by the Coast Inspector in his comments on the former despatch.

...sed erection of
...er for Boatman
at mouth of river.

      The Boatmen we send down river, to pilot steamers in, have rather a hard time under inclement weather conditions. It is very unfair that they should sometimes be obliged to spend the night in an open sampan. The hut for their shelter at the mouth

FRANCIS AGLEN, K. B. E.,
Inspector General of Customs,
   PEKING.

2.

mouth of the river, as proposed in my despatch No. 3782 is, to my mind, an absolute necessity. In my S/O. No. 281 of 27th August I asked if a refund of $30 could be made to the Boatman-pilot for loss of his personal clothing, etc., on pilotage duty during a typhoon, but this was disallowed. If there was a shelter provided for him, he would not be obliged to run into danger of this kind.

ed settlement of
e of Kuangtung
or silver coins.

I am sorry I have not yet been able to carry out the instructions of your despatch No. 1201/96,705 to melt the Kuangtung silver coins seized on the 31st August, and on the 10th instant I wired you to the effect that postponement of melting is again requested pending further appeal by the Chamber of Commerce through the Chekiang Governor.

In the meantime I have melted the coins seized in all other cases since that time but there have been some complaints.

Would

3.

Would it not be much easier to hand over all confiscated coins to the Superintendent to be dealt with in the same manner as in the case of Copper Cents? There is always a lot of discussion over this melting business, and it takes up a lot of our time; for instance, to melt the 36,960 twenty-cent pieces, in the case outstanding, will require 21 men working for 2 whole days on small charcoal braziers, the only method available in Wenchow. The melting, moreover, has to be supervised by a Customs Officer, whose services are thus lost for the two full working days! The cost of melting would be about $80, and the loss by meltage would be over $1,000 - rather a heavy penalty for using locally current coinage in an independent province.

*an Stamp Duty
*sted by Superin-
dnt.

The Superintendent called yesterday to say good bye as he is going to Shanghai for two months and also intends to visit Hangchow. He made rather an ingenious

suggestion

4.

suggestion that the Customs might advantageously introduce a Customs Stamp Duty System, whereby passengers carrying small sundries might be allowed to affix a special Customs Duty Stamp, to be issued in values of 10 cents, 50 cents and $1, to all small sundries not exceeding $100. in value and charged _ad valorem_ duty, thus saving trouble to the public and Customs as well. I said I would mention it to you and ask your opinion on the feasibility of the scheme, which, to my mind, seems to have some possibilities.

nous Rice for wine lling purposes.

I have received official notice from the Superintendent that the Provincial Governor has given permission to the Wine and Tobacco Bureau to import glutinous rice from inland ports of Chekiang under a Certificate (採運釀料憑證), issued by the Bureau, and I understand that there will be quite a lot of movements. The point now arises that exemption from duty will be claimed,

claimed, and the fact is that it is not the practice to levy Native Customs duty on rice. I told the Superintendent that this rice is not like ordinary rice and is used for industrial purposes for manufacturing a luxury, and therefore it should come under the heading of unclassed articles paying *ad valorem* duty.

Native Customs Practice.

I have just found out that shells for lime-making, young pigs, as well as rice and grain, are passed free of duty at the Native Customs, though there seems to be no authority for this practice. I am going to take up this question, together with various other reforms I consider necessary, and will send you a report on the working of the Native Customs, with suggestions for improvement, but I shall not be in a position to get it into shape until after the Annual Trade Returns and Reports are despatched. It will be the first non-routine work I shall tackle in the new year.

Brigadier

...ents of Officials.	Brigadier General P'an Kuo-kang (潘國綱) returned to Hangchow on the 5th instant.
	The new Magistrate Hsü Lin-hsiang (徐麟祥) called on me on the 12th inst., and I found him very pleasant.
	The Superintendent of Customs left for Shanghai today. During his temporary absence his Secretary Mr. Shen Ming will represent Customs interests on his behalf.
...tion of famine ...f surtax.	The 1/10th famine relief surtax on the duty collected by the Native Customs extra 50-li stations was removed from the 1st instant, by instructions of the Civil Governor.
...es of Asiatic ...eum Company.	In the summer of 1922 the Asiatic Petroleum Company decided that their present site on the main river was unsuitable for the construction of an oil installation, and therefore selected a location just inside the North River, a tributary of the Wenchow River,

7.

River, and asked for my approval, which of course I was unable to give until they obtained the sanction of the Chinese authorities. They do not wish to apply to the Chinese authorities as they are afraid of being squeezed too much, nominally on the price of the land, so I advised them to get an option on the sale, but that if they did not get authority from the Chinese officials I was unable to assist them in any way or give them my approval. The Company's Marine Superintendent came here and spent three weeks in surveying, and I put him up and lent him my houseboat, and I also provided accommodation for one of their office assistants for several months. I thereafter received many requests to supply the Company with soundings of the main river and North River, and these requests came so frequently that eventually I had to refuse to supply any further soundings as the Tidesurveyor could not be spared to go out all day working for other concerns on so

many

many occasions.

In June the Shanghai Manager of the Company wrote informing me that their large Motor Vessels "Fu Kwang" and "Wu-kiang" will be employed for the transportation of kerosene oil in bulk and/or drums and/or cases, and he further stated:

"We assume that no objections to the passage of the above named vessels for a mile to 1½ miles up the North River would be raised by the Customs and Harbour Authorities, and that as no objections could be sustained by the Chinese on reasonable grounds we could rely on your support to withstand any objections they might put forward."

To this letter I replied that the matter would be considered when the installation site is approved by the Chinese authorities.

Towards the end of last month I received a telegram stating that the Company's S.S. "Fukwang" was proceeding from Shanghai to Wenchow with case oil, etc. for

Wenchow

Wenchow and Haimen, and asking if the Haimen cargo could be left on board as it would be examined at Shanghai. I replied that this could not be allowed. The "Fukiang" arrived however from Haimen with no cargo, and presented a nil manifest. She had on board a small motor boat which was unloaded without permission and taken up the North River for two or three days. The "Fukwang" was in possession of a Tonnage Dues Certificate and an Inland Waters Certificate authorising her to ply from Shanghai to Haimen. No documents were received from the Shanghai Customs, and I believe she landed cargo at Haimen. The motor-boat, I hear, she picked up at sea outside Chinhai.

Seizures.

A seizure of opium was made recently on the Junk "Chin Hsieh An" (金協安), after which the junk cleared without permission. As the vessel was registered at Foochow, I wrote to the

Foochow

10.

Foochow Commissioner asking him to try and trace the owner or guarantor and fine him Tls. 100 for smuggling opium. This may be an unusual procedure but it might work. In connection with this seizure an accusation was laid against the searching party by a certain individual, who claimed to have given information of the case, to the effect that, of the amount seized, a certain amount was retained privately. I found that he was not an informer, but an agent for the safe delivery of opium from ship to shore, and I told the Superintendent so! In another case the opium smuggler was arrested and handed over to the Chinese authorities; his rather large family laid siege to me in my office and asked me to let him off, but it was too late.

ological.

The month began with windy weather, which gave place to heavy rainfall, interfering a good deal with the shooting, which is quite good this year.

Yours truly,

S/O

INSPECTORATE GENERAL OF CUSTOMS,
PEKING, 17 December 1923

Dear Mr. Williams,

I have duly received your S/O letter No.288 of the 1st instant.

Guarantees for inland steamers.

Yes : a despatch is going forward on the subject.

Outward Transit Procedure : objection to restriction of Wenchow Rules to 31 articles : proposed cancellation of list.

Better leave this alone for the present. The question will right itself in time.

Revenue increase.

Good : Wenchow is looking up.

Yours truly,

A S. Williams, Esquire.
WENCHOW.

CUSTOM HOUSE,

S/O NO. 290.   Wenchow, 29th Dec. 1923.

Dear Sir Francis,

_opment of Custom
_ and communications.

The local District Assembly held a special series of meetings from the 15th to 26th instant for discussion of next year's plans for local administration, etc., and the development of the port as a trading centre was also brought up. The extension of the bund in front of the Custom House for construction of an Examination Shed, and the improvement of communications from the river to the South Gate (vide my despatch No. 3749 of 27th June, 1923, Enclosure, Scheme C) were also approved, and a proposal made that I should be asked to

draw

FRANCIS AGLEN, K. B. E.,
Inspector General of Customs,
    PEKING.

2.

draw up a working scheme. The Superintendent of Customs has asked me to draw up the scheme required, of which I shall submit you a copy for approval before passing it on.

:ial Furniture.

I am revising the official furniture inventories, which have got into rather a confused state owing to the number of alterations and additions made since they were last drawn up, and to the necessity for the discarding and sale of many worn out articles (vide my despatch No. 3783). There are no inventories of office furniture, so I am going to make some. It has often occurred to me that some definite standard form of office furniture would be useful, if only to serve as a guide when having new articles made. The only standard article at present is a card-index cabinet. I have done what I can to improve the appearance of the local existing office furniture, and make it more practical. To my mind, the sectional principle, as

applied

applied to book-cases and archive-cabinets, is the most advisable in case of fire. The usual open dust-trap on the top of the ordinary book-case is, moreover, very objectionable and the closed-in sloping roof form is more sanitary. A table with a long drawer is useful for charts, and flaps to pull out on each side of the desk are of great advantage. I am also an advocate for standard binding of archives; brown leather back and corners with black cloth sides work up into a strong and good appearing volume, and I am having the Wenchow archives bound in this style; nothing had been bound here since the opening of the port in 1877.

Japanese Boycott.   The local students, having ascertained that Japanese piece goods were still being imported, held a meeting on the 20th, at which eight representatives of the piece goods merchants attended to give their views on the matter. As the merchants' explanations were considered unsatisfactory, the students

4.

students seized the eight representatives, arrayed them in red sashes, and forced them to parade the streets as a punishment for buying Japanese goods. This procedure incensed the piece-goods dealers, and a free fight ensued, the eight men being rescued, and many of the students injured. The cloth merchants then declared a strike, which, however, was ended in two days at the request of the Magistrate, Chief of Police, and President of the Chamber of Commerce.

...ments of Officials.

Colonel Hao Hsü-tung (郝旭東), left for Hangchow on the 15th and returned on the 27th instant. He is now Commander-in-Chief of Wenchow, Chuchow, and Taichow.

*...u seizures: Customs
...fier summoned to
...r to give evidence*

Whenever we hand over an opium smuggler to the Chinese Authorities, the local court calls for the seizing officer to attend the trial and give evidence. I always say he cannot be spared from his duty and send a written deposition instead

(vide

(vide my Summary of Non-Urgent Chinese Correspondence, December, 1923).

Yours truly,

C.A.S.Williams

1924 年

INSPECTORATE GENERAL OF CUSTOMS,

PEKING, 8 January 1924

S/O

Dear Mr. Williams,

I have duly received your S/O letter No. 289 of the 15th of December.

Proposed motor launch for Wenchow.

The question is being studied but economy is necessary.

Proposed erection of shelter for boatmen-pilots.

Can you give me an approximate estimate of the yearly earnings from Pilotage made by these boatmen?

Melting inferior silver coins.

This melting is giving trouble elsewhere. I think we shall have to wash our hands of it

Suggested introduction of Customs Stamp Duty System.

This would mean that the "Merchant" could value and assess duty on his own cargo! and pay according to his own assessment - which would be a very great temptation to evade the proper payment of duty.

Glutinous Rice

Williams, Esquire.
WENCHOW.

Glutinous Rice : should pay <u>ad valorem</u> duty as an unclassed article.

If the Provincial authorities insist on exemption, I fancy we shall have some difficulty in maintaining collection !

A.P.Co.'s steamer unloads small motor boat without permission.

A motor boat, carried as cargo, ought not to be landed without a permit from your office. I don't see how you can ignore this and the Company's attention should be drawn to the irregularity.

Yours truly,

INDEXED

CUSTOM HOUSE,

S/O NO. 291.   Wenchow, 15th January, 1924.

Dear Sir Francis,

robberies.   At midnight on the 13th instant a gang of about 100 men, said to be members of a secret society known as the Ch'ing Hung Pang (青紅幫), with their faces painted black, and armed with knives, raided the Jun Yüan bank (潤源錢莊) outside the East Gate, and made off with various articles of clothing and some money, afterwards entering the house of the Li family near by, wounding the son of the owner, and purloining a quantity of money and jewellery, etc. They escaped with their plunder, valued at over $4,000.00, and the police, who seem to have been either powerless or neglectful

of

FRANCIS AGLEN, K.B.E.,
Inspector General of Customs,
    PEKING.

2.

of their duty, have offerred a reward of $100.00 for the arrest of the leader of the gang and $50.00 for apprehension of each of his followers.

ase of tonnage.
On account of the increased demand for timber and charcoal in Japan since the earthquake, a large number of Japanese vessels are plying to this port for carrying out these commodities.

On the 10th instant there were nine steam-vessels in port - a record number - of which three were Japanese, and another Japanese ship arrived on the following day.

For the first time for 12 years, the port was visited by a French Gunboat, the "Algol", which came up to investigate certain rumours of hostilities between the Chekiang and Fukien forces. The "Algol" arrived on the 8th and left on the 11th; my wife and I lunched with the Commander, and the children also had tea on board on the 9th; the Commander and Officers dined

with

with us on the following day.

The Chinese Gunboat "Chao Wu" also arrived on the 3rd with one lien of artillery (133 men). On the 6th, while swinging at their moorings, the "Chao Wu" and S.S. "Kenkon Maru" collided, and the davits of the "Chao Wu" were damaged, the repairs being carried out, under Customs supervision, at the cost of the "Kenkon Maru". The "Chao Wu" left on the 9th for Haimen.

On the 11th the C.M.S.N.Co's "Kwangchi" arrived from Ningpo with 300 soldiers from Haimen.

On the 13th a new steamer of 610 tons, the S.S. "Hua Feng", arrived from Shanghai. This vessel has been chartered by a local merchant.

ing Revenue Stamps.

A notification has been issued by the Magistrate to the effect that the new Chekiang Revenue Stamps are to be used from the 5th instant, and those in possession of government stamps should go to his Office to exchange

exchange them for the new ones. The Chekiang stamps are now being affixed to petitions handed in to this Office, and I should like to enquire if this affects the instructions of your Circular No. 2631.

...and settlement of ...ve of Kuangtung ...or silver coins.

With reference to my S/O letter No. 289 of 15th ultimo, I gather from the Superintendent that the owners of the Kuangtung inferior silver coins, seized on the 31st August last year, have not been able to enlist the assistance of the Chekiang Governor in their protest against melting, and are now addressing the Shui-wu Ch'u on the matter! The Currency Bureau, the author of the original instructions for melting such coins, has, I hear, been abolished.

...burning.

On the 8th instant 244 catties of native raw opium and 7 tins of anti-opium pills, seized during the preceding quarter, were burnt publicly, the Superintendent of Customs being present at the time. The burning

5.

burning occupied from 10 a.m. to 2 p.m.

Treatment.   With reference to my despatches Nos. 3789, N.C.No.329, and 3790, N.C.No.330, and your despatches Nos. 1211/97,093, N.C.No.188, and 1212/97,094, N.C.No.189, Native Customs duty is now being collected on oyster shells, young pigs, and glutinous rice. There was a slight protest on the levy of duty on the oyster shells, but the Superintendent and myself are successfully enforcing the tariff.

...e of Detonators.   I received an anonymous Chinese letter on the 10th instant, informing me that dynamite was being smuggled from Tai-chow by Japanese, and on the 12th instant, we made a seizure of 38 detonators from a Japanese passenger, said to be a Diver, on S.S. "Yungchuan", but have not found any traces of dynamite.

...igs of Boatmen-
...t.   In your S/O Letter of the 8th, you ask for an approximate estimate of the yearly

6.

yearly earnings from Pilotage made by the Customs Boatmen employed in this work.

The total receipts in the Pilotage Account for the last five years are as follows:-

	Hk.Tls.
1919	950.66
1920	274.67
1921	1,221.97
1922	604.66
1923	2,216.67
Total:-	5,268.63
Average:-	1,055.73

Two Boatmen are employed as Pilots. Sometimes one goes out and sometimes the other. They are our two best boatmen, and we should not like to lose them. The service allows the steamer companies to use them at their own risk, but they know the river, and the system works well. When a Boatman goes out to pilot a vessel, he supplies a substitute to carry on his Customs duties.

7.

duties. Up to September 1921 all the receipts were given to the Boatmen-Pilots; after that date they have only received 3/5ths. Of the other 2/5ths the Service pays the sampan hire and retains the remainder.

I have calculated that the earnings of the two Boatmen-Pilots together average about Hk.Tls. 60 a month. The No. I Boatman goes out more frequently than the No. II, and I suppose the former draws about Hk.Tls. 45 and the latter Hk.Tls. 15 a month. These sums are insufficient to tempt outsiders to engage in pilotage work, and moreover the present increase of tonnage will not be maintained after the Japanese demand for Wenchow timber and charcoal is reduced.

The average net profit to the Service from pilotage at present is about Hk.Tls. 360.00 per annum, i.e. after deduction of sampan hire and 3/5th collection paid to the pilots.

Yours truly,

A. E. Williams.

INSPECTORATE GENERAL OF CUSTOMS,

PEKING, 16 January 1924

Dear Mr. Williams,

I have duly received your S/O letter No. 290 of the 29th of December.

<u>Opium seizures : requests for attendance of seizing officer at local court.</u>

So long as the Court will accept a written deposition this is satisfactory. But we cannot <u>refuse</u> attendance if it is insisted on when we are the initiators of a prosecution.

Yours truly,

A. S. Williams, Esquire.
    WENCHOW.

CUSTOM HOUSE,

S/O NO. 292.   Wenchow, 31st January 1924.

Dear Sir Francis,

s of Seizing
r to court to
vidence of opium
ing.

        In my S/O letter No. 290 of 29th ultimo, I informed you that whenever we hand over an opium smuggler to the Chinese authorities the local court summons the seizing officer to attend the trial and give evidence and I always send a written deposition instead. In your letter of 16th instant in reply, you say that we cannot <u>refuse</u> attendance if it is insisted on when we are the initiators of a prosecution. Can we, however, be said to be the initiators of the prosecution, i.e. the plaintifs, seeing that we only hand over the offenders at the request of the Chinese Government? Again, is it in accordance with the spirit of

RANCIS AGLEN, K. B. E.,
spector General of Customs,
    P E K I N G.

of the treaties that <u>foreign</u> seizing officers should be haled before a Chinese court of an unmixed variety, even if only to give evidence? Am I to understand that in future I am to instruct foreign Tidewaiters to go to the court if called upon?

...wu Ch'u mission to to obtain Customs ...rmation.

I hear that Mr. Wong Hsiu Sing (黄厚诚), 2nd (Chinese) Assistant, A, detatched to the Shui-wu Ch'u, has been deputed to the various ports to obtain information about the working of the Customs on behalf of the Ts'ai-chêng Pu, and that he is now at Foochow, and is expected here shortly. I saw a notice of Mr. Wong's appointment to this duty in the Shanghai Shun Pao about three months ago, and in my S/O letter No. 285 I enquired if I may give him the information he requires, but Mr. Bowra, in his letter of 31st October, 1923, in reply, only said that he was not sure that this appointment would materialise on account of lack of funds. As it appears
that

that the appointment has now materialised. I would again enquire as to what attitude I am to adopt in case Mr. Wong should apply to me for inside information about Customs affairs. I gather it is the desire of the Ts'ai-cheng Pu to prepare a general handbook of Customs office organisation and Service practice at each port, for purposes of study, in order to devise means of increasing the revenue, but it seems to me that the revenue interests are sufficiently well looked after by the Customs administration, and that more could be accomplished by the Government by stimulation and development of the industries of the country. My information of Mr. Wong's expected arrival originated in this way. Mr. Wong's brother was formerly in charge of the Native Customs here, and was transferred to Santuao where he died recently. His widow wrote to her brother Mr. Liu Chün-t'u (劉駿周), Examiner in the Native Customs at this port, and stated that Mr. Wong Hsiu Sing would arrive at Wenchow shortly and asked if Mr. Liu could arrange for some books belonging to the

4.

the deceased to be disposed of by Mr. Wong.

Relief work.

I have had a good deal to do during the year in my capacity of Co-Chairman of the Wenchow Branch of the International Famine Relief Committee, and Mr. K'o Yu-p'ing, 2nd Clerk, B, who is a member of the Committee, has been of great assistance to me in secretarial matter. I have had to round up the missionaries in the neighbourhood and get them to investigate and report on famine conditions, etc., and I have drawn up various schemes for improving the economic condition of the country districts, which have been adopted by the Committee. My colleague, the Taoyin, seems to be pleased with what I have been able to do to help in the matter.

Exemption of oyster and cross-stitch

With reference to previous official correspondence, and especially to my recent despatch No. 3803, proposing that the indefinite exemption of oyster shells from Native Customs duty be restricted to a fixed period, and

and requesting instructions re levy of Liang T'ou Dues on vessels carrying this article of commerce, the Chinese version of this last despatch is carefully worded so as not to offend the Shui-wu Ch'u, but I was rather surprised to find that the Ch'u accepted the merchants' petition without question, in spite of the joint notification issued by the Superintendent and myself. This petition had already been dealt with by the Superintendent, and the merchants would have paid the just and legal duty without any further protest, had it not been for the gratuitous exemption accorded by the Ch'u. If the Ts'ai-chêng Pu want to increase the revenue, this is not the way to do it! The temporary exemption of cross-stitch work from Maritime Customs duty (I.G. Circular No. 3454) is another case in point. The manager of the cross-stitch establishment here, runs a kind of sweat-shop, and has made his fortune. He certainly does not require any encouragement from the Government. In these two cases the Shui-wu Ch'u

6.

200

Ch'u has deliberately refused to support the Customs, to the detriment of the standing and authority of the Service and the revenue of the government. It would be advisable to fix a limit for exemption of cross-stitch work as well.

...e of scissors.

With reference to your despatch No. 1207/96,873 asking for a report on the seizure of 42 pairs of foreign scissors from Mr. S.C. Hsia (of the British-American Tobacco Company), who complained to you of unjust treatment, it occasionally happens that Chinese employees of foreign firms are rather dictatorial in their attitude towards the Customs, and demand preferential treatment in the hope that the Customs will show them unusual consideration on account of their foreign connections. Mr. Hsia had no excuse for behaving in such an improper manner, and has now apologised. I shall report the matter to you officially as directed.

...y along the coast.

In accordance with the instructions of

of your despatch No. 1206/96,872, I sent Mr. Ch'ên Pai-ch'üan's petition proposing measures for checking of piracy along the Chekiang Coast, together with a translation of the same, to the Coast Inspector, who has notified me that he has forwarded the petition to Rear Admiral Hsü, Director of the Hydrographic Department of the Chinese Navy, who has in hand the matter of organising a Coast Guard Service. Quite a number of small Water Police Gunboats have been dropping in at this port from time to time, since the petition was taken up, and attention called to Wenchow.

ats of Officials. The Taoyin, Mr. Shen Chih-chien (沈致堅), left on a visit to Hangchow on the 26th instant.

Yours truly,

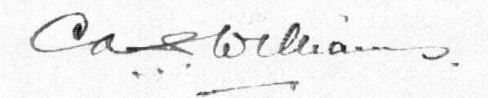

Ca. & Williams

INSPECTORATE GENERAL OF CUSTOMS,

PEKING, 1 February 1924

Dear Mr. Williams,

I have duly received your S/O letter No.291 of the 15th of January.

Issue of provincial Revenue Stamps.

As a Central Government organ, we can't enforce the use of these provincial stamps : nor, in the circumstances, can we insist on the Government ones being used. We must simply ignore them for the time being.

Superintendent and Commissioner are successfully enforcing tariff duty on oyster shells in spite of slight protest.

The Shui-wu Ch'u, without reference to me, overruled the Superintendent and yourself - this was Mr. Sun Pao-chi's own doing. I hope the Superintendent will make a strong protest. I consider the Ch'u decision quite wrong !

Boatmen-Pilots : profits to Service from Pilotage.

This

Williams, Esquire.
WENCHOW.

This net profit might be expended in giving the pilots facilities but nothing more. They seem to be fairly well paid.

Yours truly,

INSPECTORATE GENERAL OF CUSTOMS,

S/O

PEKING, 11 February 1924

Dear Mr. Williams,

The Shui-wu Ch'u has been informed that the Chekiang Tuchun Lu Yung-hsiang has bought from Germany through a Japanese agent 100 cannon, worth Tls.500 each, which are to be imported as machinery. Please let me know whether anything is known about this at your port.

Yours truly,

S. Williams, Esquire.
    WENCHOW.

CUSTOM HOUSE,

S/O NO. 293.   Wenchow, 15th February, 1924

Dear Sir Francis,

Seizure Rewards.
It has occurred to me that it would be easy to provide funds for provision of rewards for seizure of opium by means of inflicting a fine on the smuggler of the amount of the reward due, and issuing the reward from the fine without going through the somewhat cumbersome procedure of advancing it from Account $\underline{D}$, and recovering it at some future time from the interest accruing on your Loan Service Accounts (Circular 2793), and I believe you have some difficulty in providing the necessary funds from this source.

FRANCIS AGLEN, K.B.E.,
Inspector General of Customs,
　　PEKING.

2.

Of course it is not always possible to arrest the smuggler, but we can generally detain the vessel and make the master responsible. For instance on the 9th instant we made a seizure of Piculs 2.23 of Raw Opium, and Piculs 0.16 of Prepared Opium, total value Hk.Tls. 4,940.00, from the Junk "Chin Te Hsing" (全得興), when we handed over five members of the crew to the Police, and fined the Laodah Hk.Tls. 300.00, which has been duly paid without demur. The Seizing Officer's and Informant's rewards amount to $408.00, a sum which could be well covered by the fine. This is not the first time I have fined a vessel for smuggling opium.

Customs Proceeds Fines and Confiscations not uniformly o?ed in the Returns.

In accordance with the instructions of your Circular No. 2268, the net proceeds of Native Customs Fines and Confiscations are credited to the Revenue Account. I notice however that some ports show the amount thus derived in their returns, but not Canton, Swatow, or Wenchow. In Mr. Tanant's memo.

memo of 3rd November, 1920, to the Statistical Secretary, he stated that fines are, by port practice, included in export duties, and suggested adding a footnote in the annual returns "Including Fines Hk.Tls........", but the Statistical Secretary in his memo of 11th November, 1920, in reply, stipulated that the Revenue Table was to be unchanged, but 10-yearly comparative figures were to be given. The total amount of the net proceeds of Fines and Confiscations accruing to the Wenchow Native Customs Revenue Account for the year 1923 was Hk.Tls. 3,073.243, which is about a thousand taels less than the Maritime Customs proceeds. I do not think it is a very good arrangement to classify all this as Export Duty, if the other ports show separate figures, but there may be some special reason for us to continue our practice.

There is a considerable lack of uniformity, moreover, in the manner of recording the fines and confiscations by the various ports. Reference to the Annual Trade

Trade Statistics, Table I, 3.° Dues and Duties collected by the Native Customs (10-yearly comparative figures), shows the following various arrangements :-

Port.	Heading.
Shanghai	Fines and Confiscations.
Ningpo	Fines.
Wenchow	Nil.
Santuao	Fines and Confiscations.
Foochow	" " "
Amoy	Fines.
Swatow	Nil.
Canton	"
Kongmoon	Fines and Confiscations.
Wuchow	(1) Fines, (2) Confiscations.
Kiungchow	Fines.
Pakhoi	Fines and Confiscations.

...ed introduction of
...or Stamp Duty

In my S/O letter No. 289 of 15th December, 1923, I informed you that the Superintendent was in favour of the introduction of a Customs Stamp Duty System, whereby passengers carrying small sundries might be allowed to affix a special Customs Duty Stamp

5.

Stamp to all such articles not exceeding $100.00 in value, and liable to ad valorem duty, but in your S/O letter of 8th ultimo in reply you remarked that assessment and payment of duty by the cargo owner would be a temptation to evade the proper amount due. I now append a copy of a despatch which has been forwarded by the Superintendent to the Cabinet, Wai-chiao Pu, Ts'ai-chêng Pu, and Shui-wu Chu, advocating the adoption of his proposals in this connection, and you will note that he suggests that a procedure be drawn up by you. I told him of your views in the matter, but he had already sent the despatch.

The Superintendent has very little to do here and spends most of his time in Shanghai. He is a man of some intelligence, and rather wasted at this port. I suppose he wants to assert himself. Hence his Stamp Duty System.

The fact of the matter is that the great object of travellers is to avoid paying freight. If they declare to the Customs they

6.

they get caught by the steamer companies for freight. Their chances of escape from seizure are about ten to one, and they can well afford to pay the usual fine of twice duty for foreign goods and four times duty for native. By sticking stamps on their goods they would advertise them as freightable articles. I am afraid the stamps would not be **very** popular!

prospective Native Customs Office.

On the 13th instant I went with the Superintendent of Customs to point out a suitable position on the river bank for the prospective new Native Customs Head Office. There is one very good place next to the Pao Hua S. N. Co's wharf, but it would require some filling in and bunding. There is an excellent alternative site a little further down stream, which is already filled in and bunded. So far the highest tender for the old office is $3,500.00, and either of the owners of the above mentioned sites is willing to exchange with us, but I consider that a sum of money should be

paid

paid to us in addition, as our old office is estimated at Hk.Tls. 16,000.00 less 10 % annual depreciation since January 1923, though this is generally considered to be much too high an estimate. The Superintendent's Secretary, Mr. Shen Ming (沈 銘), a very able man, is handling this matter at present, and I am also interviewing persons interested. The sites we have in view are about 2 mou each, and quite adequate for our requirements. Nothing definite will be arranged without your instructions, which I shall apply for in due course.

Tariff Questions.   I sent off my first Tariff Question for your decision on the new form (B.-30), in accordance with the instructions of your Circular No. 3464, on the 2nd instant. It was despatched to the Shanghai Commissioner for transmission to you after comment. I presume no covering despatch is necessary for these documents, which I am keeping on a special file, but card-indexing with Inspectorate correspondence. May I enquire if the Tariff

Question Forms return to the Ports via the Shanghai Commissioner?

...imported as ...ery.

With reference to your S/O letter of the 11th instant enquiring if anything is known here of the report that the Chekiang Tuchun Lu Yung-hsiang has bought from Germany through a Japanese agent 100 cannon, worth Tls. 500 each, which are to be imported as machinery, I have made careful enquiries and have been unable to ascertain any details of this matter up to the present. No heavy machinery has been imported lately.

...nts of Chinese ...als.

Hao Hsü-tung (郝旭東), Commander-in-Chief of the Wenchow, Chuchow, and Taichow forces, left by S.S. "Yungchuan" on the 11th instant.

Yours truly,

C. A. S. Williams

APPEND

APPEND.

録飭海關監督胡惟賢原呈

呈為關員稽查漏稅行旅受累擬請發行海關印花稅票以便商民而裕國課仰祈

鑒核施行事竊自通商以來凡海關進出口貨稅定有專章行之既久商民稱便而有一最不便民之事莫如旅客行李帶有應納稅品如新購一器物布一足綢一端衾一襲及攜花草一二盆種類不勝枚舉照章皆應報稅而旅客方面有失於檢點者有存心偷漏者有不諳關章者有不知報關手續不得其門而入者有限於時刻或值封關輪開在即不及完納者關上搜查洋員往往在開船之頃傾篋倒簏術例搜尋一經查出變賣充公爭之有所不能控之萬難邀准其有因公往還者或先期請發護照或事後說明情由亦有從寬驗放而三等艙客無一次不被搜查無一人可

以俾免纍纍雜物堆積岸旁定期拍賣所值無幾作為罰欵提成充賞國稅不見其增行旅深受其累惟賢前任新加坡總領事有年南洋英屬大小各商埠均為自由口岸貨物便於取攜商務因之發達自民國七年冬內調始權廈關繼調蕪湖令移甌海從事關務六載於茲目觀國內情形商民不免兩困慮與各本關稅務司商議咸以定章不能擅改防弊惟有從嚴惟賢以為稽查漏稅在關員寶為應盡之職而苛細病民在國家宜籌改良之策今各關奉行之吏莫甚於檢查行李克公罰辦平民屈抑莫伸商旅困苦益甚欲定劃一之法俾有信守之方莫如創設一種海關印花稅票分一元一角三等發由海關郵局及各商店銷售按照稅則刊發簡章俾民周知除大批貨物報關納稅悉仍舊章外所有零星應稅之件照關章計值科徵粘貼此項印花海關查驗員隨時查銷貼不足者罰加二倍

補貼免其充公如此則行入無艱阻之虞貨物無走漏之弊即論國課實增一大宗之收入今以全國四十關計如每關每日平均得印稅百元之譜則每年可增稅歀一百五十萬元推行日廣年年可以加增惟賢 為利便商旅兼裕國課起見擬請

鈞院會商

稅務處飭下總稅務司詳議辦法施行是否有當伏乞

訓示祇遵除呈

外交部

財政部

稅務處外謹呈

國務院

甌海關監督兼溫州交涉員 胡惟賢

TRUE COPY:

INSPECTORATE GENERAL OF CUSTOMS,

S/O

PEKING, 19 February 1924

Dear Mr. Williams,

I have duly received your S/O letter No.292 of the 31st of January.

<u>Summons of foreign seizing Officer to court to give evidence of opium smuggling. Is this in accordance with the spirit of the Treaties ?</u>

A Chinese Court of law presumably has the right to call witnesses and in cases arising out of Customs action, if our staff is in a position to give testimony, the Court could reasonably expect no obstacle to be put in the way of the officer attending. The Court cannot, of course, sub-poena a foreign extra-territorialised subject but it can request his presence as witness through the officer's Chief and, if the Court insists, permission to attend could not be withheld !

<u>Shui-wu Chu mission to ports to obtain Customs information. Commissioner asks instructions.</u>

Give him any information he wants that is not of a confidential nature.

Williams, Esquire.

WENCHOW

<u>Famine</u>

Famine Relief work : Commissioner's activities.

Good work !

Duty exemption of oyster shells and cross-stitch :
Ch'u over-rules Commissioner and Superintendent.

The present Premier, Mr. Sun, decided the Oyster case off his own bat. It is not usual now for the Ch'u to rule on petitions without referring to me, more especially when Superintendent and Commissioner are in accord locally, but in the Oyster case Mr. Sun allowed his kindness of heart to overrule his judgment. I have pointed out that there was no hurry and that the petitioners could have been told their case would be looked into and, meanwhile, the Customs side of the question could have been asked for - through Superintendent and Commissioner respectively. I don't think they will trip up over the cross-stitch, and if you can get your Superintendent to propose a time limit to the Oyster shell exemption you should do so.

Yours truly,

INDEXED

CUSTOM HOUSE,

S/O No. 294.   Wenchow, 29th February 1924

Dear Sir Francis,

atory Notes on Articles.

With reference to the explanatory notes on articles of the Revised Import Tariff of 1919, given in your Circulars Nos. 2948 and 2952, I venture to suggest that these notes be adapted by the Shanghai Appraising Department to the Tariff of 1922, and printed in octavo size, with interleaves, as a Service Publication for use with the latter Tariff.

ration of Rice
ukien.

In my Summary of Non-Urgent Chinese Correspondence for January, 1924, N. C. No. 2, you will see that the Superintendent asked me

IR FRANCIS AGLEN, K. B. E.,
    Inspector General of Customs,
        PEKING.

2.

me to propose a procedure for the treatment of rice imported from Fukien, and I suggested that it might be covered by a Huchao issued by the Taoyin of place of provenance and should pay duty. According to local practice cereals and potato cuttings exceeding 10 piculs are imported and exported free under Taoyin's Huchao to and from places <u>in this district</u>, but it is a new idea to bring it in large quantities from Fukien, and, in point of fact, I doubt whether it will actually come from that province. I now append an extract from the local press from which it appears that it is desired to import the rice free of duty and without Huchao, and the matter is being referred to the Shui-wu Ch'u. I suppose this will mean yet another exemption. In view of the wholesale profiteering in rice in 1922, I am rather inclined to be suspicious about the traffic in this article. If the persons concerned are going to make money out of it, why should we not have some of the profits in the form of duty?

There

3.

Consular Property.   There is a hitch in the purchase of H.B.M. Consular property for Out-door staff quarters here, as the Divisional Architect has informed me that the question has been raised whether the authority from H.M. Government for the sale of the property, covers the sale under the terms now proposed by H.M. Crown Advocate, which are believed to have been communicated to me by Mr. Bowra, and the matter has been referred to London. This leaves me completely in the dark, as you have not informed me what these new terms are, and I still hold Mr. Bowra's power of attorney to purchase on the old terms.

A surveyor is coming here shortly to make an accurate demarcation of the land owned and the land rented by the British Government. The "measurement in perimeter" in the deeds is very indefinite, and the Chinese local officials have lost all their records of the matter!

S for the Tupan.   With reference again to your S, letter

4.

letter of 11th instant, re the reported acquirement of 100 cannon by the Chekiang Tupan, it is very unlikely, if secrecy is to be observed, that they would be landed at a treaty port. There are places on the Chekiang coast where munitions of war could be easily landed from gunboats.

ctive sale of ead Office.

About a quarter of the Native Customs Head Office property consists of a temple dedicated to the God of War, containing the usual objects of worship, and having a theatre in front. The value of the N. C. Head Office was estimated at Hk. Tls. 16,000 in December, 1922, and 10 % is allowed for annual depreciation. Thus the present value of the entire property may be said to be Hk. Tls. 14,400. The main property measures 22,600 sq.ft., or about $3\frac{1}{4}$ mou, the temple 3,580 sq.ft., and the theatre 2,900 sq.ft.

It appears that, as the temple and theatre is occasionally used by the public on festival days, it will be difficult to

dispose

5.

dispose of them by sale: therefore, deducting their value, i.e. a quarter of the value of the whole property, Hk.Tls. 3,600, the value of the remaining offices is Hk.Tls. 10,800. On the basis of this value, the Superintendent is calling for tenders for purchase, but our estimate should be lowered according to the existing value of local property on the market. The temple and theatre are no good to us in any case, and might be eventually relinquished. At present they are kept up by public subscription, and we seem to be constituted as custodians vested with the right of excluding the public if we like.

…ed Stamp Duty

With regard to the proposed introduction of the Customs Stamp Duty System referred to in my S/O letters Nos. 289 and 293, it has occurred to me that foreign merchants and/or passengers might raise some objections to it.

… Meteorological
… Gauge Readings.

To my Trade Report for last year

I

I have appended graphic diagrams showing the highest, lowest, and average monthly readings of the barometer, thermometer, rain-gauge, and tide-gauge at this port during the year, prepared from office records by Mr. J.W. Ryden, Tidesurveyor, B. I hope the Statistical Secretary will not exclude them, as I often have questions from people about these matters, and I think the information will be of real use.

of Staff.

Mr. I.S. Brown, 4th Assistant, B (on probation) has been down with a slight touch of influenza, but is better now. The rest of the staff are all well.

ear Commis-
e s House.

On the 25th instant, there was a fire near the south-east corner of my compound at 9 a.m. The Customs fire-hose and hand-pumping apparatus was brought with some difficulty and helped considerably to subdue the flames, which were under control by 11 a.m. In my despatch No. 3749, N.C. No. 315 of 27th June, 1923, I requested authority to apply

7.

apply to the Works Department for three patent fire extinguishers, as recommended by that Department, as fires are constantly occurring in the neighbourhood of the house I have not received any reply to this request. It takes a long time to bring up the Customs pump, and the fire-extinguishers would be very useful as a stand-by.

Exemption of
Oyster-shells.

With reference to your suggestion that if I can get my Superintendent to propose a time limit to the oyster shell exemption I should do so, I regret to say that the Superintendent does not like to oppose the Ch'u in the matter, but says that if you send on my despatch No. 3803 to the Ch'u, and the matter is referred back to him, he will then support my contention. The Superintendent's policy is generally one of "masterful inactivity".

Wireless Installations
on Steamers.

In my Summary of Non-Urgent Chinese Correspondence for December, 1923, M.C. No. 6, you will see a copy of a despatch from the

Superintendent

8.

Superintendent transmitting Ch'u instructions that steamers over 500 tons are to carry a wireless installation, which I am to see to (查照辦理). Is there anything I can do in this matter, and should I notify the steamer companies of these requirements?

Yours truly,

Ca S Williams.

Append

APPEND.

録二月十八日新甌潮日報

咨請取消運米新章

甌海道尹以內地運米領照納稅妨害民食呈請省長轉呈稅務處取銷新章茲悉省公署已據情電咨稅務處云北京稅務處鑒據甌海道道尹呈承嘉米粮全賴鄰境輸入前月閩省福安福鼎縣商船接濟被東關扣留入官致米斷絕入口近悉甌海關新定章程進口米粮概令納稅據該縣轉報經函甌海關稅務司核後准函本省米粮內地流通十石以上定有由道刊發護照辦法外省運甌米粮請咨鄰省道尹行行發給護照至徵收稅課係根據常關則例內所載未定稅則各件按照新關值百抽五例折半徵收等語該縣上年風水為災收成歉薄似此外來米粮均令領照納稅妨礙民食實甚請予轉咨辦理前

来查商人运输米粮出境為防止漏海起見是以酌給護照以便稽查運米進口無慮再致漏海若責令領照徒多周折使商人裹足不前至於米粮收稅雖據根據常關則例惟常關則不自今始該關對於進口米粮向不聞有照則例收稅之事現又在頻年災荒民食缺乏之時此等新章更難承認請速電飭該關取消新章照常放運以資接濟張載陽印

TRUE COPY:

S/O No. 295.　　　　　　　　　Wenchow　15th March, 24

Dear Sir Francis,

There are five Japanese steamers in port loading charcoal in large quantities, as at the end of the month import duty on charcoal at the rate of 42 sen per 100 lbs will be levied in Japan. It is taking the Staff all their time to attend to these shipments, and I confiscated and resold a consignment found in excess lately.

Chinese Staff.

I find that our two Chinese Tidewaiters are doing good work, but the Watchers, who often have to perform Tidewaiter's duties, do not produce such good results, and, their pay being so small in comparison, they are exposed to the temptation of releasing cargo for a consideration of, say $12 - or a month's wages. It would be

better

SIR FRANCIS AGLEN, K.B.E.,
　　Inspector General of Customs,
　　　　　P E K I N G.

better to have all Tidewaiters here and no Watchers at all.

Han   With reference to the postscript of my despatch No. 3808 of 25th ult., enquiring whether the so-called "Precious Swords" from Lungch'üan (龍泉) should be classed as arms or curios, on the 5th inst. I received a despatch from the Superintendent transmitting the Shui-wu Ch'u's ruling that the swords are to be classed as arms, but that the matter of the sword-sticks is under consideration. Tradition has it that Kan Chiang (干將) of Wu State, a celebrated swordsmith of old, inaugurated the manufacture of magic swords at Lungch'üan, which were dipped in the waters of a certain lake, and became so well tempered that they could cut stone. Owing to this story, and to the fact that the sword is the auspicious emblem of Lü Tung-pin (呂洞賓), one of the Eight Immortals (八仙) of Taoism, these ornamental Lungch'üan swords are valued as curios, and hung up in houses for good luck. If the swords are
                                        allowed

allowed to be sold as curios, perhaps there would be no harm, though it might be a bad precedent, but the sword-sticks should certainly be prohibited.

at Native   On the night of the 11th inst., thieves broke into the Seizure Room at the Native Customs Head Office, and carried away some piece goods, etc., valued at Hk.Tls. 100.00. They made a hole through the western outer wall, forced open a door, and broke the lock of the seizure room. Repairs will cost $11.00. I fined the Watchman Hk.Tls. 2.00, and requested the Superintendent to ask the Police to take steps to recover the stolen goods. It would be well, as already suggested, if we could build a new office and godown of a more substantial nature, and in a more suitable position on the bund.

Customs   It becomes more and more evident that
y Public. there is a regular traffic in Import Passes and Transit Passes obtained from the Customs. Goods are continually arriving under E.C. when it is

clear

clear that a Pass has been bought on the Shanghai market to fit the goods on which duty is to be evaded; the trouble is that it does not quite fit, and this is not the fault of the local importer, who, most unfairly, has to suffer the penalty of fine or confiscation, if the case should be discovered, but of the Shanghai exporter. When goods are re-exported from Shanghai by a firm which is not the original importer, the goods should be examined at Shanghai. The duplicate copy of the Re-export Application is, of course, a great help, and it would be a good plan if copies of the export applications could also be sent instead of the Cargo Certificates, which are so hurriedly, incorrectly, and inadequately written out.

Transit Passes are much in demand for use in evading payment of inland taxation. I have heard indirectly that the Standard Oil Company's local agent takes out Transit Passes for oil and candles imported, and makes a tidy profit on selling them to other merchants when the

the goods are consumed locally and the Passes are not required. Old kerosene oil tins filled with opium, silk, socks, handkerchiefs, etc., can thus be conveniently transported to the interior entirely free of all dues and duties!

...oner's N.C.
...gly levied
...ntendent's

In my Summary of Non-urgent Chinese Correspondence for last month you will see that the Superintendent made the tentative enquiry whether eggs from Yotsing (one of the Superintendent's Stations) have to pay duty at the Native Customs on arrival at Wenchow if not covered by documents issued by his Puchi station. I saw by this that the Superintendent was evidently desirous of collecting duty which should be collected by us, so I replied on the 4th instant, that according to existing practice, all goods imported from neighbouring districts should pay duty at Wenchow. On the 10th instant some eggs came from P'ingyang (another of the Superintendent's Stations) under D.P.C., so I immediately sent the document to the Superintendent asking him to instruct his P'ingyang Office to refund the duty, and I collected duty on deposit here

here from the importer, who is the agent for the American firm Ames Bird Company (班達公司); if the Superintendent does not refund the duty, I shall go and see him personally about the matter and try and arrange it in a friendly way. Diversion of duty by Superintendent's Stations is attempted with every change of Commissioner in the hope of establishing a precedent unnoticed. Mr. Tanant, in his despatch No. 3252, N.C. No. 181 of 1917, brought a similar case to your attention, and proved conclusively that the Superintendent has no authority to collect duty on goods for Wenchow.

accused of excessive fees.

The owner and charterer of the Lorcha "Chin Yüan Hsing" (金源興) have had recourse to the law to settle the question of responsibility and share of the profits and running expenses of the vessel. The charterer's name appears on the register, and I refused to supply the owner (not knowing anything about him) with details of Customs duty and fees paid by the charterer, unless in the latter's presence. The owner lost his law-suit, and has now complained to all and sundry

sundry, including the Shui-wu Ch'u, that we have levied excessive duty and fees, and not accounted for the same. I have acquainted the Superintendent with all the details of duty and fees charged, and I hope you will not be troubled with the matter by the Ch'u, as it is only a spiteful diatribe on the part of the man who lost his law-suit, and cannot afford to pay the damages or suffer the loss of money or face, whichever the case may be.

Kwangtung coins.

I have just received, through the Superintendent, with some relief, the Ch'u's ruling, in agreement with your proposal, that inferior silver coins seized are to be handed over to the Superintendent and reward claimed. I suppose you will issue a Circular instructing how the reward is to be calculated, or whether we are to rely entirely on the Superintendent for the calculation after he has melted the coins. We shall only be certain of the number of the coins, and it would therefore be much better if the reward was fixed according to the

number

number, as in the case of copper cents, and not according to the meltage result, which we shall no longer be in a position to verify.

With reference to the seizure made by this Office some time ago and still outstanding, I have just received a letter from the local Chamber of Commerce proposing release of the coins under a guarantee made by the Bank of China to pay any sum fixed upon later as a penalty, but I naturally replied that without special instructions from you I was unable to agree to this procedure. Would you wish me to report this officially, or can I expect to have your instructions for final settlement of this evergreen case in reply to my despatch No. 3802 of 25th January ? I do not think it would be easy to enforce any such guarantee, which would only prolong the agony !

[margin: t:n from timber s:d by t: te.]

The Magistrate asked me to give duty exemption for certain timber for construction of dykes at Ying Fu (膺符), and is now applying to the Shui-wu Ch'u through the Superintendent, but I have just found out that the timber was

seized

seized by the Native Customs, as it was being taken out of the port, in the form of a raft, without permission.

Supplementary on kerosene A Supplementary Tax is to be levied on kerosene oil by order of the Provincial Authorities. The new tax office is styled the Chekiang Kerosene Oil Supplementary Tax Office (浙江省煤油補征局). The tax is 15 cents per case (2 tins), or 12 cents per case if covered by tax receipt issued by the Kiangsu Kerosene Oil Tax Office. The Head Office is situated at Hangchow, and Sub-offices will be established at Ningpo, Wenchow, Haimen, Wuhsing, and Shanghai. There will also be numerous checking and collecting offices at different places. Oil which has paid the tax will be exempted from T'ungchüan and Yangkuang-chüan, but loti dues is leviable on goods transported through the interior.

Yours truly,
C.A.S. Williams

INSPECTORATE GENERAL OF CUSTOMS,

S/O

PEKING, 26 March 1924

Dear Mr. Williams,

I have duly received your S/O letters Nos. 293 and 294 of the 15th February and 29th February. <u>Opium seizure rewards. Suggestion that smuggler should be fined the amount of the reward.</u>

The Courts also fine in opium cases and we might find complications if we made it a practice. The rewards are a scandalous waste of money but I have no difficulty in providing it, and I can't yet see my way to abolishing them !

<u>N.C. Fines and Confiscations not uniformly recorded by ports in their Returns.</u>

Send me a Memorandum with your suggestions please, and the matter will be gone into !

<u>Customs Stamp Duty System : Superintendent in favour of.</u>

Your Superintendent is a brother of Mr. Hu Wei-te, sometime Minister of the Shui-wu Ch'u. He has influence here and can obtain a ready hearing for suggestions of this kind. I don't think much of the scheme and want you to smother it - <u>nicely</u>.

<u>Wireless</u>

Williams, Esquire.
WENCHOW.

Wireless Installations for steamers : shall Commissioner notify steamer companies of Ch'u instructions ?

You need not do anything until you receive instructions from me !

Yours truly,

S/O No. 296.　　　　　　　Wenchow　　1st April, 24

Dear Sir Francis,

The Revenue for March Quarter again shows an increase of nearly ten thousand taels, and I hope similar results will be obtained in the future, though I am rather afraid that a decrease will be registered in further trade with Japan, on account of the raising of tariff rates in that country.

I had a visit on the 21st instant from an American representative from Shanghai of the American firm Amos Bird Co., who protested strongly against - as he called it - our unreasonable contravention of the treaty stipulations, in refusing issue of transit passes for eggs, and I informed him that I had no

authority

SIR FRANCIS AGLEN, K.B.E.,
　Inspector General of Customs,
　　　P E K I N G.

authority to issue transit passes for eggs or any other article not covered by the local transit pass regulations. He stated that he would refer the matter to his Minister through his Consul, and I told him that he was quite at liberty to do so if he wished. This matter has already been brought to your notice in my despatch No. 3781 of 29th November, 1923, and you informed me in your S/O of 17th December, 1923 - in reply to my S/O No. 288 - that the question will right itself in time, and, meanwhile, it should be left alone.

With reference to my last S/O Letter, declaring my suspicions that duty on eggs from Yotsing had been wrongly collected by the Superintendent's Weiyüan at that place, I found, after all, that it was rather difficult to maintain Mr. Tanant's rather tenacious attitude on this question, seeing that the eggs are now proved to be local produce and not carried through in transit from elsewhere. I have, however, instructed the Chinese Assistant at the Native Customs to make sure, in future, that the eggs are actually local produce of the place of

alleged

alleged provenance, before accepting the Superintendent's Duty Paid Certificates, and I also asked the Superintendent to request his Weiyüan to specify on the Certificates in future that the eggs are local products, in order to avoid misapprehension.

of Cargo ks.   On the 21st instant, the cargo of five junks, loaded without permission, was confiscated. It was worth about Hk.Tls. 4,000.00, and I have decided to resell it to the owners for half value. The case is giving some trouble as a certain Yang Chên-hsin (楊振炘), a member of the local District Assembly, has a finger in the pie, and is exerting his influence for reduction of the penalty to a small fine, but I am unwilling to reduce the penalty any further, as if I do, it will only encourage others to go and do likewise. At the Superintendent's request, I agreed to resell at two-thirds of the value, but later reduced it to half. I shall be glad when this particular case is settled, as we have no place to store all this cargo safely under

cover

cover, and the weather is very wet.

Stamp Duty for I judge, from your despatch No. 1229/97,938, that you are strongly opposed to the introduction of the Stamp Duty System for Passengers' Luggage, as proposed by the Wenchow Superintendent. On receipt of the Ch'u's instructions to investigate the details in consultation with me, and <u>then</u> to draw up a suitable scheme for consideration, the Superintendent returned post-haste from Shanghai, where he spends most of his time, and he came to see me about the matter today. He informed me that the Shanghai Chinese Chamber of Commerce approves of the scheme, which he is now engaged in drawing up, and will show to me later. We discussed the question at some length, and I handed him a memorandum in Chinese, containing a number of views and queries, including all those mentioned in your despatch, together with a description of the present duty treatment of luggage, as laid down in your Circular No. 3434. I was careful to avoid being too pessimistic, but I told him

frankly

frankly that there are many objections from a revenue standpoint to the introduction of a stamp duty assessed by the owners of the goods themselves; I hope he will not take offence at the attitude I am adopting, as I have always maintained most cordial relations with him up to the present, and there are several other questions on the _tapis_ in which I am enlisting his assistance at this time.

tion of Property to by

With reference to my S/O No. 294 of 29th ult., Mr. Groves, Architect in the British Works Department of Shanghai, duly arrived here on the 28th instant to plot out the ground plan of the Consular Property we intend to buy, and he is our guest during his visit on account of the lack of suitable hotel accommodation. Mr. Handley-Derry, the Ningpo Consul, is also coming here shortly in connection with the same matter. The original plan of (I believe) 1877, is truly a fearsome and wonderful contrivance, being coloured bright red, interspersed with pictures of temples and pagodas!

Native

Native
Subordinate
Outdoor Staff.

The Native Subordinate Outdoor Staff, from Watchers downwards, have enquired whether their petition for increase of pay has been considered. This petition was submitted, with remarks and recommendations, in my despatch No. 3764 of 19th September, 1923.

Photograph for I.G.'s
...ph by
...of Wenchow
...Library.

The Customs Library has just been colourwashed, the furniture repaired and revarnished, and the books properly classified and arranged. The Members have expressed a wish to possess an enlarged photograph of yourself — head and shoulders — to hang up in the Library, and I therefore venture to ask if you would be so kind as to have a photograph taken for this purpose, which I shall have pleasure in paying for myself.

Local
...of Oil,
...es, &c.

The Ningpo Manager of the Asiatic Petroleum Co., Mr. Hopkyn-Rees, told me the other day that British merchants, in their protests against provincial taxation of oil, cigarettes, etc., will not be supported by their Consular or Diplomatic Representatives for the next five years,

which

which is tacitly agreed to be a kind of period of truce, to allow the Chinese Government a chance to acquire some stability and control, after which determined action will be taken.

     Yours truly,

     C. A. Williams

S/O

INSPECTORATE GENERAL OF CUSTOMS,

PEKING, 10 April 19 24

Dear Mr. Williams,

I have duly received your S/O letter No.295 of the 15th of March.

<u>Tidewaiters rather than Watchers suitable for Wenchow.</u>

No doubt! But Staff is not unlimited and there must be subordinate work which Watchers can perform!

<u>History of Lungch'uan Swords.</u>

This sounds something like "Excalibur".

<u>Commissioner thinks that sword-sticks should certainly be prohibited.</u>

So I think but the Ch'u will rule.

<u>S.O.Co. sells Transit Passes when goods consumed locally which facilitates transport of dutiable articles in kerosene tins to the interior.</u>

I hope the barriers will get on to this!

<u>Supplementary tax on Kerosene.</u>

There will be a lot of these extra taxes soon, I am afraid!

Inferior

Williams, Esquire.
WENCHOW.

Inferior Kwangtung silver coins. Despatch No 3802

As the Chamber of Commerce has again referred to the Ch'u, I can't move of course till the Ch'u decides. I will, however, try to get a decision.

Yours truly,

INDEXED

S/O No. 297.   Wenchow   15th April, 24

Dear Sir Francis,

Stamp
tem.
       I am about to send you an official report of my negotiations with the Superintendent regarding the Customs Stamp Duty System for Passengers' Luggage proposed by him. I have done all I can to discourage this system, but I am afraid it has become an *idée fixe* with the Superintendent, who is determined to push it through if possible, and has proposed six rules of procedure for my consideration. I am taking the stand that these rules, though of some advantage to passengers in certain respects, present insurmountable objections from the Customs point of view, and would necessitate the appointment of more foreign Tidewaiters, who are very scarce, and shroffs for detecting the large amount of bad money in circulation; the pay

of

SIR FRANCIS AGLEN, K.B.E.,
   Inspector General of Customs,
      PEKING.

of the additional staff required would probably be less than the duty collection in most ports. The Superintendent is basing his rules on the present Canton procedure, which, as reported in my despatch No. 3719 of 1st February, 1923, is not suitable to Wenchow, on account of lack of sufficient staff, etc.

Seizure   In your S/O letter of 26th ultimo you remarked, with reference to my suggestion that opium smugglers could be fined the amount of the reward when possible, that the Courts also fine in opium cases, and complications might arise if we made it a practice. I feel sure, however, that a fine by the Customs, to provide money for a reward, would be regarded as logical by the Chinese government, as there would then be no necessity for the Courts to issue the inadequate rewards, which they occasionally send us, and which are not used for purposes of reward at all, but are brought to account after special reference to you in each case. Moreover, the Court

Court fines for infringement of the law, and the Customs fines for breach of Customs regulations — two separate offences. No objections have ever been made by the Court to the procedure of the Customs, which does not come under its sphere of control.

Re of cargo ju ts. The case of seizure of the cargo of five junks, loaded without permission, and referred to in my last S/O, was duly settled by confiscation and resale of the goods at half value, Hk.Tls. 2,072,125.

Acts. According to the instructions of I.G. Circular No. 187, II Series, of 1882, Enclosure, § 10, Commissioners should report quarterly to the local Superintendent all protests noted, notarial acts performed, and fees collected; if copies of documents are required for transmission to other yamêns, they should be supplied. This port has been open nearly 50 years, and no reports of this kind have ever been made to the Superintendent.

I

I propose to continue the practice of not reporting to the Superintendent, unless he should require any copies of documents, etc.

Dr. E.T.A. Stedeford has applied for one catty of confiscated prepared opium for the use of the Blyth Hospital, Wenchow, so I asked the Superintendent to obtain authority from the Shui-wu Ch'u for the presentation of this quantity, the remainder of our stocks having been burnt yesterday.

I made a tour of inspection of the guaranteed godowns yesterday. The Pao Hua, Yung Ch'uan, and Yung Hing S.N. Co's godowns seemed to be in good order, but the China Merchants godowns are very unsatisfactory; though that Company's import godown has been recently repaired at my request, yet it is far too small for the present volume of trade, and a considerable percentage of the import cargo has to be stored in the export godown, which is really a collection of open sheds, in a very unsafe

unsafe and dilapidated condition. I shall threaten to withdraw the China Merchants' guarantee if no further improvement is made, but I shall be careful not to rush matters.

The District Assembly reopened its session on the 1st instant. The Superintendent has enquired when I can provide the details for the scheme for development of Customs offices and adjoining communications, but as you forbid me to enter into any further proposals beyond financial methods (I.G. Despatch No. 1232/98,214), I am rather at a loss how to satisfy the District Assembly, which requires a **fully-worked-out scheme** for consideration. If the Customs relinquishes interest in this matter at this juncture, I fear the hopes of future port development are none too brilliant, and the deplorable conditions, which have existed for so long, will continue indefinitely.

Yours truly,

C.A.S. Williams

INSPECTORATE GENERAL OF CUSTOMS,

S/O

PEKING, 28 April 1924.

Dear Mr. Williams,

With further reference to your S/O letter No.294 of the 29th of February last :

H.B.M.Consular Property : Commissioner is unaware of the new terms proposed by H.M.Crown Advocate. Information regarding those terms requested.

On inspection of the title deeds for this property it was found that they were only copies. Reference to the Ningpo Consul elicited the information that the originals, with the exception of a lease for a part of Conquest Island, could not be found, but that certain relevant documents bearing on early negotiations for this property with the Chinese Authorities were in existence and that rent had been regularly paid and accepted. The question of what rights these existing documents would confer was then raised, seeing that they were so worded as to lead to the conclusion that the land at present leased by the Consular Authorities had been obtained by the British Government for specific use as a
Consulate.

Williams, Esquire.
WENCHOW.

Consulate. Transfer to the Customs might, therefore, be objected to by the local officials either now or later. The following two ways of surmounting any difficulties were discussed with the British Consul at Peking : (a) Local arrangements at Wenchow for the issue of new deeds, and (b) Payment of purchase price on condition that, if transfer of land were disputed, this price would be refunded by H.B.M.'s Government. It was feared that, were the local authorities approached concerning local arrangements for transfer on the assumption that there was doubt as to the right of H.B.M.'s Office of Works to transfer the land, trouble would be likely to be precipitated. The British Consul at Peking accordingly undertook to bring up the question of conditional payment and you were notified by telegram of 2nd August 1923 as follows :-

"My despatch No.1177 : Consular title not clear. If "purchase price not paid await further orders".

Between this date and the 22nd October 1923 when your despatch No.3773 left Wenchow, nothing further was heard from the British Consul at Peking. Since in that despatch you stated that you believed that arrangements might be made through the Superintendent to

compound

compound the rental and obtain a clear title, it was decided here after consultation with the British Consul that it would be best to arrange locally for the transfer, leaving recourse to a conditional Deed of Transfer for future consideration if need arose.

  The instructions of my despatch No. 1204/96,857 were therefore conveyed to you and, as no new terms were in question, it was hoped that the matter would be speedily settled. It would now appear from your S/O No.294 that H.B.M.'s Office of Works have not understood that the Conditional Deed of Sale was intended as an <u>alternative</u> method of transfer, and that this has caused the hitch to which you refer. As, however, the Consul at Peking is in communication with them on the subject, this difficulty should soon be removed and, provided that my instructions are carefully adhered to, I do not anticipate that further difficulties will arise.

         Yours truly,

INDEXED

S/O No. 298.   Wenchow 1st May, 24

Dear Sir Francis,

's
ar   The acquisition of H.B.M.'s Consular
ty.   Property at this port for Outdoor Staff Quarters,
      with an absolutely clear title, is by no means
      so simple a matter as your Despatch No.
      1204/96,857 would imply, but the negotiations are
      proceding satisfactorily, though with a certain
      amount of circumlocution. I have had to do a
      considerable amount of entertaining, both of
      Chinese and foreign officials, in connection with
      this matter. Mr. Groves, British Works
      Department Surveyor, stayed with us for a week,
      and Mr. H.F. Handley-Derry, H.B.M. Consul for Ningpo
      and Wenchow, has been our guest for the last ten
      days, during which time I have exchanged dinners
      with the various Chinese local officials and chief
      gentry. The Consul is now engaged in packing up
                                                                his

SIR FRANCIS AGLEN, K.B.E.,
    Inspector General of Customs,
            PEKING.

archives and furniture, which he intends to remove from his Office in the Consulate in the course of the next few days; in this we are rendering all possible assistance.

.P.C. ank lation.

The Consul has today succeeded in obtaining the approval of the local Chinese authorities of the site for the Asiatic Petroleum Company's new Oil Tank Installation at this port. As soon as I am notified officially by the Superintendent and the Company I will submit proposed forms of bond, license, etc., for your consideration. There will be two tanks and a godown, and the Company intends to keep fairly large stocks here.

dewaiter 's Army n.

Mr. P.W. Coxall, 1st Class Tidewaiter, has previously been obliged to go to Shanghai monthly, or at least quarterly, to draw his British Army Pension. The fare is $40 (ridiculously high), Mr. Coxall's pension is very small, the return trip cannot be made in less than a week, and as he is the only Foreign Tidewaiter we have, he cannot be be continually spared, so I agreed to witness his signature and transmit his pension once a quarter for the time being. This procedure is now in operation. As there is no consular charge for witnessing such signatures, I do not feel justified in charging a notarial fee, especially as it is really a convenience to us. I trust you have no objection.

tory Notes ff s.   With reference to my despatch No. 3817 in which I suggested that the Shanghai Appraising Department were in a position to revise the explanatory notes on tariff articles given in your Circulars Nos. 2948 and 2952, I see that Mr. Lyall remarks that the Appraising Department has too much non-routine work to attend to. I should like to make it clear that I had no intention of thrusting any very laborious work on the Appraising Department, but this Department contains specialists who could revise these notes in a few hours far better than anybody else, and it therefore seems reasonable to refer the matter

for

for their expert treatment.

tive orks.
A Company is being formed to lay on water in Wenchow, and those who send in their names _now_ as willing to have it will not be charged for the installation. I think we ought to support this movement. It would be useful to have water in the Commissioner's House, Tidewaiters' Quarters, and Custom House compound, as the wells ocasionally run dry (in this connection _vide_ my S/O Letter No. 277 of 30th June, 1923). If the water rate is not much higher than the rates in other ports, it might be worth while to consider the matter, but the difficulty is that the promoters of the company are unable to make any definite statement as to the cost of the supply until they can obtain a sufficient number of guaranteed subscribers. Would you care for me to report this for your official decision, or can I register the Customs as a prospective subscriber?

Light
An additional set of machinery, value Hk.Tls. 40,000.00, was imported today for the local Electric Light

Light Plant. This machinery is much needed, as the current has been extremely inadequate for some years. The importation had to be made in a special vessel of larger tonnage than usual, and will take some time to discharge. We have examined it carefully to see that no arms and ammunition were concealed in the cases. It will require at least six months to install this new machinery.

Yours truly,

C.A.S. Williams

INSPECTORATE GENERAL OF CUSTOMS.

S/O

PEKING, 6 May 1924

Dear Mr. Williams,

I have duly received your S/O letters Nos.296 and 297 of the 1st and 15th of April.

Native Subordinate Outdoor Staff ask for increase of pay.

It is impossible to take the question up piecemeal. If and when convincing evidence of the necessity for an increase becomes general, the matter can be taken up.

Customs Club request photograph of the I.G.

I am very much flattered but I am afraid that I cannot undertake to be photographed specially. The Rembrandt Photo Co. 3.North Soochow Road, Shanghai, took, by special request for publication purposes, a couple of shots of me in my office at Shanghai when passing through last November. The results were not bad. They might be willing to enlarge one of them for you !

Opium Seizure Rewards : suggestion that smugglers should pay same in the form of a fine.

So far as I know, there are no instructions prohibiting fine in addition to confiscation of the opium : but be careful.

District

S Williams, Esquire.
WENCHOW.

<u>District Assembly : request for fully-worked-out scheme
for development of Custom House and communications.
If Customs relinquishes interest, future of port is
none too brilliant.</u>

     I don't want you to relax interest but finance is the bedrock of the whole scheme and it is just there that most of these schemes break down. Customs requirements are one thing, port development another, and it seems to me that you run the risk of biting off more than you can chew.

     Yours truly,

INDEXED

S/O No. 299.　　　　　　Wenchow　　15th May, 24

Dear Sir Francis,

Inspection   With reference to your Despatch No. 1240/98,588, calling for a report on the local Tea Inspection Bureau, may I remind you that a report on this Bureau was submitted to you by Mr. Tanant in his despatch No. 3202 and also 3211 of 1917, to which you replied in your despatches Nos. 721/64,903 and 729/65,214, but I am making enquiries as to whether the constitution of the Bureau is still the same or not. It seems to me that it will be difficult to ascertain if the tea produced for export is really that covered by the Bureau's Certificate or not. According to "The Peking Daily News" of the 9th inst., America evidently has a poor opinion of China tea, and the Chinese Chamber of Commerce in New York advocates measures to improve its quality and to encourage the trade.

Revenue

SIR FRANCIS AGLEN, K. B. E.,
   Inspector General of Customs,
      P E K I N G.

e Stamps for
gers'
e.

When I last saw the Superintendent, he told me he was afraid it would be rather difficult to introduce his Revenue Stamp System for Passengers' Luggage, but that it was only an idea of his which he felt inclined to submit for the consideration of the Government. My despatch No. 3824, reporting my negotiations with him over this matter, goes forward to you today. I rather think my very numerous objections have produced some effect on the Superintendent's mind, but he does not want to lose face, and will probably propose the modus operandi he suggests to me.

r
g ing Silver

I am glad to say that the seizure case of last August, involving 36,960 inferior Kwangtung 20-cent pieces, is now settled in accordance with the instructions of your Despatch No. 1238/98,502, N.Q. No. 200, and the coins were duly melted on the 6th instant in ten hours on ten charcoal stoves!

Removal

l of
s and
ure from
's
ate.

On the 7th inst., at the request of H.B.M.'s Consul for Hangchow, Ningpo, and Wenchow, who was here at the time, a number of books and documents, previously filed in the local Consulate, were burnt by the Tidesurveyor. The Consul offered me an old copy of Giles' Dictionary, but as I have one I suggested his giving it to Mr. I.S. Brown, 4th Assistant, A, who accepted it with much appreciation. All the Consular records and furniture have now been removed from the Consulate, and the keys of the strong room and jail have been handed over to me.

on Customs

On the 4th inst., Mr. P.W. Coxall, 1st Class Tidewaiter, seized four leather trunks, for which no permit was forthcoming, and was attacked by three coolies, one of whom struck him with a bamboo carrying-pole, with the object of regaining possession of the trunks. With the aid of two policemen, the trunks were, however, brought to the Custom House. The

permit

permit was produced on the following day, and I inflicted a fine of Hk.Tls. 5.00 for the assault.

ower.
The new lawn mower, supplied for my use by authority of your Despatch No. 1237/98,385, is greatly appreciated, and it gives a fine close-cut surface to the lawns - a very great advantage when playing tennis. I notice the Engineer-in-Chief has sent up some spare parts for this machine, and I have requested your official sanction for their supply, as he suggests.

ntendent's
s of Fines
iscations.
I have heard indirectly that Superintendents are being instructed to remit their 3/10ths of the proceeds of the Fines and Confiscations to the Ts'ai-chêng Pu in future, but I am unable to verify the truth of this report. I have incidentally noticed that the Superintendent is now rather inclined to suggest the reduction or cancellation of penalties for breach of Customs rules, and to support the contentions of the

public

ers.

public rather than the Customs.

Wenchow is occasionally visited by destitute Russians from Shanghai desirous of proceeding to southern ports, where they hope for better chances of employment. They invariably come to me for the money for their fare. Commercial travellers of the same nationality are also regularly arriving. They have an imperfect knowledge of English, plead ignorance of Customs regulations, and are often found to be carrying unmanifested piece goods for sale in Ningpo, Haimen, and Wenchow.

in I.G. at 1.

I.G. Despatch No. 1259 has not yet been received, the last to hand being No. 1243.

Yours truly,

Ca___

S/O No. 300.　　　　　　　　Wenchow　　2nd June, 24

Dear Sir Francis,

tive
e of
s
r
y.
　　　　The local deliberative bodies are still discussing the advisability of selling the site of H.B.M.'s Consular Property to us outright, as we propose, and the matter has been aired in the local Chinese newspaper "Sin Ngau Chau" (新甌潮), the Editor of which seems to be in favour of the sale, being evidently struck with my argument that the Customs is really a Department of the Chinese Government, so the land is not being sold to outsiders.

tn it of
en ers'
ng.
　　　　I rather fancy the Superintendent is now convinced of the impractability of his Revenue Stamp System for Passengers' Luggage, but he thinks duty ought to be collected from the passengers by us, instead of the passengers having to take the trouble to pay at the Custom House, or through a
　　　　　　　　　　　　　　　　　　　Broker

IR FRANCIS AGLEN, K.B.E.,
　　Inspector General of Customs,
　　　　　PEKING.

Broker, and suggests our following the Ningpo system. I find, however, that the Ningpo method only applies to <u>outward</u> luggage, and <u>three Tidewaiters</u> are employed to collect only about <u>$3 per diem</u>. I shall report to you officially on this matter.

ovement
ent
tion of
l.

The local gentry have petitioned the Provincial Governor to arrange for the prohibition of the exportation of charcoal, which, until quite recently, has been shipped away wholesale to Japan, resulting in the raising of the price of local commodities.

o ment of
s ioner's
n

I have taken a great interest in the gradual laying out of my garden - largely at my own expense - and I am very satisfied with the results. In fact I doubt if we have many gardens as good elsewhere. The only thing required to complete it is a slightly higher east wall, where it is overlooked by certain shabby looking

looking houses, and does not afford sufficient protection to the green-house, which is regularly damaged by the typhoons sweeping in from this direction. When I built the wall I did not realise it would be too low on the east side, and in my despatch No. 3825 I have now applied to you for permission to raise it a little, and I hope you will have no objection as it will only cost about $80.

Absence y intendent. Superintendent Hu Wei-hsien (胡惟贤) is going to Shanghai for two months, and leaves tomorrow with his Secretary Mr. Shên Ming (沈铭). Mr. Ou-yang Pao-fu (欧阳保福) will be in charge until the return in two weeks of Mr. Shên Ming, who will then assume temporary charge.

Despatch missing. The missing I.G. Despatch No. 1239, referred to in my last S/O Letter, has not yet arrived, all other numbers being complete to No. 1246.

Yours truly,

C. A. S. Williams.

INSPECTORATE GENERAL OF CUSTOMS.

S/O　　　　　　　　PEKING,　　9th June　19 24

Dear Mr. Williams,

I have duly received your S/O letters Nos.298 and 299 of the 1st and 15th of May.

<u>British Consular Property : negotiations proceeding.</u>

Good. I would like to have this matter settled.

<u>Mr. Coxall's Army Pension : Commissioner will not charge fee for witnessing his signature to monthly claim.</u>

No objection !

<u>Prospective Water Works : may Commissioner register the Customs as a prospective subscriber or shall he report officially ?</u>

Report officially.

<u>Superintendent fears that Stamp Duty System is not possible.</u>

We must think up some way of giving him "face" but his proposals are unworkable.

<u>Report that Superintendents have been ordered to remit their share of Fines and Confiscations to Peking.</u>

If they are not given a share of the proceeds they will naturally lose all interest in

S Williams, Esquire.　　　　　　　　　Confiscations
WENCHOW.

Confiscations and Fines. It is bad policy but the
Provinces are detaining so much that belongs to Peking
that this move of the Ts'ai Cheng Pu is perhaps under-
standable. I doubt, however, whether the Superintendents
will remit. They will probably confine their action
to reporting figures and fall back on Tuchun's orders !

Yours truly,

INDEXED

S/O No. 301.   Wenchow   16th June, 24

Dear Sir Francis,

of Customs.

When I arrived here two years ago I found it rather difficult to acquire a good knowledge of the Native Customs situation at this Port, more especially as no attempt had ever been made by any of my predecessors to keep the working memorandum up to date in accordance with the instructions of your despatch No.645/60,165, N.C. No.57, though it is quite likely that, for various reasons, they were not able to give the matter their attention. In course of time I gradually became acquainted with the work and effected the very necessary revision, incorporating all the various changes in local practice, which have occurred during the last eight years since the memorandum was written; and I forwarded you the result on the 14th instant in my Despatch No. 3833, N.C. No. 345, together with certain recommendations for the benefit of the revenue, etc., for your consideration.

Treatment

SIR FRANCIS AGLEN, K. B. E.,
　　Inspector General of Customs,
　　　　PEKING.

nt of ers'

As you remark in your S/O Letter of the 9th instant, some method must be devised for the restoration of the Superintendent's dignity, in view of the fact that his proposals for Stamp Duty of Passengers' Luggage are considered unworkable. I am thinking the matter out, and I shall have some proposals of my own to make very shortly, which I hope will prove acceptable both to you and the Superintendent.

n of Foreign Vessel.

The Agent of the Portuguese Motor Schooner "Kimboh" wishes to extend the route of this vessel to Haimen, and to ply from Amoy to that place *via* this Port. Her Inland Waters Certificate was deposited at Amoy when she cleared from that Port for Wenchow. I wrote to the Superintendent asking him to enquire from the Ningpo Superintendent if there was any objection to Haimen being included in the authorised route, as that place is in his district, so I suppose he will set the proper machinery in motion. In the meantime I refused clearance to Haimen, and I trust you approve of my action in the matter.

Piracy

as Excuse
posal of
y Lorcha

The Lorcha "Chin Pao Kang" (金寶康) from Shanghai reported being pirated on the 25th ultimo at Tach'ihmen (大赤門) with a loss of cargo to the value of about $1,000.00, and again pirated on the following day at Likang (瀝港), one member of the crew being said to be killed. The cargo owners argue that the vessel arrived at Chusan on the 29th ultimo and left on the 3rd instant without reporting to the authorities there, and accuse the crew of the Lorcha of disposing of the cargo on their own account, and then making up a cock and bull story about the piracy. The Superintendent asked me whether I thought the Lorcha should be detained or not, but she has already cleared.

Trade

I notice that my Trade Report for last year has been published by the North China Daily News on the 2nd instant. The Hunchun Report has also appeared in this paper.

C. Oil
tion.

Mr. R. West of the Asiatic Petroleum Company arrived here from Shanghai on the 2nd
instant

instant, and asked me for information about local prices for reclaiming, bunding, building, etc., in connection with the Company's projected oil tank and godown installation. I supplied him with the required data, but stated that I could not guarantee that my estimates would be absolutely correct. He also asked for details of tides, sand-banks, etc., which were provided by the Tidesurveyor. Construction will commence on the selected site in two months' time, and I now hear that there will be three tanks. The agreement proposed by the local authorities was submitted for your consideration in my Despatch No. 3829 of the 24th ultimo.

elle to

Mr. Reiss, a Russian subject, whose wife is at present in Peking, is appointed here as Salt Inspector, and arrived on the 12th instant. I understand the Gabelle is opening Wenchow as a Sub-Office of Hangchow, and there will be two Salt Launches stationed here. I may be able to rent quarters to Mr. Reiss when we take over the Consular buildings. I hear the Fukien authorities have

have laid their hands on the Salt Revenue, and made an attempt to seize various Salt Launches as well, but these Launches escaped and were to have been escorted here today by the British Sloop "Bluebell", but I have just received a telegram to say that this arrangement is temporarily postponed.

spatch for me.
The missing I.G. Despatch No. 1239 - referred to in my last two S/O Letters - has not yet arrived, all other numbers being complete to No. 1248.

Yours truly,

Ca S. Williams.

INSPECTORATE GENERAL OF CUSTOMS.

PEKING, 1st July 1924

Dear Mr. Williams,

I have duly received your S/O letters Nos. 300 and 301 of the 2nd and 16th June.

<u>Commissioner reports I.G. despatch No. 1239 missing.</u>

The "missing" despatch was forwarded in a Registered Cover together with No. 1238 which you appear to have received. Moreover the vouchers enclosed in the "missing" despatch (No. 1239) have been receipted and 'witnessed' in your office (as instructed in the despatch covering them) and returned to the Inspectorate ! You had better look into the matter at your end !

<u>Portuguese Motor Schooner wishes to extend route to Haimen. Commissioner has refused clearance pending reply to letter to Superintendent. Is this approved</u> ?

Yes ! It will be best not to let these motor schooners go too far without having their movements regularised, seeing that they are somewhat of a new departure !

Yours truly,

Williams, Esquire.
WENCHOW.

INDEXED

S/O No. 302.   Wenchow   1st July, 24

Dear Sir Francis,

British
Salt
&c.
The British Sloop "Bluebell" arrived on the 19th ult., escorting the Salt Launches "Chi Ssu" and "Ssu Nam", which were short of coal and water. It was very nice to see the British flag again. I called with Commander Smithwick, D. S. O., of the "Bluebell", on the local Commandant, Taoyin, Magistrate, and Commissioner of Foreign Affairs, who were, I think, very gratified. The last time a Gunboat (French) came in, I heard that the territorial officials were rather hurt at not being called upon. The "Bluebell" left with the Launches for Ningpo on the 21st.

Transfer
hü Kam Po,
Ch.)
t, A.
You will notice that, in my Staff Return: Chinese Assistants and Clerks (F.- 40), posted yesterday, I suggested the transfer to Shanghai, for family and educational reasons, of Mr. Chü

IR FRANCIS AGLEN, K. B. E.,
    Inspector General of Customs,
        PEKING.

Chü Kam Po (朱金甫), 3rd (Chinese) Assistant, A, in charge of the Native Customs. This suggestion was made at Mr. Chü's own request. He is a Cantonese with four children, and there are very few of his fellow provincials in this port. Fukienese get on much better here than Cantonese, so it would be advisable to replace him with a native of Fukien if possible.

Consul informa-
re steamer
iis, &c.

The Shanghai American Consul General asked me for a list of steamer companies registered at Wenchow, steamships, termini, and ports of call, which I supplied.

e ustoms
ra ration.

As you have seen from my recent despatches I have gone rather closely into the Native Customs situation at this port in all its aspects I suppose the time is not far distant when the Native Customs will be separated from the Maritime Customs in the same way as the Post Office was separated when in sound running order. Much better results could be produced if the whole of the Native Customs District, both <u>intra</u> and actual

and

and alleged <u>extra</u> 50-<u>li</u>, were controlled by one head.

tendents oms.

With reference to your S/O Circular No. 45, I have always maintained good relations with the Superintendent, and also with his Weiyüan and Secretary. The Superintendent is generally away. It has occurred to me that Superintendents would be much more in sympathy with revenue interests if they had some <u>practical knowledge of Customs work</u>. Would it not be possible to suggest that they might be recruited from the rather large list of Chinese Assistants ?

of ted Opium,

We burnt a little opium and some anti-opium pills today in the presence of the Superintendent's Deputy, to whom I suggested that some hypodermic needles and opium powder could be presented to the local Methodist Hospital if he would obtain the sanction of the Ch'u.

at oner's

Two burglars tried to break into the back of

of my quarters on the 27th ult., but were discovered by one of the chair-coolies, who, however, was unable to catch them. I informed the Police, though nothing was stolen.

es for y Use.
I released two cases of medical stores for military use on deposit of the duty on the 28th ult., pending telegraphic application for the formal authority through the Superintendent, whom I duly notified.

10-cent Mint.
The Superintendent has informed me that the Chekiang Mint is about to mint a quantity of 10-cent pieces, which are to be accepted as local currency.

b ion of t f o.
According to the local press the Provincial Authorities have prohibited the export of charcoal, but I have not been officially informed.

al Light an
In your Despatch No. 1076/38,344 of 1922 you instructed that we are to keep an eye on the Unofficial Lighthouse on Middle Island, Sampwan

Sampwan Group, and report from time to time how it is working. With the inadequate means of conveyance at our disposal, however, it is not easy to get out to this Lighthouse, but if the Motor Boat, applied for and recommended in my Despatches Nos. 3775, 3782, and 3799, is granted, we shall be able to go there pretty often, and carry out all manner of other work as well. I am wondering if the missing I.G. Despatch No. 1239, referred to in my last three S/O Letters, is perhaps in connection with the Wenchow Motor Boat question, and may possibly have been sent out under flying seal to the Coast Inspector?

Yours truly,

Ca S Williams

S/O No. 303.   Wenchow   15th July, 24

Dear Sir Francis,

The Maritime Customs Revenue Collection amounts to Hk.Tls. 61,917.234 for the half year, showing an increase of Hk.Tls. 5,724.499 over the figures for the first half of last year, but the Native Customs Duty has fallen off Hk.Tls. 1,256, so I hope we may be able to tighten up our control of the Native Customs, if you will allow me to effect any of the reorganisation I have suggested in my recent official correspondence.

atment of rs'

The Acting Superintendent seemed to be very pleased when I told him we were going to try to carry out his suggestion to collect duty on passengers' luggage at the steamer wharves (in accordance with the authority of your despatch No. 1254/99,385), so I think any loss of dignity he may have felt in regard to my objections to

his

R FRANCIS AGLEN, K. B. E.,
    Inspector General of Customs,
        P E K I N G.

his undesirable stamp duty system is now satisfactorily regained. I sent him joint notification drafts for the Maritime and Native Customs relating to the matter a couple of days ago.

ised Passes.

The American Amos Bird Company (班鳩公司), of Shanghai, enquire if I have received instructions from Peking to recognise their Transit Passes, issued by the Shanghai Superintendent of Customs, for eggs and poultry from certain Chekiang inland places *via* Wenchow to Shanghai. I replied that you had not sent me any such instructions. In this connection *vide* my despatch No. 3781 of 29th November, 1923. The list of articles entitled to Transit Passes under the Wenchow Outward Transit Procedure should be formally extended to include eggs and poultry before these products can be accorded transit privileges under the Wenchow Rules. No doubt you are being approached in this matter.

Visit

of Colonel
. Ruxton.

On the 6th instant Colonel Ruxton, accompanied by Mrs. Ruxton, arrived at this port on a visit of inspection in connection with the administration of the Salt Gabelle. I had tiffin with them on board the S.S. "Hsinchi". My wife invited them to go and stay with her in the hills, but they had no time.

ties to
ts &
rs of
al Yamens.

I occasionally invite local Chinese Officials to tiffin or dinner, and they bring a number of retainers with them to whom it is customary to give gratuities. There is a recognised tariff of 40 cents for t'ingch'ai and 20 cents for each soldier or chair-coolie. On the occasion of my last invitation the retinue was distributed as follows :—

<u>Commandant</u>: 2 t'ingch'ai, 6 soldiers, 4 chair-coolies
<u>Taoyin</u>:   2   "   4   "   4   "
<u>Superintendent</u>: 2   "   4   "   4   "
<u>Magistrate</u>:   2   "   4   "   4   "
<u>Weiyuan</u>:   1   "   2   "
<u>Manager, C.M.S.N.Co</u>: 1 "   2   "

Thus the gratuities amounted to $11.20. I.G. Circular

Circular No. 185 seems to give authority for payment of gratuities to such t'ingch'ai, soldiers, etc., and does not specify that they are only to be paid at New Year. As a matter of fact we do not issue any gratuities at New Year, so I venture to enquire if I may pay gratuities, under the authority of the above mentioned Circular, to servants, etc., on the occasion of the entertainment of Chinese Officials, such entertainment being absolutely necessary as good policy to maintain friendly relations in effecting any Customs work which requires collaboration with the Chinese authorities.

The Chinese Maritime Police Boat "Hsin Pao Shun" (新寶順), is reported to have captured 27 pirates off Langhu (狼湖海面) recently. I hear that Sun Shou-t'ien (孫受天), of the Hydrographical Board of the Chinese Admiralty, has come here to interview Mr. Ch'en Pai-ch'uan (陳百川) about his suggested anti-piratical measures (vide my despatch No. 2778 of November last). It is proposed in the local press that the

the Native Customs Junk Dues shall be used to provide funds for the suppression of piracy.

3. This is the typhoon season, and we have had some very gusty weather lately, with heavy rain and freshets, the tide gauge registering 17 feet this morning. The China Merchants S.N. Co's S.S. "Kuangchi", bound for Shanghai, had her upper deck structures partly washed away off Shihp'u on the 12th inst., with some loss of life, but full details are not yet to hand.

e how
e: Company.   A new concern, the Fu Chang Steamer Company (福昌商輪公司), has lately been established at this port to run the S.S. "Fuan" between Wenchow and Shanghai every ten days.

Assembly.   The District Assembly re-opened on the 11th instant.

Yours truly,

C.S. Williams

INSPECTORATE GENERAL OF CUSTOMS.

PEKING, 31st July 1924

Dear Mr. Williams,

I have duly received your S/O letters Nos. 302 and 303 of the 1st and 15th instants.

<u>Proposed transfer of Mr. Chu Kam Po, Chinese Assistant, and replacement with Fukienese.</u>

Noted.

<u>"I suppose the time is not far distant when the Native Customs will be separated from the Maritime Customs..."</u>

Why have you reason to suppose this? On the contrary, I think the Maritime Customs in the future will be brought into closer contact with provincial finance. Separation would have much the same effect as the severing of the Siamese Twins : one of them would certainly die - perhaps both !

<u>Suggestion that Superintendents be recruited from list of Customs Chinese Assistants.</u>

Superintendents are not recruited ! They are political appointees. Such a suggestion would be ignored, of course !

<u>Gratuities to servants and soldiers of official guests.</u>

I

S. Williams, Esquire.
WENCHOW.

I never give authority for expenditure by S/O letter.

Yours truly,

INDEXED

O No. 304.   Wenchow 1st August, 24.

Dear Sir Francis,

irqical
ame ts.   With reference to my last S/O Letter, Mr.
Sun Shou-t'ien (孫受天), of the Chinese Navy, came
to see me on the 18th instant. He informed me
that (in accordance with my original suggestion to
you and the Superintendent soon after my arrival
at this port in 1922) a Wireless Station will be
established possibly at Taichow, or perhaps at
Wenchow, and three fast motor vessels, fitted with
wireless and armed with machine guns, will be
provided for use in suppression of piracy. I
suggested that the submarine chasers employed durin
the war would perhaps be a good type to procure
cheaply from foreign governments, but Mr. Sun said
the boats would be constructed in Shanghai. It
seems to me that three craft will hardly be
sufficient to patrol the coast of Kiangsu, Chekiang
and Fukien, and if the allowance from the Junk
                                                                    Dues

SI FRANCIS AGLEN, K. B. E.,
    Inspector General of Customs,
            PEKING.

Dues A/c is to be Hk. Tls. 200,000 per annum, as reported in the paper, it would surely be possible to provide for a fleet of at least a dozen in course of time.

tment of Planks.

With reference to my Despatches Nos. 3834 and 3843, I see by the local press that the Chinese Government will not take up the matter of reduction of the tariff on Chinese softwood planks until the Wenchow Shipping Guild is formally registered at the Chiao-t'ung Pu.

o New ustoms f ce

The necessity for a new and more conveniently situated Native Customs Head Office - as recommended in my Despatch No. 3835, N.C. No. 346 - is all the more evident now on account of the fact that so much more work will fall on the Native Customs Staff on the steamer wharves in view of the instructions of your Despatches Nos. 1254/99,385, N.C. No. 204, and 1258/99545, N.C. No. 207 regarding duty treatment of passengers' luggage and J.W.S.N. cargo carried between treaty ports

ports via inland places. I should like to take up the matter further with the Superintendent, but I await your instructions before doing so.

Wenchow
rintendent.

On the 30th instant Mr. Shen Ming (沈銘), K'ochang in the Superintendent's Office, informed me that he had received a telegram to say that the Wenchow Superintendent Mr. Hu Wei-hsien (胡惟賢), died suddenly at Shanghai on the 29th. His death will be reported by Mr. Shen to the Shui-wu Ch'u and the Provincial Authorities; I have reported his death officially too and requested instructions as to the issue of the Allowance. Mr. Hu was in good health when I saw him last on the 2nd ultimo, but I hear he had recently been suffering from a slight cough. He was formerly Consul in Singapore and was appointed Superintendent at this Port in December, 1921. He held various decorations including the Ta Shou Pao Kuang Chia Ho. His brother Mr. Hu Wei-te, was at one time Minister of of the Shui-wu Ch'u. In 1923 he was sent by the Provincial Authorities to Singapore to collect subscriptions from Chinese residents for famine relief in China, and returned in a short time with $60,000. He spent his time chiefly in Shanghai, though one of his wives was generally in residence here. He built himself a foreign-style residence in Shanghai for Tls. 40,000. He was noted locally for his geniality and leniency when appealed to by the merchants.

I sincerely hope his successor will take more interest in Wenchow Customs affairs. Mr. Chen Ming has always dealt with me in the continual unofficial absence of the Superintendent, and I am on very cordial terms with him. He is a Graduate of the Customs College, and was formerly a Chienhai in the Shanghai Customs, speaks and writes English very well, has a good knowledge of local affairs, is young and progressive, and in full sympathy with revenue interests, and would make an excellent Superintendent in Mr. Hu's place. If it is in any way possible for you to suggest to the Shui-wu Ch'u that

that Mr. Shen Ming should be appointed Superintendent at this Port on account of his peculiarly suitable qualifications, I feel sure that, working with him, I can do a great deal of useful work.

Export
I should be grateful if you can let me know if the Wenchow procedure for treatment of tea declared for ultimate export abroad, as reported in my Despatch No. 3828, N.C. No. 343 of 21st May, meets with your approval or not.

vement of
ng and
mitions.
I enclose, for your information, a copy of an extract from the local paper stating that the District Assembly has discussed my scheme for bunding and municipal improvements, and have decided in favour of a collection of Wharfage Dues on imports by the Customs to be handed over to a Sub-committee (參事會) for use in carrying out all manner of improvements to the town, and that I am to be consulted only in the matter of the bund in front of the Custom House. This arrangement has obvious drawbacks, which will no doubt

doubt suggest some revision. To my mind it is important that the Wharfage Dues should not be used in improper ways, and only improvements to the bund and immediately adjoining roads should be allowed, for these Dues are a tax on the importers who enjoy the use of such facilities for the more convenient landing of their goods. Moreover the funds should be administered by a properly constituted Board of Works consisting of the Superintendent, Magistrate, Commissioner, Chief of Police, and a Member of the District Assembly, and accounts should be prepared by the Customs for the inspection of the Consuls when required. You will remember, however, that you informed me that the initiative of the scheme should be left entirely to the local Officials and Merchants, and I have followed out the instructions of your Despatch No. 1232/98,214, N.C. No. 198, by confining myself merely to the provision of financial details as required. I have not yet been officially approached in the matter, and you may perhaps be approached through other

other channels yourself.

Proposal *re* **Junks'** ...

The various provincial guilds at Wenchow have proposed that all junk masters should report direct to them and hand over their ship's papers on arrival, these papers to be retained by the guild concerned until the clearance of the vessel. If this is allowed, the guilds state that the entry of bad characters into Wenchow will be checked. The real reason for this move, however, is that the guilds want to get money out of the junk people. You will see in my Summary of Non-urgent Chinese Correspondence for last month that I have opposed this arrangement, which is detrimental to Customs control and routine, and was refused before in 1914 in a joint proclamation issued by the Superintendent and Commissioner.

Respective has of H.B.M. Consular Property.

I am reporting officially how matters stand as regards negotiations for transfer of H.B.M. Consular Property to us. I understand that the alternative

alternative arrangements suggested by Mr. Bowra have now been agreed to, and I hope you find them satisfactory. The best way will be to conclude the purchase of the buildings, with the proviso added to the deed to the effect that we shall be reimbursed if evicted (I do not know the exact wording), and, in any case we shall not be evicted, as I have written assurance from the Superintendent. It may still be possible to obtain possession of the land, but as the Taoyin unfortunately handed the matter over to the District Assembly for settlement, and the Assembly continues to delay discussion, no definite decision is in sight. If we do not buy the buildings now, however, I am afraid we shall lose the opportunity altogether.

Yours truly,

Ca E Williams

Append.

Append.

錄新汕潮日報 本年七月二十四二十五兩日

擴充關廠及改良道路案之修正

頃海關擬擴充關廠及改良道路案各情早誌本報現查此案業經縣議會審查結果具書報告今將原書錄下查是案業經大會委託雲龍等審查茲查得原案所擬各節間有未盡妥洽之處相應將辦法予以修正是否有當尚希公決 修正辦法（一）關於改良計劃認定原案丙種圖樣最為適宜（二）關於收買民房民地以及改良道路建築公共碼道等事宜均由參事會辦理編列預算案交由本會議決惟建築海關堤岸暨貨廠等應由參事會與頃海關協商辦理（三）收買民房民地應由參事會估定價格援照收用土地章程辦法（四）關於建築工程應由參事會製定投票辦法交由本會議決施行（五）關於經費部分（元）俟碼頭捐實行征收後

奉办毋庸借垫款项(亨)关於带征码头捐事宜委托瓯海关办理之前项带征手续费以及办理征收人员薪给纸张笔墨等项开支由带征码头捐项下提出百分之五支给之(利)捐款收入按月悉数提存瓯海关监督署转交参事会提支(贞)是项码头捐所有进口货物依原案所议税率酌量征收至出口货物一律免捐以恤商艰(六)是项码头捐等充整顿市政经费不得移作别用(七)本办法如有未尽事宜得提交本会议决修正之特务审查员陈一民押戴萱庭押周文石印朱景尹押叶云龙押

INSPECTORATE GENERAL OF CUSTOMS,

S/O

PEKING, 13th August 1924.

Dear Mr. Williams,

I have duly received your S/O letter No. 304 of 1st August, 1924.

Anti-piratical arrangements.

This is a question of Coastguard which cannot be dealt with locally. The Navy is, I think, going ahead too fast.

Death of Wenchow Superintendent: appointment of new Superintendent: *Supplies & intervention:*

I don't touch questions of this kind. Just as the Shui Wu Ch'u does not intervene in Customs appointments, so the I.G. is particularly careful to avoid any appearance of intervening in appointments of Superintendents.

Guilds' proposal to handle Junks' papers.

This would be a dangerous precedent to establish!

Yours truly,

A.S. Williams, Esquire,
  Wenchow.

No. 305.   Wenchow   15th August, 24.

Dear Sir Francis,

On the 10th instant a Japanese torpedo, landed by a fishing-boat, which found it at sea, was seized on information, and while being conveyed by us to the Custom House, was taken away by a detachment of the local soldiery. It is rumoured that the crew of the fishing-boat were arranging to sell the torpedo to some Japanese in the Mitsui Bussan Kaisha for $2,000, but some Japanese standing by at the time stated that they only intended to report the find to the Japanese Consul at Shanghai. I notified the Superintendent's Office of the circumstances of the case, and claimed the usual seizure and informant's rewards. The late Superintendent's K'ochang Mr. Shên Ming came to see me and admitted that the action of the soldiers was rather premature, and asked for my advice as to
                                                    the

R FRANCIS AGLEN, K.B.E.,
    Inspector General of Customs,
            PEKING.

the international law concerning salvage of
torpedoes, so I read him some relative extracts
from pages 344-351 of J.H. Ferguson's "Manual of
International Law."

It is reported that the China Merchants
S.N. Co's S.S. "Kwangchi", which was put on the
Wenchow-Ningpo run to compete with the other
three Steamer Companies, has now been bought off
this route by these three companies for $34,000,
and will now run to Shanghai. I hear, however,
that later on she will ply from Kuaot'ou in the
Pingyang district carrying alum direct to
Shanghai, which will seriously affect our
Maritime Customs revenue, as this alum has
always come here for shipment up to the present.

The local Police have received instructions
from the Provincial Authorities to collect a tax
on advertisements. Mr. Li Shih-hao (李師浩),
sometime Minister of Finance, has been organizing
an Industrial Exhibition at Hangchow, the
expenditure of which is estimated at $2,000,000,

to

to be raised by a loan on the security of an additional tax of $0.20 or $0.30 a picul on salt from the 1st instant.

nt of
ndent &

Mr. Ch'in Ping-lin (秦炳臨), K'ochang of the incoming Superintendent, called on me on the 13th inst., and told me that the new Superintendent Mr. Chiang Pang-yen (蔣邦彥) was expected by the next steamer from Shanghai. The new appointment is not popular as it is rumoured that, in his position of Salt Commissioner at Hangchow, he made continual misappropriations of funds. Mr. Shên Ming, K'ochang of the late Superintendent, asked me to issue the Superintendent's Allowance to him for this month up to the day on which the new incumbent takes over charge, but I told him I would be guided by your instructions which I shall receive in reply to my Despatches Nos. 3845/6, and that I shall be unable to issue any allowance, either to him, or to the new Superintendent, without authority. I asked Mr. Shên if the new appointment was approved by

the

the Central Government, and he said that although the appointment was made by the Provincial Authorities, he believed a formal application had also been made to the Shui-wu Ch'u.

of H.B.M. Property.

I have received your telegram of the 11th instant, authorising me to conclude the purchase of H.B.M.'s Consular Property, and I expect Mr. H.F. Handley-Derry, British Consul for Ningpo, will come here to effect the transfer and registration on his return from Peitaiho, where he is spending a short holiday. The matter of the annual or perpetual lease of the land will be taken up with the new Superintendent when he arrives, and I hope he will put the business through promptly.

Yours truly,

C.A.S. Williams

No. 306.   Wenchow   1st Sept.,   24

Dear Sir Francis,

There are rumours that the adjoining provinces are anxious to find a pretext to pick a quarrel with Chekiang ever since the Generals Tsang Chih-p'ing (臧致平) and Yang Hua-chao (楊化昭) and their soldiers were given a haven of refuge and enrolled in the provincial army. There is now a preponderance of Anfu men in this province, and this is regarded as somewhat of a menace. Objections have also been raised to the inability of the provincial authorities to deal satisfactorily with piracy and brigandage.

Every effort is therefore being made to guard the frontier, and any overstepping of the boundary will precipitate trouble at once. Perhaps Mr. Sun Pao-ch'i, in his new role of mediator, will be able to arrange for a neutral zone to be interposed between Kiangsu and Chekiang. On the 26th ultimo 500 soldiers were brought in on the
                                                    Chinese

FRANCIS AGLEN, K. B. E.,
    Inspector General of Customs,
            PEKING.

Chinese Gunboat "Chaowu, on the 29th 100 more, with machine guns and ammunition, arrived by the Salt Launch "Kungshun", and 250 men came in today by S.S. "Yungning", and they all proceeded up river towards the border. It is probable that all the Wenchow troops, about 1,500 men, will be transferred to Ch'uchou (處州), and the Ch'uchou Gendarmerie (警備隊) will be brought to Wenchow in exchange. It is to be hoped that our weakened defences will not lay us open to attack from the coast.

I hear that the Shanghai banks are rather apprehensive of trouble and have therefore refused to cash remittances forwarded by Wenchow merchants. This policy will probably bring the local trade to an immediate standstill. Owing to the possibility of a shortage of ready money, both the Haikuan and Shanghai Taels have considerably declined.

...ts of new ...ntendent.

The new Superintendent, Mr. Chiang Pang-yen (蔣邦彥), called on me on the 16th ultimo. I found him very affable, and he declared that he intends to encourage the local trade and develop the

the port to the fullest extent, etc., etc. I returned his call on the 18th, but, to my surprise, on the 29th - after drawing the August Allowance - he left Wenchow by S.S. "Haean" without troubling to notify me of his intended absence, so I called at the yamen and asked to see the K'ochang in charge. I was received by Mr. Shen Ming (沈铭), who informed me that the Superintendent had gone to Hangchow in connection with the political situation, and that a Mr. Hsiung (熊) would be in charge for about a month. I requested that I should be officially notified of such changes in future. I then discussed other matters, such as the necessity for Huchao covering movements of rice, the irregularity in the importation of military equipment by Salt Launches without covering documents, etc. Correspondence still continues to arrive from the Superintendent's yamen, however, bearing the Superintendent's name, so he evidently regards his absence from duty as unofficial.

    I understand Mr. Shen Ming is related to Mr.

Mr. Hu Wei-te (胡惟德), Chinese Minister in Japan, who has recommended his retention as K'ochang in the Wenchow Superintendency.

The new Superintendent, I hear, has been forced by the provincial officials to appoint about 60 so-called Advisers (諮議) at from $6 to $12 a month, who are attached to his yamen but do no work at all. The Superintendent is said to have been given his own appointment on condition that he found sinecure positions for these hangers-on, who, I believe, are all members of the Anfu party, and consider themselves as being of some official standing. The Taoyin is said to support 200 of these gentry in his establishment.

On the 29th ultimo a notice was posted up outside the Superintendent's yamen to the effect that a famine relief surtax of from $3 to $20 and upwards would be collected from holders of Chiao-t'ung Pu Certificates according to the tonnage of the vessels concerned.

out   I have had a lot of trouble lately with
                                                    rice

rice imported without Huchao from neighbouring districts. The farmers say they cannot afford to pay the high fees demanded in the Taoyin's yamen for issue of this necessary document, and I have asked the Superintendent's K'ochang if he can drop a hint to the Taoyin's staff to make the issue of Huchao a little easier for these poor peasants.

gchun on engrs' age;

The T'ungchüan Chü (old Likin), having noticed that we are now collecting duty on Passengers' Luggage on board steamers and at the wharves, has attempted to start a collection in a similar manner on its own behalf, and I have had to protest through the Superintendent against any such collection until after the goods have been passed and released by the Customs, in order to avoid confusion.

how tea ection au.

With reference to my despatch No. 3852, N.C. No. 353, although the Wenchow Tea Inspection Bureau has been in existence for some years, I do not think it has ever been formally

recognised

recognised or registered by the Nung-shang Pu. The danger is that this Bureau, on account of the desire of its officials for lining their own pockets, may eventually become a menace to the tea trade, which is in a bad enough state already. It should not be altogether discouraged, however, and it will be quite sufficient if it is allowed to control tea exported through the Native Customs.

Cargo ed between y hrts via d laces.

With reference to my telegram of 30th ult., and Ningpo despatch No. 5106, N.C. No. 343, requesting your instructions regarding the change of the Ningpo and Wenchow practice of levying Maritime Customs duties on goods destined for a Treaty Port and carried by I.W.S.N. vessels via Inland Places, seeing that a number of Ningpo merchants have protested against it to the Shui-wu Ch'u through the Ningpo Superintendent, I have received a semi-official letter from the Amoy Commissioner complaining of the delay in enforcement of the instructions of your Circular No. 3489, but it is

impossible

impossible for me to carry out the new procedure without the co-operation of Ningpo. Nearly all the Wenchow steamers will be affected by this change, as with few exceptions they run under I.W.S.N. Rules and carry cargo between Treaty Ports *via* Inland Places, and there is no doubt that the local trade will be affected almost as much as that of Ningpo; in fact it may turn out to be a real death-blow to this small port, which is ill-eqipped to resist such misfortunes, more especially at this time of political unrest.

Mr. P.W. Coxall, 1st Class Tidewaiter, detached to the Native Customs, wishes to get married to a Nurse in the Shanghai Victoria Nursing Home in January, and has asked me if I can arrange for his transfer to a larger port where he can more conveniently be married and set up house. I told him that I would mention the matter to you in case you might consider his wishes in this respect. Mr. Coxall, the only foreign Tidewaiter we have here, is a very good Officer, and he would be a decided loss to the Native Customs, where he is the

the mainstay of the Outdoor organisation, so I am not at all in favour of his transfer. His present quarters over the fish market are certainly not well situated, but I could house him quite well on the island when we take over the Consular property, and if the new Native Customs Head Office and Tidewaiter's Quarters are built, as proposed in my despatch No. 3851, N.C. No.352, he will have an excellent residence. His marriage can be easily arranged with the British Consul at Ningpo, and he will not be the only married man on the Outdoor Staff, as the Tidesurveyor is also married.

Yours truly,

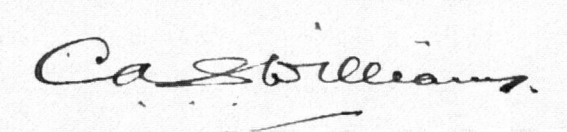

Ca. S. Williams.

S/O

INSPECTORATE GENERAL OF CUSTOMS,
PEKING, 6th September 1924.

Dear Mr. Williams,

I have duly received your S/O letter No.305 of the 15th of August.

<u>Seizure of torpedo found at sea by fishing-boat ; usual seizure and informant's rewards claimed by Commissioner.</u>

I don't understand on what principle seizure rewards were claimed. This seems to have been a case of salvage, not of smuggling ! What became of the torpedo ?

Yours truly,

A.B. Williams, Esquire.
   WENCHOW.

/O No. 307.   Wenchow   15th Sept., 24

Dear Sir Francis,

Situation.   Various proclamations of martial law have been recently issued by the local military and police authorities, and I append copies and translations for your information. On the 3rd instant 376 soldiers and equipment arrived from Haimen by S.S. "Yungning". On the 4th 350 more, with 6 machine guns arrived from Haimen by S.S. "Paohua". These troops all went forward to the frontier. The people are somewhat apprehensive of interference with their property by either defeated or victorious forces, and the Christian converts are pressing the missionaries to fly their national flags and provide sanctuary for refugees if the necessity should arise. I understand, however, that a kind of Christian banner, bearing a cross and the characters 耶蘇教堂, has been devised in order to distinguish the missionary establishments. The Military Commander

FRANCIS AGLEN, K. B. E.,
    Inspector General of Customs,
        P E K I N G.

Commander in Chief Hao Hsü-tung (郝旭東) has moved his men to Ch'uchou (處州), and Wang Wên-pin (王文彬), Chief of Ch'uchou Gendarmerie, has brought 400 men to Wenchow. There are 210 police here, 50 of whom are armed. The local defence force is therefore not strong. As no theatres or fire-crackers are allowed the town is unusually quiet. The censoring of letters has not yet been applied to my official mail, but only to suspected communications. A telephone service from Wenchow to Juian (瑞安) has been inaugurated for military purposes. The general administration of both civil and military officials appears to be very good at present, and steamer traffic is not yet interrupted to any great extent. A good many people are leaving Wenchow, especially the wives and families of the officials. I hear the Fukien forces are entrenched in a very strong and commanding position not far from P'ingyang (平陽), but this news has not been confirmed, and it is very difficult to obtain reliable information owing to the censorship. Ch'ingyüan (慶元) is also said to have been taken by Fukien.

Seizure

of Torpedo.   With regard to our seizure of the Japanese torpedo mentioned in my S/O Letter No. 305, the military authorities allowed the Mitsui Bussan Kaisha to take delivery of it on payment of $250, and it was taken over by the Japanese Destroyer "Sugi" on the 10th instant. I applied for a reward, but the military authorities are not inclined to part with any of the proceeds, and the Superintendent is trying to obtain more money from the Japanese Consul at Shanghai, from which he can issue us a reward. The whole thing has been very badly managed, as a very much higher salvage of one third of the value should have been obtained from the Japanese government. The value of torpedoes runs up to $20,000.00. I suppose independent actions by independent provinces are, however, inevitable.

New stems ce.   With reference to your Despatch No. 1261, in reply to my No. 3835, and the Engineer-in-Chief's comments on my No. 3851, on the one hand you instruct me to reduce my estimates for the land

land purchase, bunding, and construction of the proposed new Native Customs Head Office, and on the other hand the Engineer-in-Chief insists that these estimates are too low, and I do not think he realises that building is so cheap in Wenchow, as he probably judges by Shanghai standards. The best way to arrange matters would be for a Works Department Architect to be sent here to make a personal investigation of the local conditions and requirements, after which a workable scheme, illustrated with technical blue prints, can be submitted for your consideration.

of
oreign
essel. With reference to my S/O Letter No. 301, and your S/O Letter of 1st July in reply, regarding my refusal (which has your approval) to clear the Portuguese Motor Schooner "Kimboh" to Haimen, pending official extension of her route to that place, the Superintendent now informs me that it is not desirable to extend the route of this vessel to include Haimen. As the "Kimboh" is now plying between Amoy and inland places, I

informed

informed the Amoy Commissioner of the Superintendent decision.

lief

A surtax of 10% for famine relief is being collected by the Superintendent's extra 50-li Native Customs Stations from the 1st instant.

... of Mr. Coxall, 1st Tidewaiter.

In my last S/O Letter I informed you that Mr. P.W. Coxall, 1st Class Tidewaiter detached to the Native Customs, wishes to be transferred to a larger port in view of his impending marriage. He is very anxious to know if Service requirements would permit of his transfer so that he can make the necessary arrangements. If you decide to move him, he should be replaced with a capable man of equal seniority, as he has very responsible duties.

...t of ...ions.

With reference to the extract from the local paper sent you in my S/O Letter No. 304, relating to the discussion by the District Assembly of my scheme for bunding and municipal improvements, I have just been notified by the Superintendent that

that this scheme has been further revised, and the Chamber of Commerce has been asked to draw up a suitable Wharfage Dues Tariff on all goods. As soon as I know the particulars of this Tariff I will report officially to you before going into the revised scheme with the Superintendent. I notice that a translation of the extract from the paper referred to above appeared in the North China Herald of 9th August under the caption "Wenchow's trade held up by bad access. Customs recommendations for much needed improvements and how to find the money." The introductory comments are very true.

Clerical.   Wenchow has been free from serious typhoons so far this summer, so there is every prospect of our escaping altogether from such unpleasantness as was experienced last year and the year before. There was strong wind from the 5th to 7th inst., and exceptionally heavy rain from the 11th to 13th. My family returned from the hills, where it was beginning to get quite cold, on the 15th, and the temperature here is now under 80°.

Yours truly,

C.A.C. Williams

P. S.

I have just received your S/O Letter of the 6th inst., saying that you do not understand on what principle seizure rewards were claimed in the case of the salved torpedo. The seizure was made by us on information as the torpedo was being landed clandestinely. The fact that it had been previously salved did not obviate the necessity for declaring it on arrival, and the person who salved it should have notified the Customs instead of landing it and attempting to sell it privately.

The Superintendent informs me that all the available rice is reserved for the use of the Chekiang Army, and is to be exported under Huchao issued by the Taoyin. Do you wish me to make any formal protest, or simply to pass the rice in the manner required?

APPEND

APPEND NO. 1.

PROCLAMATIONS ISSUED BY WENCHOW
MILITARY AND POLICE AUTHORITIES.

浙江溫處防軍兼戒嚴司令官郝佈告

為宣佈戒嚴事案奉

督辦令開任令本司令官為溫處防軍兼戒嚴司令官等因業經通告在案茲因閩贛方面紛調軍隊希圖謀浙業已調集隊伍分赴各邊界防禦惟對於溫處兩屬本司令官有維持治安之責應時機之必要認為警備地域依照浙江戒嚴施行條例第六條及第七條第二項之規定宣告戒嚴合行抄發戒嚴條例仰爾軍民人等一體知悉自宣告戒嚴之後除對於該條例第二十五條各節隨時派員檢查及監視外如有違犯第二十六二十七兩條各款情事定即按照軍法分別辦理不稍寬貸其各凜遵切切

附抄浙江戒嚴條例

第二十六條戒嚴司令官對於地方人民之禁令如左

（一）入會結社之有妨碍時機者禁之

（二）新聞雜誌告白傳單之有妨碍時機者禁之

（三）居民有物品可供軍需之用者或因時機之必要禁止其輸出（但除特許者之外）

（四）人民私有之槍砲彈子武器火具及其他危險物品應令呈報或因時機之必要令其呈繳

（五）人民以密碼通信之件沒收之

第二十七條戒嚴司令官對於軍警各隊應先宣告臨時軍律如左

（一）任意擄掠者槍斃

（二）強姦婦女者槍斃

10.

322

(三)焚殺良民者槍斃
(四)無長官命令竊取名義擅封民產者槍斃
(五)硬搬良民箱籠及銀錢者槍斃
(六)勒索強買者論情治罪
(七)私鬬殺傷人者論情治罪
(八)私入良民家宅者罰
(九)行窃者罰
(十)賭博者罰
(十一)縱酒行兇者罰
(十二)有類以上滋擾情形者酌量罰辦

中華民國十三年九月二日

浙江溫處防軍兼戒嚴司令官郝佈告

為佈告事案奉

督電內開現在時局不靖亟應重申戒嚴以保治安倘有不逞之徒擾亂地方者准由各屬戒嚴司令官先按軍法就地槍決再行呈報匪徒聚眾持械抵抗者格殺勿論仰即轉飭轄區各屬嚴密防範並布告人民咸使凜遵等因奉此除電覆遵辦並令所屬嚴密查防外合行佈告仰爾諸邑人等一體知悉倘有違扡前項情事定按軍法從事勿謂言之不預也其各凜遵毋違特此佈告

中華民國十三年九月三日

永嘉警察局長陳佈告

為佈告事本月二日奉

溫處防軍兼戒嚴司令部發布命令內開茲值邊疆多故防務吃緊

緊深恐不逞之徒乘機窃發擾亂治安本司令官為維持地方秩序防患未然起見曾經宣布緊急戒嚴在案自經布告後務須查照後列各節遵切實辦理毋稍違延切切此令等因並開應行遵守各節奉此除前奉領發布告己分飭各區擇要張貼及開列各節內有關於警察應即遵行事件另令分飭各區隊切實奉行外合亟照錄關於人民應行遵守各節布告諸邑人等一體凜遵毋違切切特布

戒嚴條例錄下

一城區內外之客棧旅館茶坊酒肆各處應受軍警嚴行稽察
一城區廂內外禁止演劇
一城廂內外各民戶禁放爆竹
一嚴禁幇匪曁結黨集會者

一夜間十二點鐘後禁止夜行如有特別事故須持有燈籠方准通行

中華民國十三年九月二日

浙江憲兵隊第五區統帶兼

浙江憲兵戒嚴副司令官　王佈告嚴字第一號

為特別戒嚴奉令宣佈事近維謠諑紛起人心惶恐合境治安斯為首要本部頃奉

浙江軍務善後督辦盧卅電內開現在時局不靖亟應重申戒嚴以保治安倘有不逞之徒擾亂地方者准由各屬戒嚴司令官先按軍法就地槍決再行呈報匪徒聚眾持械抵抗者格殺勿論仰即轉飭轄區各屬嚴密防範並佈告民人咸使凜遵等諭本司令職司警備負全體治安之責為此祗奉

督辦命令宣佈特別戒嚴預飭各營縣軍警一律遵照實行以安

人心而保秩序用特將戒嚴法逐條揭出佈告通衢俾眾週知自此佈告之後如有知法故違者本司令言出法隨決不姑貸其各凜遵切切特示

計開戒嚴法十六條

一戒嚴期內不准多人自由結社聚眾一經查出以違法論

一不准自由集會設在正當事故必須聚議者先呈明本地官廳許可方可集會

一茶館酒店不准容留多人謹呼酣飲妄談軍事

一旅館客棧無論過往客人及常任者須每日登明循環簿送與該管官廳檢驗查核

一荒遠村莊為軍警檢查所不及者須各家互相查察不須存留面生可疑之人有存留者須聯名呈報官廳查究如代相

隱匿一經有違法事件發生鄰近皆以知情不發依軍法處治
一通衢大道每日夜間均於十點鐘禁止行人
一店家住戶每日夜間均於十二點鐘熄滅燈火
一水陸要口均設檢查所各界人民經過時行李包裹什物須逐件由軍警檢查不得托故阻撓致干究處
一妓館樂戶及下流社會所聚集者每日所集何人所作何事須呈明該管軍警檢查以免窩藏匪徒
一敵人奸細偵諜每以人不留意之小本負販為混身之地各處客棧於此等人須格外留意小心盤詰
一每日城門及大小集鎮開門均於天明六點鐘時開放午後九點鐘時關閉
一新聞雜誌圖畫告白等類與時事有關係妨害者不得存留

觀看

一 物品可供軍事用者禁止其輸出

一 私有槍砲彈藥兵器火具及危險物品未呈報者押收或沒收之不得攔阻

一 郵信電報認為可疑之件由軍警檢查人員拆閱不得攔阻

一 出入船舶及其他物品不論晝夜由在地軍警檢查之

中華民國十三年九月六日

TRUE COPY:
Casto

APPEND NO. 2.

TRANSLATIONS OF PROCLAMATIONS ISSUED BY
WENCHOW MILITARY AND POLICE AUTHORITIES.

Martial Law declared by Wenchow Military Headquarters.

Notice is hereby given that in connection with the proclamation notifying my appointment in command of the Wenchow and Ch'uchow Defence Force and Commander under Martial Law for the above places, I, having the responsibility of maintaining peace and order, owing to the intended invasion of Chekiang by the Fukien and Kiangsi forces, have, in addition to sending troops to the frontier for defensive purposes, to provide for the requirements of the situation, to protect my boundary, and declare Martial Law in accordance with the 2nd article of the 6th and 7th rules of the Chekiang Martial Law. A copy of the Martial Law is herewith appended for the information of military men and civilians. Since the declaration of the Martial Law, officers have been sent out as prescribed in the 25th rule of the Martial Law to watch for offenders. Any violation of the 26th and 27th rules will be dealt with in accordance with the seriousness of the offence against the

Martial

13.

Martial Law.   No mercy will be shown.

The following is the 26th rule regarding the prohibition list for civilians.

1. No meetings or societies having anything to do with the political situation are allowed.

2. Newspapers, magazines, advertisements and handbills regarding the political situation are not allowed to be published.

3. Commodities available for military use in time of need are not allowed to be exported unless specially permitted.

4. Arms, ammunition, other fighting implements and combustible materials, etc. should be declared and if necessary handed over to the Military Headquarters.

5. Private codes are to be seized.

Rule 27: the following is the provisional Military Law for troops and police:

1. He who makes unlawful capture of civilians shall be shot.

2. He who commits rape shall be shot.

3. He who commits arson and kills civilians

shall

shall be shot.
4. He who seizes property of people without orders from superior officers shall be shot.
5. He who steals personal effects and money shall be shot.
6. He who extorts money and buys things by force shall be dealt with according to the seriousness of the offence.
7. He who fights or kills others shall be dealt with according to the seriousness of the offence.
8. He who enters a civilian's house without reason shall be punished.
9. He who steals shall be punished.
10. He who gambles shall be punished.
11. He who drinks to excess and causes violen shall be punished.
12. Any similar offences shall be dealt with according to their seriousness.

Wenchow, 2nd September, 1924

Proclamation issued by Military Headquarters.

I am in receipt of a telegram from the Tupan stating:

As

As the situation is grave, it is necessary to strictly enforce the Martial Law in order to preserve peace and order. Permission is hereby given that any lawless person causing trouble shall be shot immediately, before the case is reported by the Commanders of of Martial Law of various places. Bandits who resist by force of arms shall be killed on the spot. Transmission of this order by officers to their respective subordinates with a view to taking strict precautions is expected, and this order is also to be notified for the information of the people:

and therefore, in addition to replying to the Tupan and ordering my subordinates to take strict precautions, I notify you, all grades of people. If any violation regarding the above be made, the case will be dealt with in accordance with the military law. It will be useless to say that the law has not been announced beforehand. Every one of you should strictly observe the order.

Wenchow, 3rd September, 1924.

Proclamation

21.

Proclamation issued by the Police in connection with Martial Law.

With reference to the receipt on the 2nd instant of the order issued by the Wenchow and Ch'uchow Defence Force and Martial Law Headquarters stating:

> Since many troubles have arisen along the Chekiang boundary, precautionary steps have been taken. It is, however, feared that the lawless will avail themselves of the opportunity to cause trouble with a view to disturbing peace. I, as Commander, shouldering all the responsibility of maintaining order of the place, have therefore taken precautionary measures as notified in the Martial Law Proclamation. Since the declaration, all the rules should be strictly observed and carried out promptly:

the police, beside issuing proclamations to be posted at the various important places and making copies of the rules concerning observance on the part of police to be strictly enforced by the various police sub-stations, have accordingly drawn up the rules to be be observed by the various grades of people. The following are the rules of the Martial Law:

1. All the inns, hotels, tea houses and restaurants, inside and outside the city, shall be closely watched and searched by troops and police.

2. No theatrical performances, inside and outside the city, shall be allowed.

3. No firecrackers, inside and outside the city, shall be allowed to be fired.

4. No illegal society and meeting shall be allowed.

5. No person shall be allowed to walk in the street after 12 o'clock in the night. But if on special business, he must carry a lantern.

Wenchow, 2nd September, 1924.

Proclamation issued by Commander of Chekiang 5th Gendarmerie and Vice Commander under Wenchow and Ch'uchow Martial Law.

In connection with recent current rumours which have caused panic among the people, and for which maintenance of peace is necessary, I received on on the 30th August a telegram from the Tupan to the effect that :

> as the situation is grave, it is necessary to lay stress on Martial Law in order to maintain peace. Commanders of Martial Law of the various places are authorised to deal in accordance with military law with lawless persons disturbing peace, before they report the case to the Tupan. Bandits who resist by force of arms shall be shot on the spot. This order is to be transmitted to the various subordinates of the Commanders of Martial Law and also to be notified to the people:

and, I, as Commander of the Gendarmerie, beside declaring Martial Law to be observed by the various troops and police with a view to calming people and preserving peace, have therefore issued the rules of the Martial Law for the information of the people. Hereafter intentional offenders will be dealt with according to the above without mercy. The following are the 16 rules of the Martial Law.

1. During the period of Martial Law, no society shall be allowed to be formed, otherwise punishments

24.

punishments will be inflicted.

2. No meeting shall be held, but, if necessary, the circumstances should be reported to the local Authorities, before the meeting can be held.

3. No noise and discussion on military affairs shall be allowed in the tea houses and restaurants.

4. Hotels and inns shall make out lists of both temporary and permanent guests to the local Authorities for inspection.

5. For far-off villages where there are no troops and police, a mutual inspection system shall be called for in order to give no chance to strangers to live there. If any stranger remains in the village, he should be reported to the local Authorities. The Military Law will be inflicted on the neighbours who are presumed to know the offender.

6. No person shall be allowed to walk in the street after 10 o'clock at night.

7. All shops and residences shall put out lights after

25.

after 12 o'clock in the night.

8. Inspection quarters shall be established both on land and water to inspect baggage, parcels, etc. of passengers, any refusal of which will be dealt with.

9. Brothels and singsong houses, and houses in which a low class of people live, shall report to the police all the persons who visit there and also what they did during the day, with a view to preventing bandits from hiding there.

10. Spies and detectives often disguise themselves as petty traders and therefore all the inns should pay much attention to them by means of inquiry.

11. All the city gates and village gates shall be opened at 6 in the morning and shut at 9 in the evening.

12. Newspapers, magazines, pictures, advertisements etc. having anything to do with the political situation shall not be allowed to be seen.

13. Commodities available for military use shall not be allowed to be exported.

14. Arms, ammunition, other fighting implements, fire

26.

fire materials and explosive articles, if undeclared, shall be placed under custody or confiscated.

15. Letters and telegrams of a suspicious nature shall be inspected by the censors.

16. Outgoing and incoming vessels and goods carried by them shall be inspected day and night by troops and police stationed at the various places.

Wenchow, 6th September, 1924.

TRUE TRANSLATION :

No. 308.   Wenchow 1st October, 24.

Dear Sir Francis,

Rebellion Situation.

    I have officially acquainted you with the developments of the local situation as regards the Chekiang Rebellion. I have taken measures to safeguard the Customs and Postal Staffs and their families, and have offered to help the Acting Superintendent if necessary. At the instance of the British residents I have also been instrumental in obtaining a British Gunboat. Seeing that we have also been provided with French and Japanese warships, we certainly feel that we are adequately protected for the time being. As there are no compradore shops here, the gunboats are rather badly off for provisions, but we are doing our best to help them as far as possible. Commander d'Arvieu of the French Sloop "Craonne" has been very kind in his offers of assistance at any time, and has supplied me with some signal

SIR FRANCIS AGLEN, K. B. E.,
  Inspector General of Customs,
        PEKING.

signal lights in case we should require his aid. The Fukien Commander P'êng Tê-ch'üan (彭德铨) tells me he is a native of Peking, but he does not speak very pure Mandarin; he seems very pleasant, but rather reluctant to give away much information. He has issued a notification saying that he has only come here on his way to find Generals Tsang Chih-p'ing (臧致平) and Yang Hua-chao (杨化昭), and the Wenchow people have nothing to fear. At the same time he engaged in impressing 500 coolies to carry military stores destined, it is said, for Taichow, and everybody is trying to avoid the press-gangs. This looks as though he is preparing to advance. The Laodahs of the Juian launches have brought a report today that the Fukien soldiers are not well disciplined at Juian and Pingyang and are committing rapine and pillage there; it is to be feared that these men may come on here after the present troops proceed to Taichow or elsewhere.

utions for   Two rows of ramshackle lath and plaster
operty.
               houses

houses are being constructed at the back of, and almost touching, my quarters in the city. They interfere with free access to the public well, which we also use, and are very dangerous in case of fire. I am trying to get the acting Superintendent to have them set back a little, but in the absence of the proper Superintendent it seems impossible to put anything through at all. The fire-extinguishers applied for in my Despatches Nos. 3749 and 3859 are very necessary even at ordinary times, and the more so at present, so I venture to hope that you will allow me to procure them, as the water supply is limited.

Silver Under existing instructions all inferior Kuangtung and Fukien silver coins are confiscated and handed over to the Superintendent for melting and issue of reward. I notice, however, that the amount deducted by the Superintendent as cost of melting is three or four times as much as we paid when we controlled the melting arrangements ourselves in the past. I suppose, however, that

a

a protest on this head would be hardly comme il faut. The Fukien invaders have naturally brought large quantities of Fukien money (and some Japanese yen) into the province, which rather complicates matters. The local Magistrate has issued a notification to the effect that Fukien ten cent pieces are to be accepted at 14 to the dollar and 14 coppers each.

S.S."Yatung". The Fu Ch'ang Co's S.S. "Yatung", with a cargo of charcoal from Wenchow to Japan, is reported sunk in the Japan Sea on or about the 28th of September, with a considerable loss of life.

  The Staff of this Office have behaved very well during the disturbances. Mr. J.W. Ryden, Tidesurveyor, B, has been in bed for a few days with gastritis, but is on duty again now. Mr. Ryden does very useful work here and I should be sorry if he were transferred. Mrs. Ryden does not find the place very amusing, though we do
        everything

everything we can to make things pleasant for her. My wife and I like Wenchow very much. I append, for your information, a copy of one of the certificates of identification issued to the Chinese Staff by the Foochow Office. I propose to issue similar certificates locally, in case our employees are interfered with by the military press-gangs, and I have wired to ask your permission to do so.

Yours truly,

Ca. S. Williams.

APPEND

APPEND.

Copy of certificate of identification issued to Chinese Customs employés at Foochow.

闽海关税务司

发给证书以便壹志奉公事查林占鳌系本关职员
无论居处行走幸勿擅行干涉致悮要公特给此书为凭
右证书给林占鳌收执

中華民國十一年十月
(Foochow Commr's Seal)
(Initialed) P.R.W.
十二日

This is to certify that the bearer Mr. LING CHAN NGAU (林占鳌) is a member of the Staff of this CUSTOM HOUSE, and it is requested that he be not interfered with.

(Signed) Percy R. Walsham.
Commissioner of Customs.

Custom House,
Foochow, 12th October 1922.
(FOOCHOW COMMISSIONER'S
SEAL)

TRUE COPY:

INDEXED

INSPECTORATE GENERAL OF CUSTOMS,

PEKING, 7th October 19 24.

S/O

Dear Mr. Williams,

I have duly received your S/O letter No.306 and 307 of the 1st and 15th September.

Mr. Coxall desires transfer after marriage.

Mr. Coxall has been at Wenchow since 1st April 1923 only, and, seeing that he can be given the necessary quarters, he cannot well expect a transfer now merely to suit his own tastes ! His name is noted for a transfer next year if Service requirements permit.

Rice for Chekiang troops: shall Commissioner protest?

Protests in war conditions are not much use. They only rile. Put on record what rules require and pass !

Yours truly,

S. Williams, Esquire.
WENCHOW.

S.O. 309.　　　　　　　　Wenchow　15th October, 24.

Dear Sir Francis,

ng rebellion
l Situation.　　　　The operations of the military press-gangs, referred to in my last S/O Letter, were eventually discontinued when the Chamber of Commerce guaranteed the provision of the necessary number of coolies for military transport when required. Commander P'êng remarked, when visiting the French Gunboat, that the impressing was "all a mistake"! The Gunboat gave him a salute of 15 guns, which caused great excitement and nearly broke the windows of the Custom House.

　　　　Commander P'êng has been discharging most of the local officials and putting in his own men, probably to control the financial resources. He appointed a new Likin Chief Chu Ping-chün (朱秉鈞) on the 4th instant vice Hsia Chi-yü (夏啟瑜), and compelled the Taoyin to discharge the Magistrate Hsü Lin-hsiang (徐麟祥) - a very good man -

　　　　　　　　　　　　　　　　　　replacing

SI FRANCIS AGLEN, K.B.E.,
　　Inspector General of Customs,
　　　　　　PEKING.

replacing him by Wu T'ao (吳濤), a Fukienese, on the 8th instant. Other appointments were T'ao Chên-tsu (淘振租), Head of the Wine and Tobacco Monopoly, vice Chou Tsung-i (周宗頤), on the 5th, and Ch'ên Hsiang (陳祥), vice Pan Jui-wu (班瑞五), Commander of the Salt Guards. Finally he has turned out the Superintendent's Staff, the Superintendent himself (appointed on the 16th August) having left Wenchow at the first sign of unrest on the 29th August. He has persuaded the Tuli to appoint the Juian Magistrate Yang Ch'êng-hsiao (楊承孝) as Wenchow Superintendent from the 16th instant. Under ordinary conditions a Magistrate is too junior an official to be made a Superintendent, but it is said that Yang ingratiated himself with the Commander when the latter occupied the town of Juian, and he is thus repaid, no doubt with a view to future requirements. I have wired to you to enquire as to the issue of the Superintendent's Allowance for this month, the first half of which is due to the old Staff.

On

On the 4th instant a civilian, T'ang Chih-chung (湯執中), was shot for posing as a military officer, and extorting money "for military use." T'ang was a native of P'ingyang, not far from here, and, at the outset of the civil war, he offered his services as a spy to Commander P'êng, and provided him with maps of the district. He has blackmailed numbers of people and was cordially disliked. On the 7th a soldier was shot for rape, on the 11th another was shot for desertion, and on the 14th a man was shot for wrongfully enlisting soldiers for service elsewhere. Order has been restored in the city, however, and conditions are more or less normal again.

The French Sloop "Craonne" left on the 2nd, and the Japanese Destroyer "Sugi" on the 3rd. The British Sloop "Hollyhock" will leave tomorrow, having received information by wireless that Generals Lu and Ho have fled, and the Chekiang forces are retiring from Shanghai, while the Kiangsu troops have occupied the Shanghai North Railway Station, so the rather involved situation is apparently cleared up to some extent.

Return

With reference to my Despatch No. 3863 informing you that Native Customs Watcher Liu Tzŭ-ch'un (劉子春) was granted local leave, but was unable to return on the due date on account of the civil war, and asking for instructions re issue of his pay, this employee returned to duty on the 11th instant, thus exceeding his period of leave by nine days. His baggage was stolen and his progress stopped by soldiers en route overland, so he had to return to Foochow and travel by steamer via Wenchow.

On the 8th instant I received the following telegram from H.B.M.'s Consul at Ningpo :

> Hartman British subject proceeding Wenchow should not be assisted. If he should go up country please inform me. British Consul.

On the following day the man Hartman arrived with no passport, calling himself a doctor and a **Dutch**
subject

subject, and telling an extraordinary story about his loss of luggage, how he had been cheated universally, and how he was in fear of his life owing to indiscretions committed in Shanghai and Ningpo, and how he was implicated in some difficulties with the secret service agents of the Chekiang and Kiangsu armies, etc., etc. He turns out to be quite irresponsible and addicted to morphia, and is making himself a general nuisance to the community, continually worrying us by visits at night (he takes morphia during the day) and demanding food, money, clothes, etc. He does not want to go to Shanghai or Ningpo, but has expressed a desire to go to Amoy by junk. No doubt he has heard that Amoy is the chief centre of opium smuggling, and he would probably have no difficulty in obtaining the drug he requires there. I doubt if he can get a junk to take him from here to Amoy, though he might get one to Foochow. These junks go off more or less on a roving commission by devious routes, and many of them have most unprincipled crews. I am afraid we shall have a lot of trouble with Doctor (?) Hartman as he has no more money to buy morphia

and

and is becoming desperate.

…o's Oil …ation and …t with …ficials.

The Asiatic Petroleum Company is filling in and bunding the new installation site on the North River, and now wishes to import building material, but I told the Company's Agent that (as you instruct in your Despatch No. 1250/99,183) as construction of the tanks cannot begin until the Agreement with the local authorities has been signed, I have to defer issuing authority to land materials on the proposed site. On the 13th instant I received the following telegram from H.B.M.'s Consul at Ningpo :

> Asiatic Petroleum Company inform me that you have instructions from Inspector General to prohibit landing of installation building material. Will you confirm this. Handley-Derry.

I wired in reply :

> My instructions are to defer question of landing building material until Agreement is signed.

The

The Standard Oil Co., by the way, put up their tank here three years before the Agreement was signed, but of course it could not be used until the Agreement was signed, and Bond and Licence duly executed; the Agreement, moreover, would never have been signed if I had not helped the Company over the terms of the Agreement, etc. In the Case of the Asiatic Petroleum Co., however, you do not wish me to comment - as requested by the Superintendent - on the very unfair Agreement proposed. I do not think the Chinese Government can prevent foreigners building anything they like on their own property, but of course oil or inflammable goods cannot be stored there without the Agreement. May I suggest that you may be prepared to reconsider your decision to block the building of the A.P.C. Installation by refusing permission to land the necessary building material, which, after all, is prohibited under your present treatment? There is always a lot of hanky-panky

with

with the local Chinese authorities about these
Agreements, which, according to information I have
received from Agents of the Oil Companies, are
generally made an excuse for demanding a very
high "fee" or "Compensation" - for something or
other - which goes straight into the pockets of
the said authorities. This obstructive and sordid
policy on the part of a few avaricious officials
is bad for China's trade and prestige, and it
would be much better if the Agreements were
drawn up on a uniform plan by the Central
Government, say or a printed form, and signed in
Peking without passing through the hands of the
territorial authorities at all.

Yours truly,

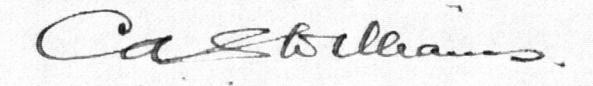

C. A. S. Williams.

No. 310.   Wenchow   1st November, 24.

Dear Sir Francis,

Wenchow is still under martial law, but local conditions are quiet at present and trade has recovered to some extent. On the 16th ultimo one ying of Fukien troops arrived from Juian, and on the following day about 1,000 men left for Taichow via Yotsing, no doubt on account of the abortive declaration of independence at Ningpo. I issued 43 badges and certificates of identification to the Chinese members of the Maritime Customs Staff, and 35 to the Native Customs, to avoid any possible interference with them by the soldiery.

The new Superintendent Mr. Yang Ch'êng-hsiao (楊承孝) called on me on the 16th ult., and I returned his visit on the 18th. He gave a
                                                              tiffin

FRANCIS AGLEN, K.B.E.,
    Inspector General of Customs,
            PEKING.

tiffin party on the 28th, to which the Ningpo Consul, local Magistrate, Customs Doctor, Chief of Gentry and myself were invited. I am wondering whether Mr. Yang's appointment has yet been ratified by the Central Government. I presume I am not wrong in recognising him as Superintendent (vide my Despatch No. 3867, N.C. No. 360).

ar ann.

Doctor (?) Hartmann, the morphia maniac referred to in my last S/O Letter, left by the Junk "Kou Shih Chun" for Amoy via Juian on the 18th ultimo - to our great relief. I informed the Ningpo Consul, who wired a warning to the Amoy residents.

Now that the winter is coming on piracy is becoming more prevalent. It is to be hoped that there will be no piracies on the Shanghai-Wenchow steamers, though it seems possible after the recent case of S.S. "Ninghsin" off Wenchow. The Junk
"Chin

"Chin Heng Hsing" was pirated near Taichow on the 14th ult., and there have also been other piracies.

British Consul.   Mr. H. F. Handley-Derry, H.B.M. Consul for Hangchow, Ningpo and Wenchow, arrived from Ningpo on the 23rd ult., and still remains as my guest. He came to effect the transfer of the Consular Property to us, and to enquire into the arrest of the Agent of the British American Tobacco Co - a Chinese who acquired British nationality - for selling cigarettes without tax stamps; he also had business with the local authorities in connection with the construction of the Asiatic Petroleum Co's Installation, etc.

P.C Instalation.   It seems that the Magistrate has demanded a fee of 6% of the value of the land before conclusion of the agreement with the Asiatic Petroleum Company relating to their proposed new Oil Tank and Godown Installation on the North River.

River. This fee has been refused, and now the construction of the Company's jetty is opposed on the pretext that it will impede navigation. As a matter of fact the jetty is essential, and will be no obstruction at all, and a pontoon or mooring buoys would not be satisfactory, while the development of the land will improve and strengthen the river frontage; this is also the opinion of the Harbour Master, who has sounded and charted the channel at various times, both at high and low water. I have navigated the North River quite often myself in my houseboat when out for pheasant shooting, and am well acquainted with the riparian and riverine conditions. I visited the site yesterday in company with the Consul, Magistrate, Harbour Master, Chief Gentry, etc., and there was a general discussion of the case, but nothing settled. I am afraid some palm-oil will have to be supplied by the Company, which is up

against

5

against a brick wall at present. The site is now being filled in and raised, and the Company is anxious to protect it by bunding while the weather is favourable, but you/ have forbidden me to give permission for the necessary building material to be landed (vide my last S/O Letter). The Consul is now taking up with his Legation the question of landing the material before the agreement is signed on the ground that the agreement only refers to tanks, and the Company wants to put up a godown for the storage of case oil before the erection of the tank. At present case oil is stored in the city, a very dangerous arrangement.

Shelter. The hut for the accommodation of our Boatmen-pilots, while waiting for incoming steamers at the mouth of the river, is very urgently needed now that the cold weather is approaching. We order our best Boatmen out for Pilotage duty and

and their health is endangered by exposure, which could be avoided by the provision of the hut in question (vide my Despatch No. 3871). This shelter will also be useful to Outdoor Officers on special duty, such as taking soundings, inspecting guiding marks, lights, etc.

Silver   You will see by my Despatch No. 3875, N.C. No. 363, that the Superintendent, to save himself trouble, wishes to over-rule the Shui-wu Ch'u's instructions, and not melt confiscated Kuangtung and Fukien subsidiary silver coins, in order to placate the local Fukien authorities, who naturally object to their own currency being interfered with, but I do not quite know how to treat the 2/10ths of the actual coins seized, which the Superintendent has returned to me as a Seizure Reward. This matter always causes trouble. Perhaps the easiest way would be for us to melt the "Reward", sell it, and distribute the proceeds to

7

to the Seizing Officers. If we accept the Superintendent's irregular procedure, the Superintendent will be regarded as a local benefactor, while we will be suspected of merely working for our own interests. It is a pity the Customs has to mix itself up in currency matters, when the simplest way would be for the issuing banks to be instructed to recall their inferior issues.

Now that we are at last the owners of the Consulate and Constable's House, I am anxious to put them into good condition as Tidesurveyor's and Examiner's Quarters (vide my Despatch No. 3872). I have not yet been informed of any definite decision on the part of District Assembly, Taoyin, or Superintendent, as regards the tenure or lease of the land, but I am pressing the matter as much as possible, and I feel assured that the matter will finally be placed on

a

a satisfactory basis. I am proposing the removal of a strong-room steel door, for use in the Tidesurveyor's Office instead of in the Consulate, for storing seizures of coins, opium, and other valuables, and for keeping petty cash monies, etc.

As local conditions are no longer disturbed it will be quite convenient for a Works Department Architect to come here and examine the specifications and building requirements in connection with the suggested new Native Customs Head Office (vide my Despatch No. 3858, N.C. No. 355), and I would most strongly urge the immediate purchase of the selected site on the bund at once, or we we shall most probably lose the opportunity to acquire it. It only costs $2,000, and is a decided bargain.

Yours truly,

C.A.S. Williams

INSPECTORATE GENERAL OF CUSTOMS,

PEKING, 7th November 1924

Dear Mr. Williams,

I have duly received your S/O letters Nos. 308 and 309 of the 1st and 15th October.

<u>A.P.C. Oil Installation : Commissioner reads I.G.'s instructions to mean that building of installation is to be blocked by refusal to permit landing of necessary building material pending signing of Agreement.</u>

I have given no decision to block the building of the proposed A.P.C. installation and I have given no instructions to refuse permission to land the necessary building material. The instructions of my despatch No.1250 were that you should defer issuing authority to land materials on the proposed site: that is to say that you should be careful not to go ahead of the local authorities who were apparently not in accord with the A.P.C. on the question of the Agreement to be signed. I assumed that the Agreement would be signed shortly ! We cannot of course refuse permit to import and land building material which is not contraband, but landing of goods outside Harbour limits requires special

Customs

S. lliams, Esquire.
CHOW.

Customs authority and payment of Out-of-Harbour limit fee. We have to avoid any appearance of prejudging a question which does not concern us, and to issue prematurely a general authority to land in a particular spot building materials for an installation which forms the subject of an Agreement likely to be in dispute might give colour to such appearance. The arrival of the goods brings the matter to an issue. The Company naturally wants to land them on the site, which you state has the approval of the Territorial Authorities, to avoid expense hereafter. You may therefore permit the landing of the materials but you should inform the Company that such permission does not imply any permission to construct the tanks.

Yours truly,

No. 311.   Wenchow   15th Nov., 24.

Dear Sir Francis,

Situation.   The Chekiang Civil Governor Hsia Ch'ao
(夏超) appears to be somewhat out of sympathy
with the Tuli Sun Chuan-fang (孫傳芳), and is
trying to recruit soldiers at Tsingtien (青田),
his native place, and at Wenchow. This plot
has been discovered by the Tuli who has sent
orders to the Fukien Commander here to nip it
in the bud, with the result that a large number
of arrests have been made locally from among the
outward passengers on the steamers, and they are
to be tried by martial law. Hsia Ch'ao was
formerly Provincial Chief of Gendarmerie, and has
a considerable following, but I do not think he
will be able to stand long against the Tuli. He
does not approve of Commander P'êng's autocratic
appointments of territorial officials, and has

                                              ordered

SIR FRANCIS AGLEN, K.B.E.,
    Inspector General of Customs,
              P E K I N G.

ordered a new Magistrate, Huang Chên (黄辰), to proceed to Wenchow, but this individual is rather chary of turning out the present incumbent Wu T'ao (吴涛) appointed by the Commander. The Police are very inefficient, and we have had robberies of stores, poultry, and garden produce recently both at the Assistant's Quarters and my own. There seems to be no proper official control over municipal affairs, and vagrants are allowed to settle in the temples or on the streets. Houses are allowed to encroach on the roads, which are also obstructed with timber, street-stalls, and general merchandise awaiting shipment. All complaints I make are referred on to the Taoyin, Magistrate, District Assembly, etc., and little results but circumlocution and waste of paper. I invited the Fukien Commander, Taoyin, Superintendent, and Magistrate to tiffin on the 6th instant, and tried to persuade them to take a little interest in municipal affairs for the

benefit

benefit of the port. The local deliberative bodies are all at loggerheads with one another, and there is considerable dissatisfaction with the recent improper election of Yeh Wei-chou (葉維周) and T'ang Kêng (唐庚) as President and Vice President respectively of the Chamber of Commerce; the merchants have, in point of fact, refused to have anything more to do with the Chamber of Commerce, and have formed a Trades Union (商界聯合會). You will therefore understand that, at the present time, I am having considerable difficulty in invoking the aid of the Chinese authorities - who are continually changing according to political events - in matters affecting Service interests, and the question of the tenure or lease of the site of the recently acquired Consular buildings, as reported in my Despatch No. 3872, is still in abeyance.

ow Anti-iation.

A local Anti-Opium Association was formed on

on the 12th instant under the auspices of the China Inland Mission. A Mr. T'ao, Chief of Staff under Commander P'êng, and Mr. Chu, representing the Taoyin, were elected Honorary Presidents, and the Committee consists of 25 members including the foreign heads of the Methodist and China Inland Missions. Have you any special views on the opium question, which you would like me to introduce at any of the meetings?

Shelter.
With reference to the Engineer-in-Chief's comments on my Despatch No. 3877 applying for authority for the construction of a shelter at the mouth of the river for our Boatmen-pilots, I can make the hut slightly larger if necessary without exceeding the margin of cost allowed for, but it is, of course, the exception rather than the rule that all three pilots are out at the same time. Arrangements can easily be made

locally

locally for safety of the few window and other fittings (fixtures) of the hut. The roof will be sufficiently well protected from typhoons by the provision of specially strong tiles firmly affixed with cement mortar. The Coast Inspector is also in favour of the construction of this shelter.

ioner's
ry:

If you authorise the supply of the much-needed tea-set and glassware applied for in my Despatch No. 3874, the inventory of the Commissioner's House will be in fairly good order with the exception of the plate and cutlery, which are worn out, but I have purposely refrained from applying for new knives, forks, and spoons, as I have heard indirectly that they are no longer supplied by the Works Department, though there is no Circular authority to this effect. I should be glad to know, however, whether my information is correct or not, or whether an application is in order.

The

ilver   The currency question is much vexed. We continually make seizures of inferior silver coins, and this action on our part causes considerable disaffection, and the Superintendent is not inclined to back us up. The case reported in my Despatch No. 3875 is unsettled pending your instructions, and two more cases have occurred since. A couple of days ago, by the way, 7,000 spurious 20-cent pieces were seized by the Police; they had been imported from Juian, where so much counterfeit Chinese and Japanese money is regularly produced.

With the approach of China New Year, fires are, as usual, of more frequent occurrence. There have been several this month, the last being on the 11th instant near the south-west gate.

The recently garnered rice crop was most satisfactory, and attempts are now being made

to

to smuggle consignments out of Wenchow in order to profit by sale at high prices in less favoured localities.

Yours truly,

C.A.ated

No. 312.　　　　　　　　　Wenchow　　1st December, 24.

Dear Sir Francis,

r silver　　　I have received your Despatch No. 1286/101,109, N.C. No. 218, instructing me to inform the Superintendent that you cannot direct me to depart from instructions laid down by the Shui-wu Ch'u with regard to seizures of inferior silver coins, but I fully explained this principle to him at the time, and it does not prevent him continuing as before, so I now await your reply to my further Despatch No. 3879, N.C. No. 364. The best way out of the difficulty would be for the Government to raise the embargo on Fukien coins in Chekiang, so long as the Fukien Military Authorities are in charge, while maintaining the prohibition of Kuangtung coins as before. As faras I am concerned, however, all I want to know is how I am to treat the coins returned to me by the Superintendent in past and future cases.

　　　　　　　　　　　　　　　　　　　　The

SIR FRANCIS AGLEN, K.B.E.,
　　Inspector General of Customs,
　　　　　　　PEKING.

The Ningpo Agent of the Asiatic Petroleum Company is now here with some of his Staff. He tells me that official objections to the Company's proposed pontoon, giving access to the new Oil Tank Installation Site, will only be removed on payment of $7,000.00 - "to pacify the inhabitants of the North River valley"; this money is, of course, a mere "squeeze." The Agent, who is a son of the late Chinese scholar Dr. Hopkyn Rees, being well acquainted with Chinese characteristics, has offerred $1,000.00 - for "travelling expenses of the North River gentry," whom he has invited to an elaborate dinner-party, and he hopes to secure good results with this policy!

In your S/O Letter of 15th February, 1923, you told me that any women and children, who appeal to the Customs for rescue in case of kidnapping, are to be assisted. On the 17th ult., Mr.

Mr. Sia Liang (謝良), 3rd Class (Chinese) Tidewaiter, B, reported that there was an evident attempt to take away some children by the Japanese S.S. "Sin Eng Maru". The Tidesurveyor boarded the vessel and found six children, from 2 to 9 years of age, who could not be satisfactorily accounted for, and, acting under my instructions, he brought them ashore and handed them over to the police for investigation.

w
piu:
ati'n.
On the 21st ultimo I was invited to become an Adviser to the local Anti-Opium Association, the formation of which was mentioned in my last S/O Letter. I attended a meeting on the 27th, at which various speeches were delivered by some of the local officials and gentry, after which a photograph was taken. A procession through the town, in demonstration of anti-opium feelings, is arranged for the 7th instant. Most of the opium comes to Wenchow by junk from Fukien, and is

landed

landed at small places along the river between Wenchow and the coast, and, until we are entitled to exercise proper control over the 5o-li zone, it is practically impossible to check the smuggling. There is no doubt that opium-smoking at this port is continually increasing.

Light   The new set of machinery imported for the local electric light plant on the 1st May, as mentioned in my S/O No. 298, is now in working order, and the lighting is extremely good. The cost of installation is now about $3.20 per lamp (including wiring) and $20.00 deposit for the meter. It is reported that electric machinery will be installed by some of the local manufacturing concerns now that sufficient current is available.

Mr. Huang Ch'ên (黄辰), appointed Magistrate at Wenchow by the Civil Governor, as stated in my

last

last S/O Letter, arrived on the 20th ult., but has not yet taken over from the present incumbent Wu T'ao (吳濤), appointed by the Military Authorities.

At 10.30 a.m. on the 23rd ultimo the newly built residence of Mr. T'ang Kêng (唐庚), Vice President of the Chamber of Commerce, was completely destroyed by fire. The loss amounts to about $10,000.00.

Yours truly,

Ca S Williams.

INSPECTORATE GENERAL OF CUSTOMS,

S/O

PEKING, 13th December, 1924.

Dear Williams,

I am directed by the I.G. to forward a letter containing accusations against 4th Class (Ch.) Tidewaiter A Lu Si Huo; to ask you to investigate the charges made and to report if the complainants can be identified.

Yours truly,

G.C.F. Hollam

Please return the letter with your reply.

C.A.S. Williams, Esquire,
WENCHOW.

北京总税务司钧鉴密查浙江瓯海关查验员卢诗和品行极不端方现与商船订约匿税每船只装有杂货等应有纳税若干而该卢诗和令各船户以多报少私自向各船户取利饱入私囊月得共洋约四五百元每逢在商轮码头搜查获有贵美物品即将此货私自暂置友人家或取回家中并面令客人到伊家或到友人家将此货赎回而赎价比海关拍卖较为廉价谈卢诗和如此营私舞弊想税务司前途大有妨碍二月间在飞鲸轮船中查获新银角子私罚洋七百元三月间升利轮中查获新角子私罚洋二百元七月间在海晏轮中查获烟土五色私取家中变卖十月二十九夜深在海晏轮船查获新角子罚洋六百五十元以上罚款都归卢诗和私自在码头处罚闻提三成与迄丁水手以致密缝此像实在情形用特电请撤革以维税收浙江瓯海公民陈大雄黄国贞吴兆龙周文璋王一庭郑起叶汉章叶凯仝叩 十三年十二月三十日

Memorandum for the Commissioner.

In regard to charges against Mr. Lu Si-nuo, Chi. 4th Cl. Twtr., brought to the attention of the Inspector General in a letter signed by, allegedly, businessmen of Wenchow, I respectfully beg to call your attention to a somewhat similar letter received by this Customs on November 20th last, accusing the same Officer of malpractices. In that case the letter proved a forgery, and the essential part of it was found entirely baseless.

In the present case the charges are more vague, only one definite date given. On November 25th (10th moon, 29th day) Mr. Sia Liang, ~~4th~~ Chi-3rd Cl. Twtr. B. was on night duty, and there is nothing in the Report-books to indicate that Mr. Lu visited the s.s."Haean" on that particular night. With second parties to transactions in question not coming forward, and with no evidence at all to hand, it is not possible to take up anonymous charges, except by directly questioning the Officer concerned, who will naturally deny anything and everything.

Mr. Lu is an intelligent and capable young man, of good manners, and has proved himself a useful Officer. His record of seizures effected is quite satisfactory, and it is possible that in the execution of his duties he has incurred the enmity of some person or other. I have made enquiries in regard to his private life, and visited his home, but in neither is there any display of large means at command. Moreover, transactions on such a large scale as alleged could scarcely be carried out amongst a crowd of passengers, and with the ship's crew and the local police constantly about, but that some rumours about them should leak out. I always make it a point of attending at arrivals and departures of the Shanghai passenger-steamers, and it would be easy for an aggrieved party or the writers of the two letters in question, to inform me on the spot and at the time of offence being committed.

As it is disquieting to have in a responsible position an Officer against whom such charges are persistently levied, I would recommend that Mr. Lu Si-nuo be transferred to a larger port, where he would be under more direct observation of a Foreign Tidewaiter or a Boat Officer, and that in his place a Foreign Tidewaiter be appointed to Wenchow. With only Chinese Officers at my disposal, I naturally have to delegate to them work, and place in them a trust, that I would not otherwise think advisable.

As for the Watcher Lin Ting-fang, his case had better be held over for future consideration.

Wenchow, December 24th. 1924.

John Sydell

Tidesurveyor B.

/O No. 313.   Wenchow   15th Dec., 24.

Dear Sir Francis,

Collection of intra Native Customs Duties by Superintendent.

The Superintendent is inclined to be somewhat unconstitutional in his policy - as you have noticed in his treatment of seizures of inferior coins. He is now making efforts to collect Native Customs duty in the 50-li area at Kuant'ou (館頭), which, being only one of his Checking Barriers, has no business to interfere with cargo consigned to Wenchow. The merchants also object to this new duty collection at Kuant'ou, and I am now reporting the matter for your instructions, as I am afraid that if I give way to this encroachment of our authority, the thin end of the wedge is admitted, he will reach out further, and we shall find that much of our regular intra 50-li duty is being diverted to the Superintendent's duty-farmers.

Inferior

SIR FRANCIS AGLEN, K.B.E.,
　　Inspector General of Customs,
　　　　PEKING.

ilver   I have two more unsettled cases of seizure of Kuangtung and Fukien inferior silver coins on hand, but I have not yet sent these coins to the Superintendent pending receipt of your reply to my Despatch No. 3879, N.C. No. 364.

Case.   As a result of our action in the kidnapping case reported in my last S/O Letter, I have been asked to send a number of members of the Staff to give evidence in court, and I have suggested sending one Chinese Tidewaiter to represent all, but have heard nothing more about the matter.

03 Outdoor s.   In my Summary of Non-urgent Chinese Correspondence for last month you will notice certain accusations against members of the Outdoor Staff. The Customs Broker would be glad to get Mr. P. W. Coxall, 1st Class Tidewaiter, into trouble, as the latter carries out his Native

Customs

Customs examination work with strict attention to malpractice on the part of the merchants. I have, however, told Mr. Coxall to try and hit it off better with the Brokers without relaxing his vigilance. As regards the accusation against Yang Chu-ming, we have no employee of this name, but there is a Native Customs Examiner called Yang Ch'ao who may perhaps be the person implied, but I have no reason to believe that he is in any way dishonest. A good deal of cargo passes through his hands, and he is kept up to the mark by Mr. Coxall, and often sends in a seizure report. You will see my reply in this month's Summary.

Mr. Huang Ch'en (黄辰), referred to in my last two S/O Letters, took over charge of the Yungchia (Wenchow) Magistracy on the 3rd instant. Mr. Wu T'ao (吳濤), the former Magistrate, left for Hangchow on the 6th in company with Mr. Yang Ch'eng-hsiao

Ch'eng-hsiao (楊承孝), the local Superintendent of Customs. It is believed that the Superintendent has been taking part in a conference at the capital relative to the recent political innovations in Peking. The departure of the Superintendent under these circumstances generally results in the appointment of a new Superintendent, and such continual changes are very detrimental to the interests of the Service.

Anti-
tic.
A procession of 10,000 people was arranged by the newly formed local Anti-Opium Association, and the streets of the city were paraded on the evening of the 7th instant. Soldiers, students and others took part in the procession and carried banners bearing the characters 拒毒會警戒, etc. I have heard indirectly that many of the members of the Association are opium-smokers themselves, and that opium is being grown by order of the soldiers not far from Wenchow at

Luch'aoshan

Luch'aoshan (鹿巢山) and Chouyang (周垟)!

f The French Sloop "Algol", with Admiral
Frochot. Frochot on board, arrived on the 24th ultimo, and
stayed for three days. I believe this is the
first occasion that Wenchow has been visited by
an Admiral.

an
Vessel. A new vessel, S.L. "Yungfa", has recently
been put on the Wenchow run. She plies to
Chianghsia (江厦), Kuaot'ou (古鳌头), Juian
(瑞安), and other inland places.

         Yours truly,

         C. S. Williams.

S/O No. 314.

CUSTOM HOUSE,

Wenchow, 27th Dec., 1924.

Dear Sir Francis,

With reference to Mr. Holland's S/O Letter of 13th instant:

forwarding a letter containing certain accusations against Mr. Lu Si Huo, 4th Class (Ch.) Tidewaiter, A, and asking me to investigate the charges and to report if the complainants can be identified:

I notice that the letter is ante-dated 30th December, and contains no address; the signatorie moreover cannot be traced in Wenchow.

On the only definite date mentioned in the letter, i.e. the evening of the 28th November (10th moon, 29th day), Mr. Lu was not on night duty, and therefore could not have made the seizure of coins as alleged, and I do not think it is possible that the other large transactions

could

SIR FRANCIS AGLEN, K.B.E.,
 Inspector General of Customs,
  PEKING.

could have been so continuously carried out without any rumours or complaints reaching my ears. I consider that the charges are therefore groundless, or due to resentment on account of strictness of examination of cargo or luggage.

In this connection I append a copy of a further letter (signatory also untraceable), from which you will see that the alleged writer of the former letter exonerates Mr. Lu altogether, and has apparently communicated with you to the same effect.

The original letter is returned herewith.

Yours truly,

快郵代電

字第　　號

税務司鉴窃民前由申返里至碼頭受贵閩查驗員盧詩和開箱檢查甚為嚴勵帶有貨物令民指稅絕無遁融民頗有怪意次日告訴商家乃有一二商家亦被盧搜過私貨充公心極不平邀民捏名控盧而民一時性急誤聽人播弄当卯飾詞訴請懲税務司查此不料海關新頒章程帶有貨物在碼頭均須補稅於此檢查更為嚴密難怪盧檢查認真前難今民……

快郵代電

第　　字　　號

總稅務司電內謂盧獲得貴美貨物携帶變賣並私罰等款均屬子虛當時誤聽商人謬言無故控告盧詩和違法心有不安自認無理茲奉到飭查請切相信除另呈總稅務司請將此案注銷保全盧君名譽外理合聲明王一龍叩

前電陳某等均是化名合併聲明

INSPECTORATE GENERAL OF CUSTOMS.

PEKING, 31st December 1924

Dear Mr. Williams,

I have duly received your S/O letters Nos. 310, 311, 312 and 313 of 1st and 15th November, 1st and 15th December.

Formation of Anti-Opium Association.

I hope this Anti-Opium Association will not, as at many ports, be merely a camouflaged opium monopoly bureau.

Is there Circular authority re supply of cutlery for Commissioners' houses?

This article is not supplied, vide Circular No. 2123, paragraphs 6 and 7.

Yours truly,

S. Williams, Esquire.
WENCHOW.

INDEXED

INSPECTORATE GENERAL OF CUSTOMS

PEKING, 31st December 1924

Dear Mr. Williams,

With further reference to your S/O letter No. 313 of the 15th December.

Inferior Silver Coins: two unsettled cases outstanding. How shall they be dealt with?

Follow instructions of my despatch No. 1292.

Superintendent is attending conference at the Capital. Departure under these circumstances usually results in change of Superintendent, which is detrimental to Service interests.

Of course! But this is the Chinese way!

Yours truly,

S. Williams, Esquire.
WENCHOW.